New Horizons in Web Search, Web Data Mining, and Web-Based Applications

New Horizons in Web Search, Web Data Mining, and Web-Based Applications

Editors

Jing Zhang
Jipeng Qiang
Cangqi Zhou

Basel • Beijing • Wuhan • Barcelona • Belgrade • Novi Sad • Cluj • Manchester

Editors

Jing Zhang
School of Cyber Science
and Engineering
Southeast University
Nanjing
China

Jipeng Qiang
School of Information
and Engineering
Yangzhou University
Yangzhou
China

Cangqi Zhou
School of Computer Science
and Engineering
Nanjing University of Science
and Technology
Nanjing
China

Editorial Office
MDPI
St. Alban-Anlage 66
4052 Basel, Switzerland

This is a reprint of articles from the Special Issue published online in the open access journal *Applied Sciences* (ISSN 2076-3417) (available at: https://www.mdpi.com/journal/applsci/special_issues/80FX2FWBZ8).

For citation purposes, cite each article independently as indicated on the article page online and as indicated below:

Lastname, A.A.; Lastname, B.B. Article Title. *Journal Name* **Year**, *Volume Number*, Page Range.

ISBN 978-3-7258-0071-1 (Hbk)
ISBN 978-3-7258-0072-8 (PDF)
doi.org/10.3390/books978-3-7258-0072-8

© 2024 by the authors. Articles in this book are Open Access and distributed under the Creative Commons Attribution (CC BY) license. The book as a whole is distributed by MDPI under the terms and conditions of the Creative Commons Attribution-NonCommercial-NoDerivs (CC BY-NC-ND) license.

Contents

About the Editors vii

Preface ix

Jing Zhang, Jipeng Qiang and Cangqi Zhou
New Horizons in Web Search, Web Data Mining, and Web-Based Applications
Reprinted from: *Appl. Sci.* 2024, 14, 530, doi:10.3390/app14020530 1

Matthew Haffner, Matthew DeWitte, Papia F. Rozario and Gustavo A. Ovando-Montejo
A Neural-Network-Based Landscape Search Engine: LSE Wisconsin
Reprinted from: *Appl. Sci.* 2023, 13, 9264, doi:10.3390/app13169264 6

Juan Aguilera-Alvarez, Juan Martínez-Nolasco, Sergio Olmos-Temois, José Padilla-Medina, Víctor Sámano-Ortega and Micael Bravo-Sanchez
Development of a Web Application for the Detection of Coronary Artery Calcium from Computed Tomography
Reprinted from: *Appl. Sci.* 2022, 12, 12281, doi:10.3390/app122312281 25

Rongping Zou, Bin Zhu, Yi Chen, Bo Xie and Bin Shao
EFCMF: A Multimodal Robustness Enhancement Framework for Fine-Grained Recognition
Reprinted from: *Appl. Sci.* 2023, 13, 1640, doi:10.3390/app13031640 38

Zhuangyi Zhang, Lu Han and Muzi Chen
Fuzzy MLKNN in Credit User Portrait [†]
Reprinted from: *Appl. Sci.* 2022, 12, 11342, doi:10.3390/app122211342 53

Zijuan Zhao, Kai Yang and Jinli Guo
Link Prediction with Hypergraphs via Network Embedding
Reprinted from: *Appl. Sci.* 2023, 13, 523, doi:10.3390/app13010523 74

Pengfei Li, Shaoyu Dong, Yin Zhang and Bin Zhang
Predicting Task Planning Ability for Learners Engaged in Searching as Learning Based on Tree-Structured Long Short-Term Memory Networks
Reprinted from: *Appl. Sci.* 2023, 13, 12840, doi:10.3390/app132312840 83

Liting Wei, Yun Li, Yi Zhu, Bin Li and Lejun Zhang
Prompt Tuning for Multi-Label Text Classification: How to Link Exercises to Knowledge Concepts?
Reprinted from: *Appl. Sci.* 2022, 12, 10363, doi:10.3390/app122010363 96

Yi Zhu, Xinke Zhou and Xindong Wu
Unsupervised Domain Adaptation via Stacked Convolutional Autoencoder [†]
Reprinted from: *Appl. Sci.* 2022, 13, 481, doi:10.3390/app13010481 109

Kiril Griazev and Simona Ramanauskaitė
Web Page Content Block Identification with Extended Block Properties
Reprinted from: *Appl. Sci.* 2023, 13, 5680, doi:10.3390/app13095680 126

Snober Naseer, Umer Rashid, Maha Saddal, Abdur Rehman Khan, Qaisar Abbas and Yassine Daadaa
WSREB Mechanism: Web Search Results Exploration Mechanism for Blind Users
Reprinted from: *Appl. Sci.* 2023, 13, 11007, doi:10.3390/app131911007 142

About the Editors

Jing Zhang

Dr. Jing Zhang is a Professor of Computer Science and Artificial Intelligence at the School of Cyber Science and Engineering, Southeast University, China. He received his Ph.D. degree in Computer Science from Hefei University of Technology, China, in 2015. He has worked as a Visiting Scholar (Professor) at several universities and institutes, such as the University of Pittsburg (2019–2020), the University of Technology, Sydney (2017), and Zhejiang Lab (2023). His research interests include data mining, machine learning, and trustworthy artificial intelligence. He has published more than 100 articles in prestigious journals, such as *TPAMI*, *TKDE*, *TNNLS*, *TCYB*, *TMM*, and *JMLR*, as well as top-tier conferences, such as SIGKDD, AAAI, SIGIR, ICDM, CIKM, etc. He has been granted three funds from the National Natural Science Foundation of China and more than ten funds from provincial governments and enterprises. He is a Senior Member of the IEEE and serves as a Senior PC member for a number of AI-related top-tier conferences, as well as a reviewer for more than 40 international journals.

Jipeng Qiang

Dr. Jipeng Qiang is an Associate Professor and the group leader of the Computational Linguistics and Data Mining Group at Yangzhou University. He received his Ph.D. degree in Computer Science and Technology from Hefei University of Technology in 2016. He was a Ph.D. visiting student at the Artificial Intelligence Lab at the University of Massachusetts, Boston, from 2014 to 2016. His research interests mainly include data mining and natural language processing. He has over 70 publications that have appeared in several top conferences such as AAAI, CVPR, ACL, and EMNLP, as well as journals including *AIJ*, *TACL*, *TKDE*, *TNNLS*, *TKDD*, and *TASLP*.

Cangqi Zhou

Dr. Cangqi Zhou is an Associate Professor with the School of Computer Science and Engineering, Nanjing University of Science and Technology, Nanjing, China. He received his Ph.D. degree in Control Science and Engineering from Tsinghua University, Beijing, China, in 2015. From 2015 to 2017, he was a Postdoctoral Research Fellow with the Center for Intelligent and Networked Systems (CFINS) at Tsinghua University. His research interests include data mining in networked systems, graph neural networks, network representation learning, community detection, and text mining. He has published more than 40 research articles in prestigious journals and conferences. He is the P.I. of two research projects funded by the National Natural Science Foundation of China and the provincial government. He serves as a PC member for the ACL demo track and a reviewer for several international journals such as *TKDE*, *TASE*, *KBS*, *Physica A*, etc.

Preface

Web searching and web data mining constitute the cornerstone of today's diverse intelligent web applications. With the rapid advancement in digitization and intelligentization, web searching and web data mining serve as the main methods of extracting valuable information from large quantities of ever-growing network data. With the rapid development of information technology and artificial intelligence, web applications have expanded from traditional information retrieval and multimedia services to mobile crowd-sensing systems, intelligent healthcare systems, and even collaborative scientific innovation platforms. The emergence of novel applications generates massive amounts of heterogeneous data, calling on more complex and comprehensive analysis and modeling technologies for their exploration and exploitation. At the same time, the emergence of a large number of machine learning models, such as CNN, RNN, LSTM, BERT, Transformer, graph neural networks, etc., also provide more powerful tools for analyzing and modeling web data. Consequently, web searching improves the relevance and accuracy of search results by employing more complex algorithms, while web data mining helps enterprises and organizations to deeply understand customer needs and optimize their products and services. The models, algorithms, and techniques of web searching and web data mining are constantly and rapidly evolving, leading to various autonomous, proactive, content-exploring, self-learning, socially collaborative, and location-aware web applications.

To address the challenges in the development of web searching, web data mining, and web-based applications, we launched this Special Issue in September 2022, which encourages researchers all over the world to submit their high-quality original work related to all aspects of this field. After more than a year of hard work from all authors, reviewers, and editors, of the fifteen articles submitted, ten were finally accepted for publication after the peer-review process: an acceptance rate of 67 percent. The published articles cover a range of topics, from basic models and algorithms to newer applications. Although submissions to this Special Issue are now closed, the need for further in-depth research and development remains. We believe that this Special Issue, "New Horizons in Web Search, Web Data Mining, and Web-Based Applications", has addressed some significant existing knowledge gaps and aids in the advanced development of web searching, web data mining, and web-based applications. It will inspire more researchers to devote themselves to this field and make more contributions in the future.

In the end, we would like to take this opportunity to express our most profound appreciation to the MDPI Book staff; the editorial team of the *Applied Sciences* journal, especially Andy Liu, Section Managing Editor of this Special Issue; the talented authors; and the hardworking and professional reviewers.

Jing Zhang, Jipeng Qiang, and Cangqi Zhou
Editors

Editorial

New Horizons in Web Search, Web Data Mining, and Web-Based Applications

Jing Zhang [1,2,*,†], Jipeng Qiang [3] and Cangqi Zhou [4]

1. School of Cyber Science and Engineering, Southeast University, Nanjing 211189, China
2. Engineering Research Center of Blockchain Application, Supervision and Management, Southeast University, Ministry of Education, Nanjing 211189, China
3. School of Information and Engineering, Yangzhou University, Yangzhou 225127, China; jpqiang@yzu.edu.cn
4. School of Computer Science and Engineering, Nanjing University of Science and Technology, Nanjing 210094, China; cqzhou@njust.edu.cn
* Correspondence: jingz@seu.edu.cn
† Current address: Jiulonghu Campus, Southeast University, No. 2 SEU Road, Nanjing 211189, China.

1. Introduction

In today's era of rapid digitization and information technology advancement, web search and web data mining stand at the core of the technological progress of numerous web-based applications [1–3]. Web search is accompanied by the emergence of the Internet, and it continues to develop as Internet applications become increasingly diversified. It has evolved from the early days of navigating people to web pages of interest and providing people with rich content to automatically searching for relevant resources based on the user's characteristics, integrating related functions, and pushing personalized services. The root cause of achieving these exciting web application experiences is that we have a set of web data mining algorithms that continuously analyze massive amounts of web data and user-generated content [4]. They analyze large volumes of data in an automated or semi-automated manner to find hidden functional patterns like outliers, clusters, and association rules, classify targets into different categories, or link two different types of items (i.e., recommender systems).

In general, web search and web data mining are the main ways to extract valuable information from massive network data, and their models, algorithms, and techniques are constantly evolving. As a result, web applications tend to be autonomous, proactive, content-exploring, self-learning, socially collaborative, and location-aware. For example, through user click and eye-tracking modeling, search results can be optimized more accurately based on user characteristics [5]. Advanced autoencoder deep learning models make extracting information from heterogeneous contexts more efficient [6]. In web image search, semi-supervised pseudo-labeling and variational contrastive learning can be used to overcome the influence of noise and obtain better retrieval performance [7]. Embracing location-based social networks into web applications enables the users to register whenever they visit a specific point-of-interest (POI) through the so-called check-ins, or to establish social links with other users in the system [8]. Relying on multiple rounds of natural language, the interaction technology image search engine can obtain more semantically accurate retrieval results [9]. Crowdsourcing technology makes large-scale scientific research collaboration based on the web possible [10,11]. In summary, search engines improve the relevance and accuracy of search results by employing more complex algorithms, such as models based on machine learning and machine intelligence. Web data mining helps enterprises and organizations deeply understand customer needs and optimize products and services by applying complex statistical methods, machine learning, and deep learning technologies. Together with the development of cloud and mobile computing, web-based applications have become more powerful and diverse. These applications support the

operation of multiple industries such as e-commerce [12], online education [13], and remote healthcare [14]. Innovations such as blockchain technology and the application of the Internet of Things have further expanded the possibilities of web applications [15,16] providing users with safer and more personalized services.

The articles published in this Special Issue have shown that web search, web data mining, and web-based applications are in a stage of rapid development. Different research and practices from various fields indicate that with the continuous emergence and application of new technologies, these fields will continue to drive social and technological progress.

2. An Overview of Published Articles

"Predicting Task Planning Ability for Learners Engaged in Searching as Learning Based on Tree-Structured Long Short-Term Memory Networks" by Pengfei Li, Shaoyu Dong, Yin Zhang, and Bin Zhang was published in November 2023, and it proposed a new method by which to predict the task planning ability of learners using network-based search engines in the context of searching as learning (SAL). This method not only improves the accuracy of predicting the task-planning ability of learners but also provides valuable insights for web-based search engines, recommendation systems, and instructional designers. The innovative contribution of this study lies in its ability to help create personalized and efficient search interfaces and support educators in designing more effective learning experiences based on the needs of individual learners.

"WSREB Mechanism: Web Search Results Exploration Mechanism for Blind Users" by Snober Naseer, Umer Rashid, Maha Saddal, Abdur Rehman Khan, Qaisar Abbas, and Yassine Daadaa was published in October 2023, and it introduced an innovative framework for improving the accessibility of network search for blind users and addressing the challenges they face due to information exchange and cognitive pressure. This study proposes a novel WSREB mechanism, which emphasizes accessibility and navigation of web documents while reducing the cognitive load in a non-linear and integrated way. It significantly improves the availability and accessibility of network content for business units This study helps to redefine the paradigm of online search to promote inclusivity and optimize user experience for blind users, reflecting that technological development in web search increases the well-being of minority groups.

"A Neural-Network-Based Landscape Search Engine: LSE Wisconsin" by Matthew Haffner, Matthew DeWitte, Papia F. Rozario, and Gustavo A. Ovando-Montejo was published in August 2023, and it introduced a search engine, namely, LSE Wisconsin, which extends the perspectives of remote sensing research by implementing image retrieval based on terrain and vegetation features. The new method proposed in this study indicates that the VGG16 and ResNet-50 networks typically produce more favorable results, marking an important step towards developing more comprehensive and high-resolution landscape search engines. This study helps to create powerful and user-friendly digital resources for the research community and users, improving the accessibility and practicality of remote sensing data in various applications.

"Web Page Content Block Identification with Extended Block Properties" by Kiril Griazev and Simona Ramanauskaitė was published in May 2023 and proposed an innovative method for web content block recognition, which is of great significance for automatically integrating web content into other systems. The main technological advancement lies in the ability to describe, in detail, the scope and variants of each content block through text similarity and document object model (DOM) tree analysis. Compared to manual tagging and other existing methods, it can recognize more content blocks, reducing at least 70% of manual tagging work. This work led to a full understanding of the web page structure, making automated integration and transformation of web content possible.

"EFCMF: A Multimodal Robustness Enhancement Framework for Fine-Grained Recognition" by Rongping Zou, Bin Zhu, Yi Chen, Bo Xie, and Bin Shao was published in January 2023, and it proposed an innovative method for fine-grained recognition in multi-mode data. It enhances the learning ability of multimodal data complementarity by randomly deactivating modal features in the constructed multimodal fine-grained recognition model, solving challenges such as pattern loss and resistance attacks. EFCMF improves the processing of missing modal scenes without additional training. It is worth noting that compared to traditional models under adversarial conditions, it achieves significantly higher accuracy and shows a 27.13% performance improvement.

"Link Prediction with Hypergraphs via Network Embedding" by Zijuan Zhao, Kai Yang, and Jinli Guo was published in December 2022 and introduced a new link prediction method using hypergraphs and network embedding (HNE), demonstrating technological progress in the field of network analysis and providing a new perspective for studying complex relationships. Hypergraphs provide a natural way to represent complex higher-order relationships. The findings of this paper have broad implications, proposing potential applications in different fields such as online social network recommendations and bioinformatics by integrating hypergraphs and network embedding methods.

"Unsupervised Domain Adaptation via Stacked Convolutional Autoencoder" by Yi Zhu, Xinke Zhou, and Xindong Wu was published in December 2022, and it proposed a new unsupervised domain adaptation method that significantly improves domain adaptation technology by using the Stacked Convolutional Sparse Autoencoder (SCSA). It obtains higher-level representations for unsupervised domain adaptation by performing layer projection from the original data. SCSA effectively addresses the challenges of performance degradation caused by ineffective optimization and data redundancy in deep neural networks. Compared with existing methods, it shows superior classification accuracy of up to 89.3%. This research effectively improves the efficiency of using unsupervised methods to transfer knowledge in different domains.

"Development of a Web Application for the Detection of Coronary Artery Calcium from Computed Tomography" by Juan Aguilera-Alvarez, Juan Martínez-Nolasco, Sergio Olmos-Temois, José Padilla-Medina, Víctor Sámano-Ortega, and Micael Bravo-Sanchez was published in November 2022, and it introduced a novel web application that uses Agaston technology for semiautomatic quantification of coronary artery calcium (CAC). This study makes an important advancement in cardiovascular disease analysis. The innovative approach in the system provides accessibility to any device through internet connectivity, which significantly simplifies the processes of healthcare professionals and improves the practicality and efficiency of cardiovascular risk assessment. This system not only simplifies the workflow of cardiologists but may also help with the early detection and management of cardiovascular diseases.

"Fuzzy MLKNN in Credit User Portrait" by Zhuangyi Zhang, Lu Han, and Muzi Chen was published in November 2022, and it proposed an improved fuzzy MLKNN multi-label learning algorithm. The new algorithm solves the subjectivity problem caused by the discretization of credit data and provides more dimensional portraits for credit users. It weakens the subjectivity of credit data after discretization by introducing intuitionistic fuzzy numbers and better realizes the multi-label portrait of credit users by using the corresponding fuzzy Euclidean distance. Compared with traditional MLKNN algorithms, it significantly improves performance, especially in reducing one error. The method creatively combines fuzzy set theory with multi-label learning, paving the way for more sophisticated credit data analysis and potentially aiding in more accurate credit risk assessments.

"Prompt Tuning for Multi-Label Text Classification: How to Link Exercises to Knowledge Concepts?" by Liting Wei, Yan Li, Yi Zhu, Bin Li, and Lejun Zhang was published in October 2022, and it proposed a novel multi-label text classification prompt adjustment method (PTMLTC). The proposed method automatically links exercises with knowledge concepts in educational environments. Specifically, the relevance scores of exercise content and knowledge concepts are learned by a prompt tuning model with a unified template, and then the multiple associated knowledge concepts are selected with a threshold. It solves the cost and time challenges of requiring a large amount of training data in traditional multi-label text classification methods and performs significantly better than existing methods in terms of efficiency and accuracy on the self-constructed Exercises–Concepts dataset of the Data Structure course. This innovative method not only simplifies the process of connecting educational content but also has the potential for wider application in intelligent education systems.

3. Conclusions

The objectives of this Special Issue on "New Horizons in Web Search, Web Data Mining and Web-Based Applications" were successfully achieved through the incorporation of groundbreaking research in these domains. Each contribution significantly advanced the understanding and capabilities of web-based technologies, focusing on enhancing information retrieval, intelligent data analysis, and innovative application development. The collective impact of these studies is profound, aligning with the core purpose of science and research: to enhance human experiences and capabilities in the digital age. This issue stands as a testament to the potential of web technologies in shaping a more informed, efficient, and connected world.

Author Contributions: Conceptualization, J.Z.; Investigation, J.Z. and J.Q.; Writing—original draft preparation, J.Q. and C.Z.; Writing—review and editing, J.Z. All authors have read and agreed to the published version of the manuscript.

Acknowledgments: I would like to extend my appreciation to the authors for their diligent research, the reviewers for providing insightful comments and constructive suggestions, as well as the editors and proofreading team for their meticulous attention to detail, ensuring high-quality publishing in terms of both research content and printing standards.

Conflicts of Interest: The authors declare no conflicts of interest.

References

1. Hitzler, P. A review of the semantic web field. *Commun. ACM* **2021**, *64*, 76–83. [CrossRef]
2. Ristoski, P.; Paulheim, H. Semantic Web in data mining and knowledge discovery: A comprehensive survey. *J. Web Semant.* **2016**, *36*, 1–22. [CrossRef]
3. Al-asadi, T.A.; Obaid, A.J.; Hidayat, R.; Ramli, A.A. A survey on web mining techniques and applications. *Int. J. Adv. Sci. Eng. Inf. Technol.* **2017**, *7*, 1178–1184. [CrossRef]
4. Gheisari, M.; Hamidpour, H.; Liu, Y.; Saedi, P.; Raza, A.; Jalili, A.; Rokhsati, H.; Amin, R. Data Mining Techniques for Web Mining: A Survey. *Artif. Intell. Appl.* **2023**, *1*, 3–10. [CrossRef]
5. Zhang, R.; Xie, X.; Mao, J.; Liu, Y.; Zhang, M.; Ma, S. Constructing a comparison-based click model for web search. In Proceedings of the Web Conference 2021, Ljubljana, Slovenia, 19–23 April 2021; pp. 270–283.
6. Ahmad, F.; Abbasi, A.; Kitchens, B.; Adjeroh, D.; Zeng, D. Deep learning for adverse event detection from web search. *IEEE Trans. Knowl. Data Eng.* **2020**, *34*, 2681–2695. [CrossRef]
7. Yavuz, M.C.; Yanikoglu, B. VCL-PL: Semi-supervised learning from noisy web data with variational contrastive learning. In Proceedings of the 2022 26th International Conference on Pattern Recognition, Montreal, QC, Canada, 21–25 August 2022; pp. 740–747.
8. Sánchez, P.; Bellogín, A. Point-of-interest recommender systems based on location-based social networks: A survey from an experimental perspective. *Acm Comput. Surv.* **2022**, *54*, 1–37. [CrossRef]
9. Tan, F.; Cascante-Bonilla, P.; Guo, X.; Wu, H.; Feng, S.; Ordonez, V. Drill-down: Interactive retrieval of complex scenes using natural language queries. *arXiv* **2019**, arXiv:1911.03826.
10. Simpson, R.; Page, K.R.; De Roure, D. Zooniverse: Observing the world's largest citizen science platform. In Proceedings of the 23rd International Conference on World Wide Web, Seoul, Republic of Korea, 7–11 April 2014; pp. 1049–1054.
11. Zhang, J. Knowledge learning with crowdsourcing: A brief review and systematic perspective. *IEEE/CAA J. Autom. Sin.* **2022**, *9*, 749–762. [CrossRef]
12. Tang, A.K. A systematic literature review and analysis on mobile apps in m-commerce: Implications for future research. *Electron. Commer. Res. Appl.* **2019**, *37*, 100885. [CrossRef]
13. Criollo-C, S.; Guerrero-Arias, A.; Jaramillo-Alcázar, Á.; Luján-Mora, S. Mobile learning technologies for education: Benefits and pending issues. *Appl. Sci.* **2021**, *11*, 4111. [CrossRef]
14. Pires, I.M.; Marques, G.; Garcia, N.M.; Flórez-Revuelta, F.; Ponciano, V.; Oniani, S. A research on the classification and applicability of the mobile health applications. *J. Pers. Med.* **2020**, *10*, 11. [CrossRef] [PubMed]

55. Yang, W.; Aghasian, E.; Garg, S.; Herbert, D.; Disiuta, L.; Kang, B. A survey on blockchain-based internet service architecture: Requirements, challenges, trends, and future. *IEEE Access* **2019**, *7*, 75845–75872. [CrossRef]
56. Da Xu, L.; Viriyasitavat, W. Application of blockchain in collaborative internet-of-things services. *IEEE Trans. Comput. Soc. Syst.* **2019**, *6*, 1295–1305.

Disclaimer/Publisher's Note: The statements, opinions and data contained in all publications are solely those of the individual author(s) and contributor(s) and not of MDPI and/or the editor(s). MDPI and/or the editor(s) disclaim responsibility for any injury to people or property resulting from any ideas, methods, instructions or products referred to in the content.

Article

A Neural-Network-Based Landscape Search Engine: LSE Wisconsin

Matthew Haffner [1,*], Matthew DeWitte [1], Papia F. Rozario [1] and Gustavo A. Ovando-Montejo [2]

[1] Department of Geography and Anthropology, University of Wisconsin–Eau Claire, Eau Claire, WI 54701, USA; rozaripf@uwec.edu (P.F.R.)
[2] Department of Environment and Society, Utah State University, Blanding, UT 84511, USA
* Correspondence: haffnerm@uwec.edu; Tel.: +1-715-836-2316

Featured Application: This paper introduces a neural-network-based landscape search engine tool for the state of Wisconsin. It provides several examples of how the application works and suggests avenues for future research.

Abstract: The task of image retrieval is common in the world of data science and deep learning, but it has received less attention in the field of remote sensing. The authors seek to fill this gap in research through the presentation of a web-based landscape search engine for the US state of Wisconsin. The application allows users to select a location on the map and to find similar locations based on terrain and vegetation characteristics. It utilizes three neural network models—VGG16, ResNet-50, and NasNet—on digital elevation model data, and uses the NDVI mean and standard deviation for comparing vegetation data. The results indicate that VGG16 and ResNet50 generally return more favorable results, and the tool appears to be an important first step toward building a more robust, multi-input, high resolution landscape search engine in the future. The tool, called LSE Wisconsin, is hosted publicly on ShinyApps.io

Keywords: image retrieval; remote sensing; web GIS; GIScience

1. Introduction

Deep learning (DL) has been extensively and successfully applied in the field of remote sensing for tasks such as object detection, object segmentation, and land use classification [1]. Such methods have brought about major advancements in the discipline and have been crucial to the fusion of data science and remote sensing. At the same time, however, image retrieval—that is, returning similar images given a single input image—has become an increasingly common data science task, yet its application to remotely sensed datasets has been lacking. This project seeks to fill that gap in research through the creation of a "landscape search engine" tool, designed particularly for (though certainly not limited to) location analysis applications.

To achieve this goal, the authors leverage several common DL models—VGG16, ResNet-50, and NasNet—on digital elevation model (DEM) data and combine these outputs with a traditional vegetation metric, the normalized difference vegetation index (NDVI), in creating the image retrieval tool. The authors present this as a publicly accessible web application (https://uwec-geog.shinyapps.io/lse-wi accessed on 6 August 2023) which allows users to retrieve similar landscapes in the US state of Wisconsin for a location they select on the map. Using sliders and drop-down list options, users can select a specific neural network (NN) model, the number of locations to retrieve, the relative weight on terrain or vegetation, the amount of weight to place on mean vs. standard deviation NDVI, and an optional exclusion radius from the input location. To date, this is the only landscape search tool built specifically for the state of Wisconsin, and, to the authors' knowledge, it is the only search engine tool which leverages neural network models for landscape search. Considering the increasing impact of data science on the domains of geographic information science (GIScience) and remote sensing, the development of this tool and its corresponding metrics signifies a crucial stride towards the creation of robust, user-friendly digital resources for the research community and end-users alike.

Background

Implementations of DL in remote sensing and within the broader field of geographic information science (GIScience) have been applied to a variety of tasks, such as land cover mapping [2], environmental parameter retrieval [3], data fusion and downscaling [4], object detection [5], and information construction and prediction (see [1,6,7] for comprehensive overviews). Other efforts have focused on advancing the principles of DL in remote sensing, including the integration of aerial images, and the detection of small objects on the landscape [5,8]. Yuan et al. [3], in particular, have advocated for the fusion of geographic principles into DL for remote sensing tasks, most notably Tobler's famous First Law of Geography: "Everything is related to everything else, but near things are more related than distant things". The most common and mainstream frameworks are back-propagation NNs, such as convolutional neural networks (CNNs). Indicative of their power, CNN models often produce a sizable increase in accuracy over traditional regression models, particularly when working with remotely sensed data. Further, unlike traditional learning algorithms, intrinsic features from raw input data can be extracted using a variety of DL frameworks without using manual digitizing techniques, thus reducing the need for reliance on domain knowledge [9].

Despite the significant number of remote sensing studies which utilize DL, there is a paucity of research on the particular task of image retrieval using remotely sensed data, with a few notable exceptions. Jasiewicz et al. [10] first coined the term "landscape search engine" in building a landscape similarity tool for terrain across the entire country of Poland. Using the concept of "geomorphons", this approach classifies pixels from digital elevation models (DEMs) into several types: ridge, shoulder, spur, slope, hollow, footslope, valley, pit, flat, and peak. Another landscape similarity tool, developed by Dilts et al. [11], has been applied toward location optimization of control sites based on the spatial characteristics of treatment sites. The researchers applied a moving window analysis to generate per-pixel maps of similarity between the treatment and control areas for site selections. Outside of this application, the United States Geological Survey (USGS) has a landscape search tool focusing on land treatment exploration within the United States, making use of modifiable parameters, such as soil and vegetation characteristics [12]. Through an interactive web map, it allows users to input empirical characteristics for the purpose of finding areas with similar heat load, soil properties, and climate conditions. At the time of writing, however, the two formerly mentioned studies do not have publicly available toolkits, and none of these prior implementations make use of NNs.

VGG16, ResNet-50, and the Neural Architecture Search Network (NasNet) have been used frequently in remote sensing. The Visual Geometry Group (VGG) model architecture is a standard CNN which uses a specified number of consecutive convolutional layers to extract features from image data. The input of VGG is an image with resolution 224×224, and, since VGGNet is a classification network, the output shape is proportional to the number of classes in the dataset. The model architecture consists of multiple convolution layers followed by max pooling layers, and the end of the model consists of fully connected layers followed by the final classification layer. Two common VGG architectures used are VGG16 and VGG19, which are sixteen and nineteen layers deep, respectively [13]. The VGG16 architecture, in particular, was first introduced by Simonyan and Zisserman [14] for image recognition and has been used extensively in multispectral and hyperspectral image classifications even with low resolution imagery [15]. It has also been utilized for tasks such as road feature extraction [16], sea ice classification [17], image stitching [18], and many others.

ResNet-50 falls into the family of deep residual networks and contains 50 layers: 48 convolutional layers, one average pooling layer, and one max pooling layer [19]. This model, along with small modifications to its architecture, has been successfully applied in many remote sensing applications, such as image segmentation [20], classification [21,22], and image captioning [23]. In a comparative study of several NN models for remote sensing classification, ResNet-50 indeed outperformed other models, including NasNet and VGG16 [24]. NasNet has been applied to tasks such as scene classification (e.g., see [24,25]) but has been used for remote sensing tasks less often than VGG16 and ResNet-50. This makes its use in new applications of particular interest as a comparison with more commonly utilized models.

It should be noted that the issues associated with image retrieval for landscapes vary markedly from those associated with image retrieval on traditional color photographs. Whereas a picture of a red ball against the backdrop of green grass and a blue sky exhibits stark within-image pixel differences (i.e., high contrast), the continuous nature of the Earth's surface makes such extreme differences uncommon in landscape qualities like elevation. Similarly, the variability of color in a natural landscape is much less than what is present in photos containing human objects, such as vehicles and clothing. For these reasons, it is worth exploring the utility of DL for image retrieval with landscape data.

2. Methods and Data

Due to the often long computation times incurred by using NN models and in making vector geometry calculations, the code used to create LSE Wisconsin was grouped into three stages: (a) data extraction, (b) a priori modeling, (c) and ad hoc querying. We notably take a different approach from Jasiewicz et al. [10] by using NNs rather than geomorphons, additionally utilizing vegetation data, and allowing users to select a variety of model options. Further, our work is differentiated by the fact that the models make no explicit classification of pixels into various terrain types. In addition to taking advantage of state-of-the-art algorithms, this approach adds the benefit of flexibility.

2.1. Data Extraction

Two freely available remotely sensed data sources were utilized in this project: DEM data and NDVI data (see Figure 1). The DEM data comes from the Wisconsin Department of Natural Resources (DNR), and a 30m DEM resolution was selected to produce reasonable computation times given the size of the state of Wisconsin. This data is available for direct download as a single file from the Wisconsin DNR. Using a command line utility from the Geospatial Data Abstraction Library (GDAL), this single file was retiled into individual .tif files, each 256×256 pixels. Thus, the resulting extent of each .tif was about 7.5 km $\times$ 7.5 km, which resulted in a total of 2510 observations after removing .tif files which were completely empty (i.e., those at Wisconsin's borders). This size balances ease of computation while keeping a user-friendly approach. Medium-sized cities such as Eau Claire and La Crosse can mostly be covered by 1–2 grid cells, whereas larger cities such as Madison and Milwaukee are encompassed by more cells. It also strikes a reasonable balance between substantial terrain and vegetation variation between grid cells on the application, without burdening users with an overwhelming number (i.e., tens of thousands) of small grid cells as selection options.

The vegetation data comes from the National Air and Space Administration's (NASA) Moderate Resolution Imaging Spectroradiometer (MODIS) program, specifically, the 16-Day L3 Global 250 m SIN Grid. Similar to the DEM data, this dataset is available as a single HDF5 file. Using the R Project for Statistical Computing, the single raster was cropped by each of the 2510 DEM .tif files into individual vegetation .tif files. This ensured a one-to-one spatial match of each terrain and vegetation grid cell. The vegetation data come from 5 June 2021 which was selected for several reasons. First, by this point, all of the snow has melted in Wisconsin, and plants are actively growing. At the same time, crops have been planted but are not yet fully grown. The idea behind this was to effectively separate natural vegetation (i.e., prairie and forests) from agriculture. Experiments with vegetation data from later in the growing season did not effectively show the difference between the abundant coniferous forests of northern Wisconsin and the farms commonly found farther south.

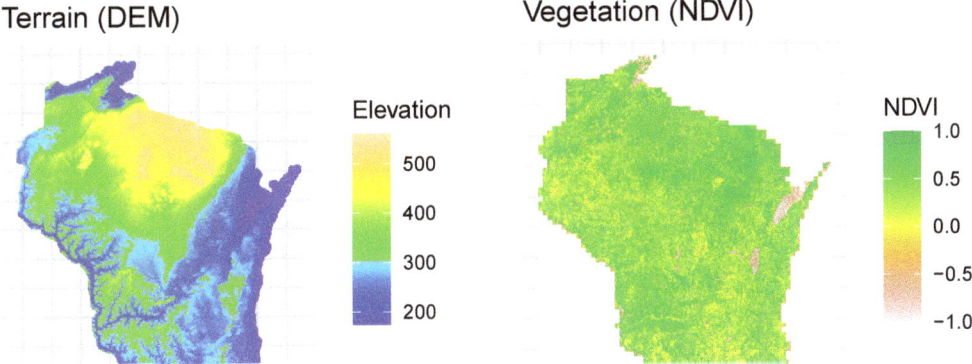

Figure 1. Map of terrain (DEM) and vegetation (NDVI) data.

2.2. A Priori Modeling

The a priori modeling—which only runs once—effectively serves as a data preparation step before the results are handed over to the web application. The majority of this a priori code was developed with Python 3.7 with a small portion being written in the R Project for Statistical Computing. The major steps for the terrain data involved (1) creating feature vectors using NN models, (2) comparing the feature vectors using cosine distance, and (3) using min-max normalization to effectively scale the results. The three NN models selected are benchmark models in TensorFlow and are commonly used in remote sensing, though other models, such as XCeption and Inception, were tested, but were ultimately not utilized due to their apparent poor performance for the task at hand. Though the authors experimented with applying NN models to the vegetation data similarity, it was ultimately discovered that more direct measures of NDVI, e.g., the mean and standard deviation, better captured similarity as the resolution of individual vegetation images was relatively low, which resulted in the NN models struggling to effectively separate these single-band observations with relatively little structural difference.

Model Metrics

In order to create feature vectors, each DEM dataset, stored as a .tif, was first read as a numpy array and resized appropriately based on the required input dimensions of each model. This resizing was accomplished with bilinear sampling. Since the DEM data is effectively a singular band containing one variable—elevation—and NN models often work with three bands (i.e., RGB) images, this singular channel was copied two more times to create an $n \times 3$ array. Each array was then processed through each NN model to create a one-dimensional feature vector.

Following this, each pair of feature vectors was compared using the cosine similarity defined as:

$$\text{cos\_sim} = \frac{A \cdot B}{\|A\| \|B\|}$$

where A is one feature vector and B is another. This is effectively a measure of the angle between two model outputs in vector space, computed by dividing their dot products by their magnitudes. This produces a single value for each pair of images.

In order to scale results between 0 and 1, min-max normalization was used:

$$\text{model\_sim} = \frac{x_{i,j} - min(x)}{max(x) - min(x)}$$

where $x_{i,j}$ represents a single pair of similarity results and x represents the aggregate of all pairs. This was separately completed for each of the three NN models, producing variables `resnet50_sim`, `vgg16_sim`, and `nasnet_sim`. These values were each stored in individual numpy arrays.

After this, the vegetation metrics were computed. The within-image mean NDVI and standard deviation NDVI were each computed, and similarities were computed by retrieving the absolute value of the difference between each pair and then subtracting this value from 1:

$$\text{mean\_ndvi\_sim}'_{i,j} = 1 - abs(\text{ndvi\_mean}_i - \text{ndvi\_mean}_j)$$

$$\text{sd\_ndvi\_sim}'_{i,j} = 1 - abs(\text{ndvi\_sd}_i - \text{ndvi\_sd}_j)$$

These were then min-max normalized to create variables `mean_ndvi_sim` and `mean_sd_sim` and were stored as numpy arrays. Distances (variable `dist`) were also calculated between each image pair and stored in a numpy array.

Finally, the results were aggregated into a SQLite database. Here, each row represents a pair of locations and their corresponding similarity metrics, producing a "tall" rather than "wide" dataset. Since there are 2510 locations in the dataset, the number of rows is equal to the square of the number of locations, i.e., 6,300,100. While this approach produces a reasonable amount of data duplication, leveraging a database in this way allows for shorter query times and more efficient memory usage within the web application. The final database size is a manageable ~450 MB.

2.3. Ad Hoc Querying

The querying of results occurs behind the scenes in the web application, which was created with R's web framework, Shiny [26]. On the application's landing page, users are given several input options:

- Exclusion radius in miles (variable `dist`, values: 0–300): following Tobler's First Law of Geography, it was expected that nearby locations would be highly similar and that users may want to exclude options within a certain distance in order to retrieve results from farther away. The default is 0, meaning that no locations are excluded due to nearness.
- Number of similar locations to retrieve (variable `k`, values: 1–10): The default is 5.
- Terrain model (variable `resnet50_sim`, `vgg16_sim`, or `nasnet_sim`, depending on using input from options "ResNet-50", "VGG16", and "NasNet"): The neural network model to use in comparing results.
- Criteria weight for terrain (variable `terrain_scale`, values of 0–1): Relative weight to use for terrain (default of 0.8). This gives end-users flexibility by allowing them to place more or less emphasis on terrain versus vegetation.
- Criteria weight for NDVI mean vs. NDVI standard deviation (variable `veg_mean_scale`, values 0–1): Relative weight to use for each of the two NDVI variables (default of 1). This allows users to place more or less emphasis on total vegetation (i.e., mean NDVI similarity) versus the amount of NDVI variability (i.e., NDVI standard deviation).

Using these input values with the similarities stored in the database, a "total similarity" metric is computed on-the-fly after a user selects input options and clicks on the "Find Similar Landscapes" button:

$$\text{total\_sim} = (\text{terrain\_scale}_u * \text{model\_sim}) +$$
$$(\text{veg\_scale}_u * ((\text{veg\_mean\_scale}_u * \text{veg\_mean\_sim}) + (\text{veg\_sd\_scale}_u * \text{veg\_sd\_sim}))$$

where

$$\text{veg\_scale}_u = 1 - \text{terrain\_scale}_u$$

and

$$\text{veg\_mean\_scale}_u = 1 - \text{veg\_sd\_scale}_u$$

Here, variables noted with the subscript "u" are either taken from or calculated by user input, whereas the others have been computed a priori and are stored on disk. Effectively, total_sim takes the similarity results and scales them based on the user's desired parameters. This metric represents the combined similarity of terrain and vegetation, enabling users to tailor emphasis on one landscape characteristic or the other to suit a specific use case. The relative weight to place on terrain (terrain_scale$_u$) is multiplied by the terrain similarity scores as computed by the NN models and the cosine distance between the feature vectors (model_sim). Similarly, the weight to place on vegetation (veg_scale$_u$)—which is the additive inverse of the weight placed on terrain—is multiplied by the vegetation similarity results. However, since vegetation similarity considers both NDVI mean similarity (veg_mean_sim) and NDVI standard deviation similarity (veg_sd_sim), the weight to place on each of these vegetation metrics is considered as a part of the larger weight placed on vegetation similarity through the inputs veg_mean_scale$_u$ and veg_sd_scale$_u$, respectively. The metric total_sim could be thought of as simply a weighted average of similarity results scaled by user input options.

Other variables are retrieved from user input and queried from the SQLite database using R's dbplyr package [27] (see Figure 2 for a visual representation of the model). Queries are accomplished quickly due to dbplyr's ability to query databases on disk rather than loading an entire dataset into memory; though users may notice a delay of several seconds, the web application currently operates with only 1 GB of memory and a single CPU core.

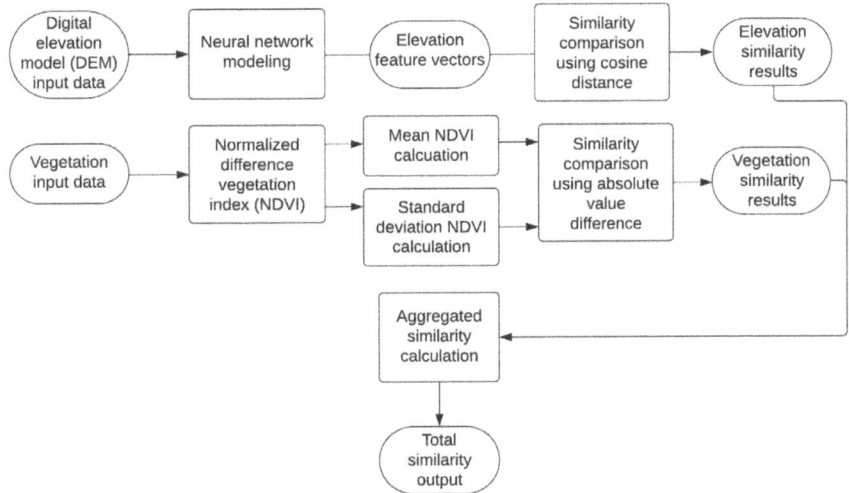

Figure 2. Similarity calculation flowchart.

3. Case Studies

3.1. Observations of General Patterns

In order to better understand how similarity scores are distributed and what the results mean, the authors aggregated the similarity scores of each location pair for every model. Then, the distributions and correlations between measures were investigated. In general, the aggregated similarity scores produced by ResNet-50 and NasNet are highly left-skewed, with NasNet scores being more leptokurtic (Figure 3). This means that these scores are generally closer to a value of 1, or deemed more similar on average. The VGG16 similarity scores, on the other hand, are far more mesokurtic and slightly right-skewed. This means that, for any given pair of landscapes, the ResNet-50 and NasNet scores are more likely to be scored as more similar, though it should be kept in mind that this is simply a function of how the models produce and compare feature vectors. Min-max normalization helps in compensating for non-normality, but, in the end, such transformations do not alter the ordering of similar images, only the way in which they are represented. The vegetation similarity scores are also left-skewed (Figure 4).

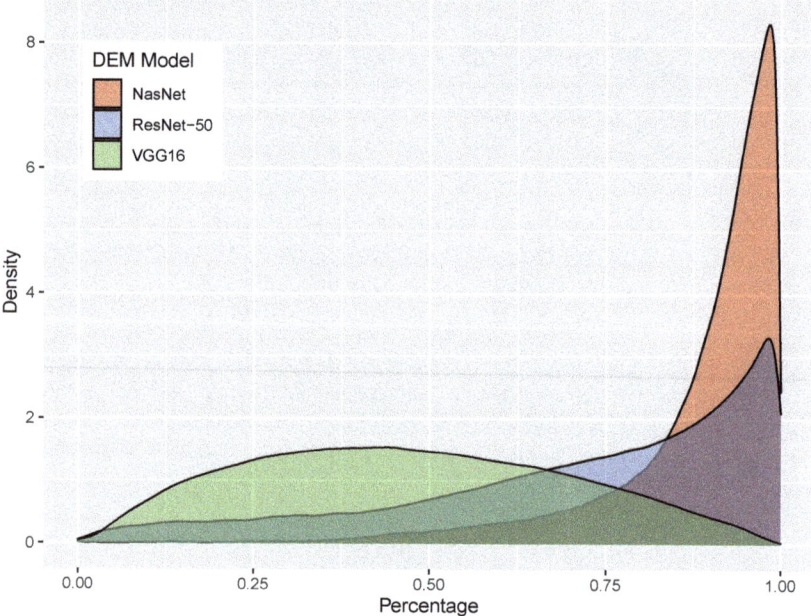

Figure 3. Density plots of neural network model similarities.

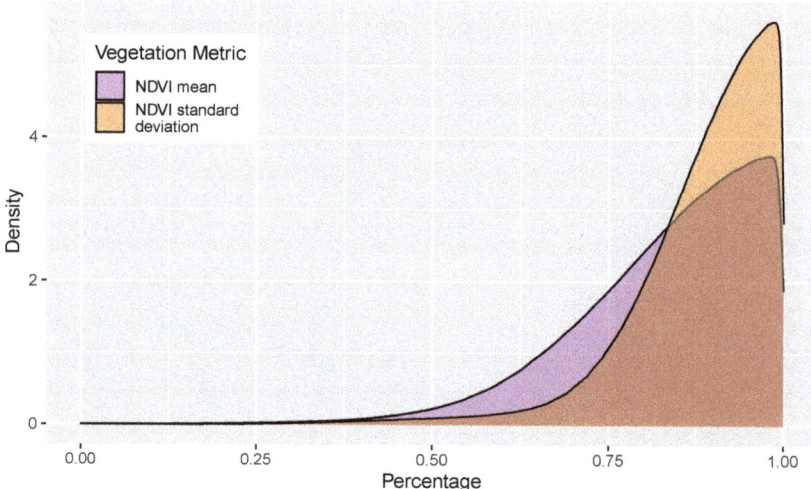

Figure 4. Density plots of NDVI similarities.

A correlogram of all variable pairs helps determine how similar model metrics are in terms of what they fundamentally measure (Figure 5). Pairs with stronger correlations exhibit a higher degree of overlap, while those with weaker correlations manifest distinctive measurements. The inclusion of distance in correlation computations also provides insights into spatial dependence. Spearman's ρ is used due to the non-normal nature of the distributions. Correlations among the variables are generally weak with the exception of the terrain variable pairs:

- resnet50_sim with vgg_16_sim
- resnet50_sim with nasnet_sim
- vgg16_sim with nasnet_sim

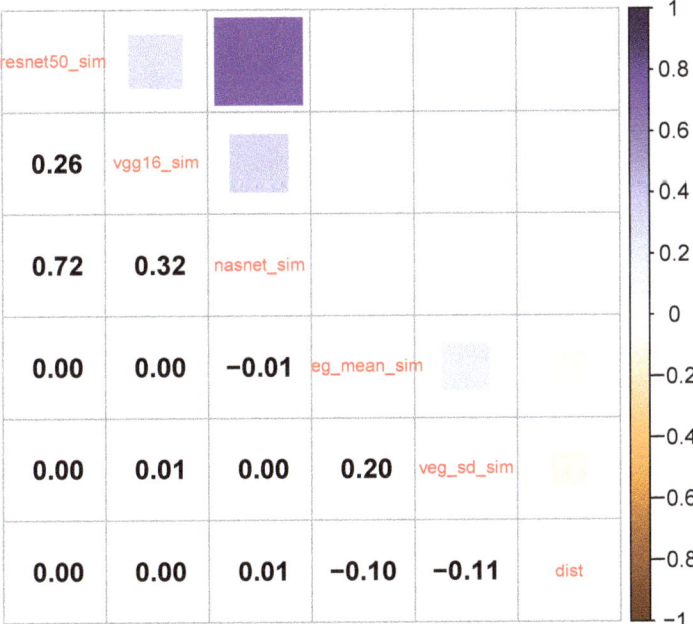

Figure 5. Correlogram of similarity results.

The strongest relationship is between resnet50_sim and nasnet_sim ($\rho = 0.72$), meaning that these variables capture similar things. In turn, this means that vgg16_sim is capturing something relatively unique. Despite the high correlations between ResNet-50 and NasNet, we keep both due to the exploratory nature of the web application. Indeed, in practice, the two do seem to function differently.

There is virtually no correlation between the individual vegetation metrics with any of the terrain metrics. On the surface, this appears counterintuitive as the amount of vegetation in a location is, to a certain degree, dependent on characteristics closely tied to the terrain: lithology, topography, and soil. However, while Wisconsin is far from isotropic, its terrain admittedly does not vary nearly as much as a state like Colorado, which straddles the Rocky Mountains. Following this, very flat locations in the state can have wildly different NDVI values—consider, for example, a location of mostly water and one of flat farmland. Further, given the right skew of most model metrics, yet the low amount of correlation between the terrain and vegetation similarity scores, using these two in tandem to produce the total similarity score is wise, as, importantly, the two combined help separate individual observations.

In general, there is a surprisingly low amount of spatial dependence in the data as evidenced by the small Spearman's ρ correlations of the variable dist with others. In fact, the relationship between dist and veg_mean_sim along with the relationship between dist and `veg_sd_sim` are both negative, meaning that nearby locations are likely to be dissimilar in terms of NDVI. While this is a little surprising given the apparent regional differences in Wisconsin with respect to vegetation, the scale of analysis is such that adjacent locations can indeed vary greatly.

3.2. Individual Locations

Below, we demonstrate the use of the application with three different locations and parameter configurations. These were chosen intentionally to demonstrate both where the search engine appears to function well and where it does not. Additionally, we retrieve similarity results for three different parts of the state with varied terrain features and vegetation types. We attempt to use a variety of different configuration options, though it is not possible to cover them all.

3.2.1. Location A: Western Wisconsin

This location is located in western Wisconsin, just south of the town of Independence Situated in the area commonly referred to as the "Driftless Area" due to its lack of evidence for glaciation, it is characterized by relatively steep ridges and dendritic drainage—that is, the terrain appears like branching tree roots (Figure 6). In retrieving similar landscapes, the following model parameters are used:

- $k = 5$
- `terrain_model` = 'resnet50'
- `terrain_scale` = 0.8
- `veg_mean_scale` = 1.0
- `user_dist` = 0

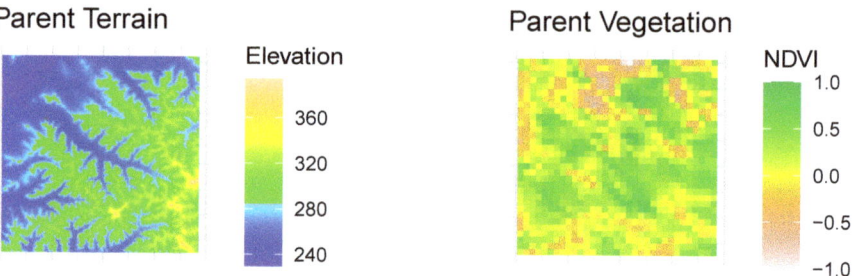

Figure 6. DEM and NDVI rasters for Location A (id = 1521).

These are the default options within the web application. So, if a user were to use the application, click on the same location, and obtain results with no modifications, the exact same result would be obtained. With these default options, the majority of the emphasis is placed on the terrain signature—80%—rather than on the vegetation. Additionally, for the 20% of metric emphasis used on vegetation, 100% is used on the total NDVI and none is used on the NDVI variability. No exclusion distance is used in this case, so results may be obtained for locations at any distance away from the parent location (see Figures 7 and 8, and Table 1 for results).

Despite the fact that matched locations are found at varied distances from the parent location—between 5 and 171 miles away—the model appears to work well with this type of location, as matched instances appear very similar, especially those ranked 1, 2, and 5. The dendritic patterns are clearly visible in these matched locations, just like the parent location. The matched location ranked 1 is also located in the Driftless Area, and the matched location ranked 2 is located in the cell adjacent to the parent location, just to the West.

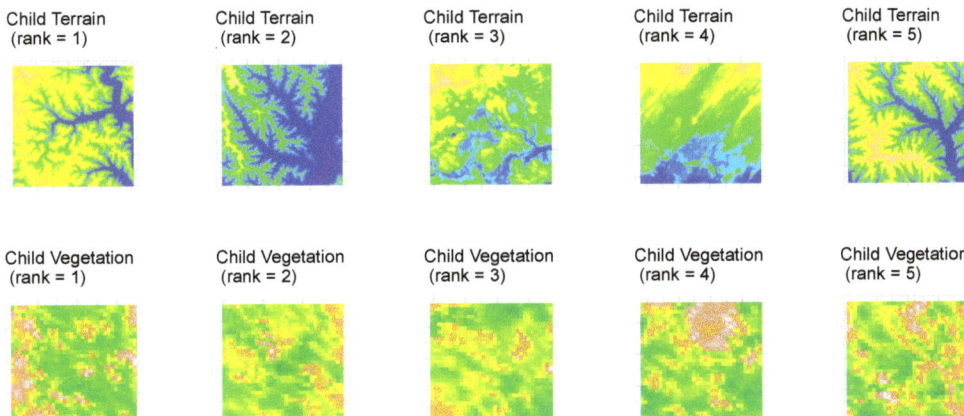

Figure 7. Matched locations for Location A (id = 1521).

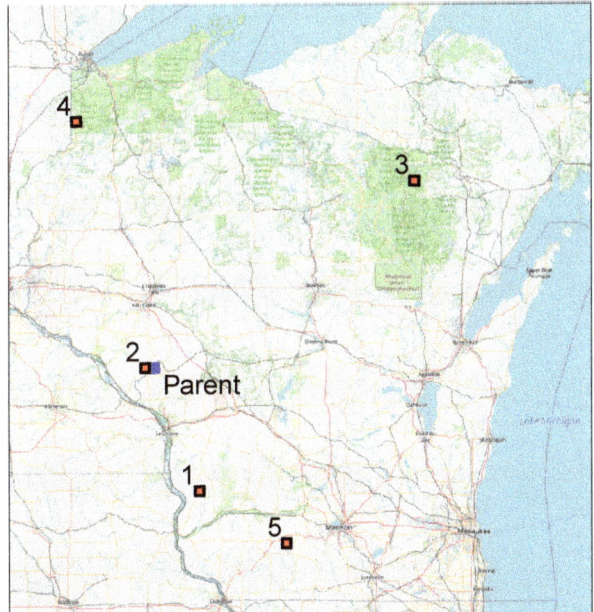

Figure 8. Map of matched locations for Location A (id = 1526, shown in blue) labeled by similarity rank (interactive web map available online).

Table 1. Similarity results from an example query (id = 1521).

Similarity Rank	Distance (mi.)	Total Similarity Score	Resnet-50 Similarity	VGG16 Similatiry	Nasnet Similarity	NDVI Mean Similarity	NDVI SD Similarity	Parent ID	Child ID
1	71	0.974	0.968	0.738	0.953	0.998	0.820	1521	2073
2	5	0.972	0.966	0.349	0.888	0.995	0.980	1521	1520
3	171	0.971	0.970	0.613	0.923	0.973	0.986	1521	450
4	139	0.970	0.967	0.676	0.952	0.985	0.797	1521	150
5	119	0.969	0.972	0.808	0.983	0.957	0.895	1521	2289

3.2.2. Location B: Northern Wisconsin

This location lies in northern Wisconsin in Bayfield County, between the towns of Hayward and Ashland. It is within the Bibon Swamp State Natural Area, and the region is characterized by glacial moraines and a plethora of lakes. While the parent DEM appears to possess significant amounts of water (Figure 9), being in a swamp, this is only the case at certain times of the year. The following model parameters are used:

- `k` = 5
- `terrain_model` = 'vgg16'
- `terrain_scale` = 0.5
- `veg_mean_scale` = 0.9
- `user_dist` = 0

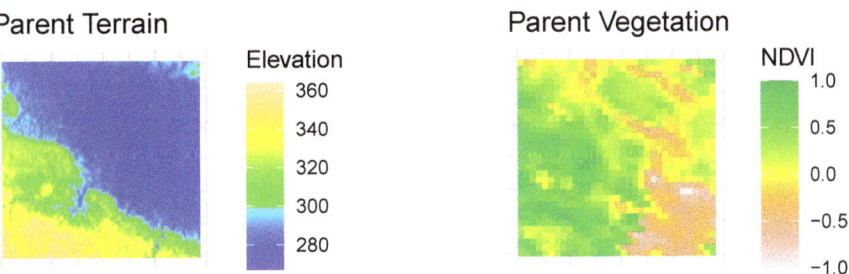

Figure 9. DEM and NDVI rasters for Location B (id = 117).

Equal emphasis is placed on terrain and vegetation, and a small amount of emphasis is placed on NDVI variability (10%). Instead of ResNet-50, VGG16 is used, and the exclusion distance is kept at 0 (Figures 10 and 11, and Table 2 for results).

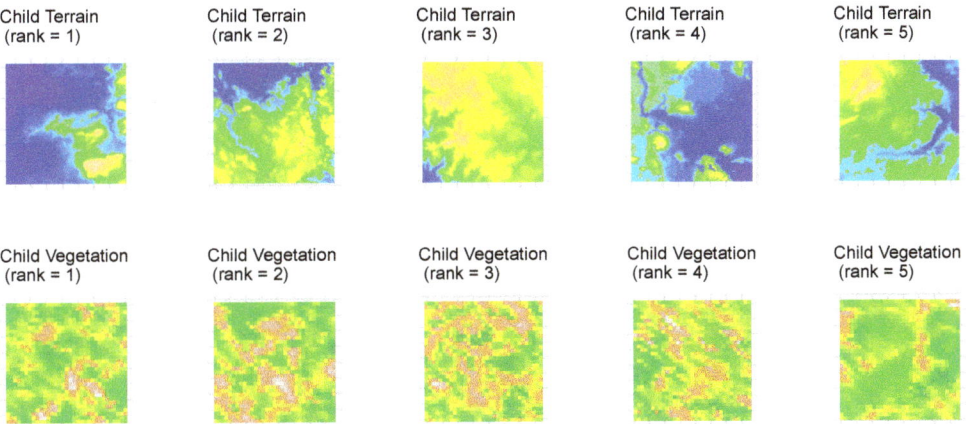

Figure 10. Matched locations for Location B (id = 117).

Table 2. Similarity results from an example query (id = 117).

Similarity Rank	Distance (mi.)	Total Similarity Score	Resnet-50 Similarity	VGG16 Similarity	Nasnet Similarity	NDVI Mean Similarity	NDVI SD Similarity	Parent ID	Child ID
1	183	0.890	0.705	0.812	0.957	0.968	0.959	117	1548
2	226	0.884	0.937	0.811	0.974	0.959	0.942	117	1772
3	124	0.884	0.953	0.840	0.949	0.921	0.983	117	1286
4	194	0.881	0.695	0.785	0.948	0.978	0.965	117	1797
5	283	0.872	0.792	0.831	0.944	0.917	0.872	117	2309

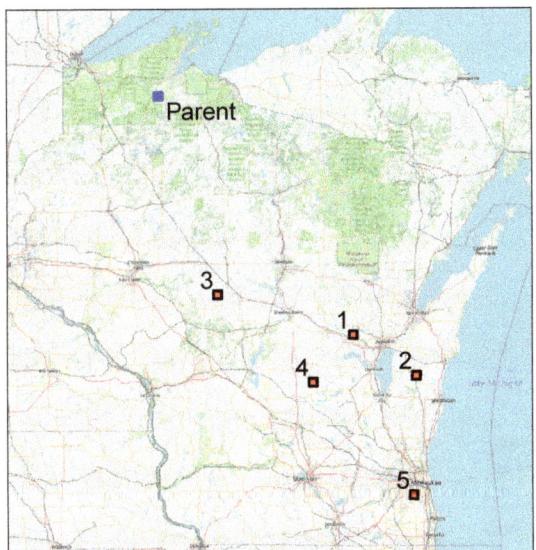

Figure 11. Map of matched locations for Location B (id = 117, shown in blue) labeled by similarity rank (interactive web map available online).

Here, all matched locations are relatively distant as the closest matched location is 124 miles away. That said, all matched locations appear materially similar to the parent location, as most are relatively flat and appear to contain significant portions of water.

3.2.3. Location C: Urban Milwaukee

This is the only urbanized location evaluated in this paper, and it lies in the southeast part of the state near Lake Michigan. The area is relatively flat with moderately low NDVI values (Figure 12). The following parameters are used:

- k = 5
- terrain_model = 'resnet50'
- terrain_scale = 0.2
- veg_mean_scale = 0.5
- user_dist = 150

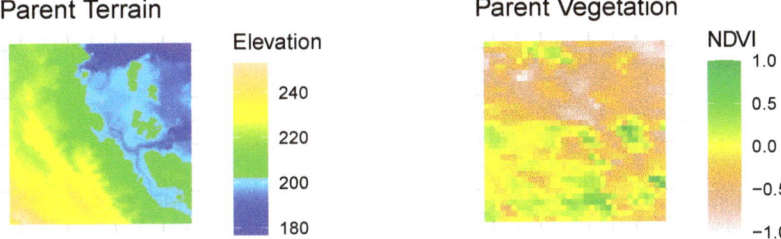

Figure 12. DEM and NDVI rasters for Location C (id = 2276).

Here, the influence of terrain is kept small compared to vegetation. Additionally, vegetation variability carries 50% of the overall vegetation influence. This example also makes use of the exclusion distance metric, as all locations within 150 miles of the parent image are excluded from the results. These results have some intriguing facets that are worth discussing (Figures 13 and 14, and Table 3).

First, the terrain images of the matched locations appear visually dissimilar from the parent location, but this is to be expected with only 20% of the overall metric emphasis placed on terrain. The vegetation images appear to be very similar to the parent location, as they have relatively low NDVI values. Notably, all five matched locations appear in a small group; the distances away from the parent location are 262, 253, 241, 213, and 214 miles respectively, ranked from most similar to least similar. While these are not urban areas they are certainly visually similar based on the criteria utilized. It is also notable that the area containing the cluster of matched locations is the one substantial area of native prairie in Wisconsin.

Though this example exhibits the difficulty in identifying urban areas as similar to other urban areas, land use is not necessarily dependent upon terrain. Further, at the time of year of this NDVI data—early June—vegetation is less dependent on land use for built-up land than later in the growing season. The inclusion of additional datasets, such as true color aerial photographs, or simply using NDVI from a different time of year, would likely change this result.

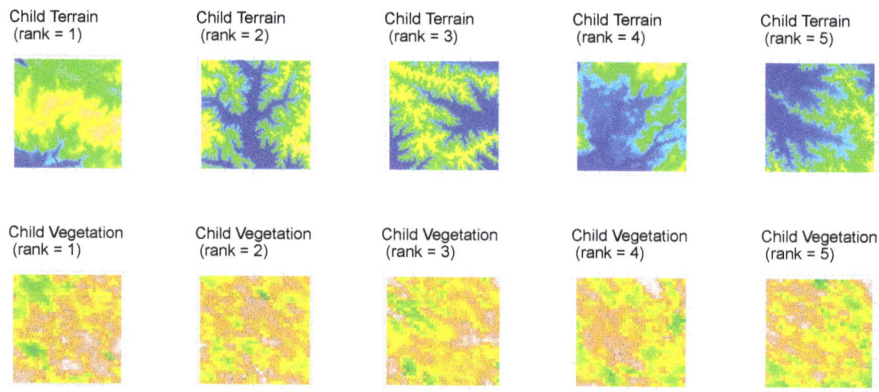

Figure 13. Matched locations for Location C (id = 2276).

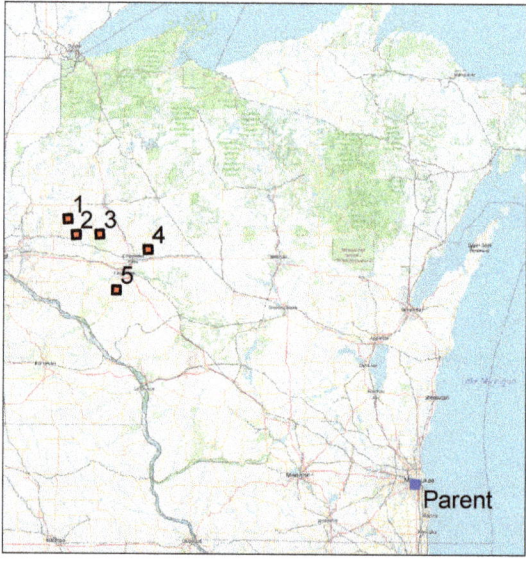

Figure 14. Map of matched locations for Location C (id = 2276, shown in blue) labeled by similarity rank (interactive web map available online).

Table 3. Similarity results from an example query (id = 2276).

Similarity Rank	Distance (mi.)	Total Similarity Score	Resnet-50 Similarity	VGG16 Similarity	Nasnet Similarity	NDVI Mean Similarity	NDVI SD Similarity	Parent ID	Child ID
1	262	0.982	0.964	0.676	0.785	0.995	0.978	2276	767
2	253	0.962	0.971	0.415	0.838	0.994	0.927	2276	873
3	241	0.962	0.916	0.194	0.921	0.971	0.975	2276	876
4	213	0.954	0.861	0.428	0.781	0.961	0.995	2276	996
5	214	0.954	0.892	0.508	0.942	0.943	0.997	2276	1274

4. Discussion

Overall, in the authors' experiments, it appears as though VGG16 and ResNet-50 work best for retrieving similar landscapes. Despite the high degree of correlation between the ResNet-50 and NasNet similarity scores, ResNet-50 nevertheless appears to work better. Due to the near infinite number of potential parameter combinations, it is not practical to demonstrate the application using every configuration option and not even with every NN model. The authors leave this further exploration up to the reader. The development of this introductory tool provides a meaningful first step in the domain of NN-based landscape search engines, but, despite the application's utility, its approach is not without drawbacks. Future implementations could improve upon LSE Wisconsin in a variety of ways, yet many of the limitations point to need for a robust, multi-input custom NN architecture designed specifically for landscapes. The subsequent discussion echoes this point.

First, higher resolution data encompassing smaller areas may allow for more tangible applications, especially given the low amount of spatial dependence in the data. Lidar-derived 1 m DEM, for instance, could be used in place of the terrain data utilized in LSE Wisconsin. This would, however, increase the end dataset size by a factor of 90, placing considerable strain on a web server equipped with 1GB of memory at the time of writing.

Second, one of the most salient limitations is that all models appear, at least to some degree, to struggle in comparing locations covered by large amounts of water. The inclusion of water as a discrete variable in a multi-input NN model would appear prudent, but there can be considerable variation in where water is actually present throughout Wisconsin, particularly in its wide-ranging marshes in the northern part of the state.

Related to this, vegetation data from multiple time periods would allow for different types of comparisons. For instance, giving users the option to select a time period later in the summer may help differentiate urban areas from agricultural land use better, as elucidated in the Milwaukee example. Indeed, such issues would be resolved by the use of a custom NN architecture with several inputs—e.g., terrain, multiple vegetation datasets, land use, aerial photography, and others—but such an approach is inhibited by the inherent subjectivity of "similarity", not to mention a lack of remote sensing test datasets for such problems. Survey-based research would be beneficial in quantifying the degree of landscape likeness. An approach such as the one implemented by Wang et al. [28] with remote sensing scientists would be useful; appropriately ranking a set of images could be used as a test dataset for a custom NN architecture.

Other more obvious extensions include applying this approach to other US states, other locations entirely, or expanding the approach to include an entire country. Such a foray would be ambitious, however, given the necessity of using large, potentially disparate datasets outside of Landsat-derived products. Another ambitious improvement would be in giving users the ability to input their own terrain and/or vegetation datasets for evaluation, though this would require feature vector comparison on-the-fly. Moreover, the increasing availability of user-derived datasets using unmanned aerial systems (UAS) presents opportunities also worth considering for additional improvements. Future work is needed by domain experts to help fine-tune LSE Wisconsin for real use cases and to direct future development.

5. Conclusions

This paper introduced a methodology for constructing a neural-network-based landscape search engine and presented a corresponding web application. This is the first tool of its kind for the U.S. state of Wisconsin, and, to the authors' knowledge, it is the first landscape search engine tool that uses NN for landscape search. Through this paper, the authors have demonstrated that benchmark NN models can indeed work for image retrieval with landscape data, and VGG16 and ResNet-50 appear to be the most promising models. Despite the models struggling in locations with significant amounts of water, as it stands now, LSE Wisconsin could nevertheless be used directly for location analysis applications. This tool marks an important step in the application of image retrieval on remotely sensed datasets, and additional domain applications are likely to emerge with time. Further, the authors hope that LSE Wisconsin ultimately pushes the research community toward a more robust, multi-input landscape search engine tool in the future.

Author Contributions: M.H. was the project lead. He created the web application, aided in a priori modeling, and participated in writing the paper; M.D. took the lead on a priori modeling and neural network conceptualization. He also participated in writing the paper; G.A.O.-M. contributed to the remote sensing conceptual framework, application testing, and writing of the paper; P.F.R. contributed to the remote sensing conceptual framework, application testing, and writing of the paper. All authors have read and agreed to the published version of the manuscript.

Funding: This project was supported by the Office of Research and Sponsored Programs at the University of Wisconsin-Eau Claire through its Summer Research Experiences for Undergraduates Program.

Data Availability Statement: The data used in this project is available at https://gitlab.com/mhaffner/lse-wi/data.

Acknowledgments: The authors would like to thank the three anonymous reviewers for their helpful comments and suggestions.

Conflicts of Interest: The authors declare no conflict of interest. The founding sponsors had no role in the design of the study; in the collection, analyses, or interpretation of data; in the writing of the manuscript; or in the decision to publish the results.

Sample Availability: The web application is available at https://uwec-geog.shinyapps.io/lse-wi/ (accessed on 6 August 2023). The source code for the web application is available at https://gitlab.com/mhaffner/lse-wi. The source code for the data extraction and a priori modeling is available at https://gitlab.com/mhaffner/landscape-search-engine.

Abbreviations

The following abbreviations are used in this manuscript:

CNN	Convolutional Neural Network
DEM	Digital Elevation Model
NDVI	Normalized Difference Vegetation Index
NN	Neural Network
NN	NasNet
DL	Deep Learning
USGS	United States Geological Survey
DNR	Department of Natural Resources
GDAL	Geospatial Data Abstraction Library
GIScience	Geographic Information Science
NASA	National Air and Space Administration
MODIS	Moderate Resolution Imaging Spectrometer
VGG	Visual Geometry Group

References

1. Ma, L.; Liu, Y.; Zhang, X.; Ye, Y.; Yin, G.; Johnson, B.A. Deep learning in remote sensing applications: A meta-analysis and review. *ISPRS J. Photogramm. Remote Sens.* **2019**, *152*, 166–177. [CrossRef]
2. Pei, H.; Owari, T.; Tsuyuki, S.; Zhong, Y. Application of a Novel Multiscale Global Graph Convolutional Neural Network to Improve the Accuracy of Forest Type Classification Using Aerial Photographs. *Remote Sens.* **2023**, *15*, 1001.
3. Yuan, Q.; Shen, H.; Li, T.; Li, Z.; Li, S.; Jiang, Y.; Xu, H.; Tan, W.; Yang, Q.; Wang, J.; et al. Deep learning in environmental remote sensing: Achievements and challenges. *Remote Sens. Environ.* **2020**, *241*, 111716. [CrossRef]
4. Xia, F.; Lou, Z.; Sun, D.; Li, H.; Quan, L. Weed resistance assessment through airborne multimodal data fusion and deep learning: A novel approach towards sustainable agriculture. *Int. J. Appl. Earth Obs. Geoinf.* **2023**, *120*, 103352. [CrossRef]
5. Wen, L.; Cheng, Y.; Fang, Y.; Li, X. A comprehensive survey of oriented object detection in remote sensing images. *Expert Syst. Appl.* **2023**, *224*, 119960. [CrossRef]
6. Li, Z.; Wang, Y.; Zhang, N.; Zhang, Y.; Zhao, Z.; Xu, D.; Ben, G.; Gao, Y. Deep Learning-Based Object Detection Techniques for Remote Sensing Images: A Survey. *Remote Sens.* **2022**, *14*, 2385. [CrossRef]
7. Li, J.; Hong, D.; Gao, L.; Yao, J.; Zheng, K.; Zhang, B.; Chanussot, J. Deep learning in multimodal remote sensing data fusion: A comprehensive review. *Int. J. Appl. Earth Obs. Geoinf.* **2022**, *112*, 102926. [CrossRef]

8. Chen, J.; Hong, H.; Song, B.; Guo, J.; Chen, C.; Xu, J. MDCT: Multi-Kernel Dilated Convolution and Transformer for One-Stage Object Detection of Remote Sensing Images. *Remote Sens.* **2023**, *15*, 371. [CrossRef]
9. Li, Y.; Zhang, H.; Xue, X.; Jiang, Y.; Shen, Q. Deep learning for remote sensing image classification: A survey. *WIREs Data Min Knowl. Discov.* **2018**, *8*, e1264. [CrossRef]
10. Jasiewicz, J.; Netzel, P.; Stepinski, T.F. Landscape similarity, retrieval, and machine mapping of physiographic units. *Geomorphology* **2014**, *221*, 104–112. . [CrossRef]
11. Dilts, T.E.; Yang, J.; Weisberg, P.J. The Landscape Similarity Toolbox: New tools for optimizing the location of control sites in experimental studies. *Ecography* **2010**, *33*, 1097–1101. . [CrossRef]
12. Pilliod, D.S.; Jeffries, M.I.; Welty, J. Land Treatment Exploration Tool. Available online: https://susy.mdpi.com/user/assigned/production_form/1c6eec251f1a7967167a5f989ab777ab (accessed on 6 August 2023).
13. Gomes, R.; Kamrowski, C.; Langlois, J.; Rozario, P.; Dircks, I.; Grottodden, K.; Martinez, M.; Tee, W.Z.; Sargeant, K.; LaFleur, C.; et al. A Comprehensive Review of Machine Learning Used to Combat COVID-19. *Diagnostics* **2022**, *12*, 1853. [CrossRef] [PubMed]
14. Simonyan, K.; Zisserman, A. Very Deep Convolutional Networks for Large-Scale Image Recognition. In Proceedings of the International Conference on Learning Representations, San Diego, CA, USA, 7–9 May 2015.
15. Ye, M.; Ruiwen, N.; Chang, Z.; He, G.; Tianli, H.; Shijun, L.; Yu, S.; Tong, Z.; Ying, G. A Lightweight Model of VGG-16 for Remote Sensing Image Classification. *IEEE J. Sel. Top. Appl. Earth Obs. Remote Sens.* **2021**, *14*, 6916–6922. [CrossRef]
16. Ganakwar, P.; Date, S. Convolutional neural network-VGG16 for road extraction from remotely sensed images. *Int. J. Res. Appl. Sci. Eng. Technol. (IJRASET)* **2020**, *8*, 916–922. [CrossRef]
17. Khaleghian, S.; Ullah, H.; Kræmer, T.; Hughes, N.; Eltoft, T.; Marinoni, A. Sea Ice Classification of SAR Imagery Based on Convolution Neural Networks. *Remote Sens.* **2021**, *13*, 1734. [CrossRef]
18. Zhu, F.; Li, J.; Zhu, B.; Li, H.; Liu, G. UAV remote sensing image stitching via improved VGG16 Siamese feature extraction network. *Expert Syst. Appl.* **2023**, *229*, 120525. [CrossRef]
19. He, K.; Zhang, X.; Ren, S.; Sun, J. Deep Residual Learning for Image Recognition. *arXiv* **2015**. [CrossRef]
20. Alsabhan, W.; Alotaiby, T. Automatic Building Extraction on Satellite Images Using Unet and ResNet50. *Comput. Intell. Neurosci.* **2022**, *2022*, 5008854. [CrossRef]
21. Jian, X.; Yunquan, Z.; Yue, Q. Remote Sensing Image Classification Based on Different Convolutional Neural Network Models. In Proceedings of the 2021 6th International Symposium on Computer and Information Processing Technology (ISCIPT), Changsha, China, 11–13 June 2021; pp. 312–316. [CrossRef]
22. Firat, H.; Hanbay, D. Classification of Hyperspectral Images Using 3D CNN Based ResNet50. In Proceedings of the 2021 29th Signal Processing and Communications Applications Conference (SIU), Istanbul, Turkey, 9–11 June 2021; pp. 1–4. [CrossRef]
23. Liu, C.; Zhao, R.; Shi, Z. Remote-Sensing Image Captioning Based on Multilayer Aggregated Transformer. *IEEE Geosci. Remote Sens. Lett.* **2022**, *19*, 1–5. [CrossRef]
24. Alafandy, K.A.; Omara, H.; Lazaar, M.; Achhab, M.A. Using Classic Networks for Classifying Remote Sensing Images: Comparative Study. *Adv. Sci. Technol. Eng. Syst. J.* **2020**, *5*, 770–780. [CrossRef]
25. Li, L.; Tian, T.; Li, H. Classification of Remote Sensing Scenes Based on Neural Architecture Search Network. In Proceedings of the 2019 IEEE 4th International Conference on Signal and Image Processing (ICSIP), Wuxi, China, 19–21 July 2019; pp. 176–180. [CrossRef]
26. Chang, W.; Cheng, J.; Allaire, J.; Sievert, C.; Schloerke, B.; Xie, Y.; Allen, J.; McPherson, J.; Dipert, A.; Borges, B. *Shiny: Web Application Framework for R*, R package version 1.7.1.; 2021.
27. Wickham, H.; Girlich, M.; Ruiz, E. *Dbplyr: A 'Dplyr' Back End for Databases*, R package version 2.2.0.; 2022.
28. Wang, Z.; Bovik, A.; Sheikh, H.; Simoncelli, E. Image quality assessment: From error visibility to structural similarity. *IEEE Trans. Image Process.* **2004**, *13*, 600–612. [CrossRef] [PubMed]

Disclaimer/Publisher's Note: The statements, opinions and data contained in all publications are solely those of the individual author(s) and contributor(s) and not of MDPI and/or the editor(s). MDPI and/or the editor(s) disclaim responsibility for any injury to people or property resulting from any ideas, methods, instructions or products referred to in the content.

Development of a Web Application for the Detection of Coronary Artery Calcium from Computed Tomography

Juan Aguilera-Alvarez [1], Juan Martínez-Nolasco [2,*], Sergio Olmos-Temois [3], José Padilla-Medina [4], Víctor Sámano-Ortega [1] and Micael Bravo-Sanchez [1]

1. Doctorado en Ciencias de la Ingeniería, Tecnológico Nacional de México/IT de Celaya, Celaya 38010, Mexico
2. Departamento de Ingeniería Mecatrónica, Tecnológico Nacional de México/IT de Celaya, Celaya 38010, Mexico
3. Departamento de Cardiología, Centro Médico Quirúrgico, Celaya 38000, Mexico
4. Departamento de Ingeniería Electrónica, Tecnológico Nacional de México/IT de Celaya, Celaya 38010, Mexico
* Correspondence: juan.martinez@itcelaya.edu.mx

Abstract: Coronary atherosclerosis is the most common form of cardiovascular diseases, which represent the leading global cause of mortality in the adult population. The amount of coronary artery calcium (CAC) is a robust predictor of this disease that can be measured using the medical workstations of computed tomography (CT) equipment or specialized tools included in commercial software for DICOM viewers, which is not available for all operating systems. This manuscript presents a web application that semiautomatically quantifies the amount of coronary artery calcium (CAC) on the basis of the coronary calcium score (CS) using the Agatston technique through digital image processing. To verify the correct functioning of this web application, 30 CTCSs were analyzed by a cardiologist and compared to those of commercial software (OsiriX DICOM Viewer).All the scans were correctly classified according to the cardiovascular event risk group, with an average error in the calculation of CS of 1.9% and a Pearson correlation coefficient r = 0.9997, with potential clinical application.

Keywords: Agatston score; computed tomography; coronary artery calcium; image processing; web application

1. Introduction

The World Health Organization indicates that 17.9 million people died from cardiovascular diseases in 2019, which represent 32% of all deaths worldwide [1]. Atherosclerosis is a progressive disease characterized by the accumulation of lipids and fibrous elements in the large arteries, and it is the primary cause of heart disease and stroke [2]. Atherosclerosis is closely related to the calcified plaque detected in coronary arteries [3,4], which is known as coronary artery calcium (CAC), and its detection is considered to be one of the strongest indicators to predict the presence of atherosclerosis in patients who do not have symptoms yet [5–7]. The most common way to detect CAC is through a cardiac computed tomography (CT) for calcium scoring (CTCS), which consists of a noncontrast enhanced CT of the heart [8], which is interpreted by quantifying the coronary calcium score (CS) in terms of the Agatston score [9–11]. CS is determined on CTCS by identifying calcified lesions that are represented on CT as pixel islands with an intensity greater than 130 Hounsfield units (HU) belonging to one of the coronary arteries: left main (LM), left anterior descending (LAD), circumflex (CX), and right coronary artery (RCA) [9].

Digital image processing provides techniques frequently used in the identification of CAC, for example, the design of automatic algorithms to obtain CS, the segmentation of coronary arteries, and the relationship between other clinical indicators and CAC. For the development of these studies, some researchers use open-source medical image processing software such as 3DSlicer [12] to manually segment lesions or regions of interest (ROIs) the manually obtained information is supplied to computed or statistical systems for analysis and/or interpretation [13–15]. Another open-source software option is ImageJ [16] which, in addition to allowing for manual operations with images, allows for developers to use predefined semiautomatic functions and the possibility of creating custom macros or plugins to automate some image process analyses [17–21]. An alternative to the previously defined software is the use of the OpenCV open-source library [21] which allows for implementing more complete image processing techniques through predefined classes and functions [22–25].

The development of applications with web technology has increased significantly because they present advantages such as (1) no installation required, (2) automatic updates and (3) universal access form any device connected to the internet [26]. Web applications have been developed in medicine [27–29] especially during COVID-19 [30–32], academia [33,34], ecology [35,36], and biology [37,38], among others [39–41]. This article presents a web application to determine the CAC on the basis of the Agatston score evaluated with digital processing techniques in the corresponding images included in a CTCS.

2. Materials and Methods

The web application uses CTCS scans to perform the semiautomatic calculation of the CS in the lesions defined by the specialist in cardiovascular medicine. Its implementation required three stages: (1) image processing and the calculation of results, (2) the programming of the web page, and (3) the deployment of the application on the Internet (Figure 1) The backend was programmed in the Python language, and the frontend was developed with the HTML, CSS, and JavaScript languages. The web application was mounted onto a virtual private server (VPS), so that users could use it from any device with an Internet connection. A physician with a specialty in cardiology and 10 years of experience in the field compared the results of the web application with the results of the OsiriX DICOM Viewer software, which is the application that the cardiologist uses daily. Two filters were proposed to remove noise from to the image, so three CS values were evaluated, Pearson's correlation coefficient was calculated for each of the assessments performed in comparison with the reference OsiriX DICOM viewer software, and the diagnoses issued by the specialist were also compared with the total CS value per scan for each developed method. Lastly, the risk of a. cardiovascular event corresponding to each of the studies according to the classification given by the CS was compared with the reference.

2.1. Calculation of the Coronary Calcium Score

For the calculation of CS in the coronary arteries, the calcified lesions represented on the CT as pixel islands with intensity greater than 130 HU located in one of the four coronary arteries (LM, LAD, CX, and RCA) are identified. Figure 2 shows an example of a lesion of each of the ROIs identified with different colors (LM: red, LAD: blue, CX: yellow, and RCA: green). In addition, pixel islands with an intensity greater than 130 HU are shown that were not part of any of the coronary arteries (such as bones); these islands were identified as None (cyan).

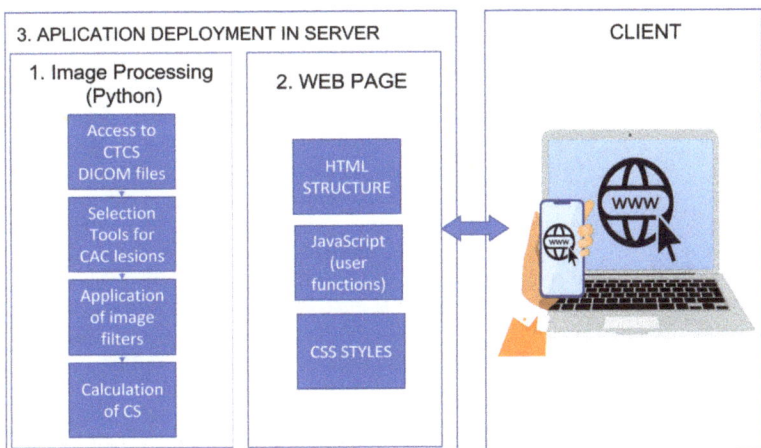

Figure 1. Stages of web application development.

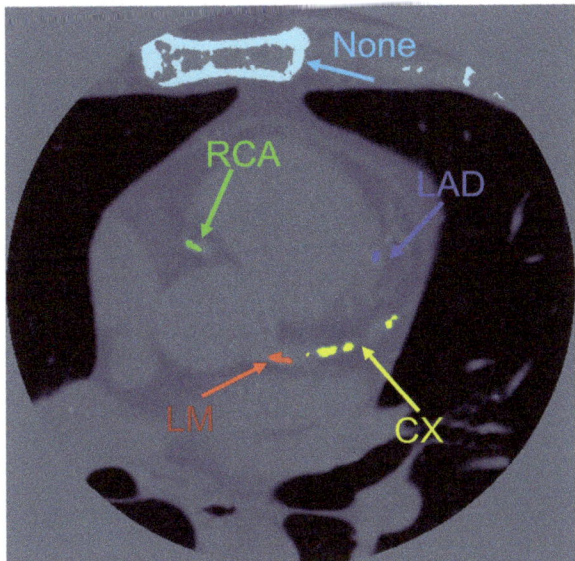

Figure 2. Example of islands of pixels with an intensity greater than 130 HU and their labels.

The CS in terms of the Agatston score is an indicator of the presence of coronary artery disease (CAD) and determines the presence of atherosclerosis in patients who do not even have symptoms [5–7].

To calculate the Agatston score, the density score (F) is used, which depends directly on the maximal HU value of the lesion. The possible values of F are (a) F = 1 if $130 \leq HUmax \leq 199$, (b) F = 2 if $200 \leq HUmax \leq 299$, (c) F = 3 if $300 \leq HUmax \leq 399$, (d) F = 4 if $400 \leq HUmax$ [9]. In addition, the area (a) of the calcified lesion in mm^2 was evaluated. Equation (1) was used to evaluate the CS, where n represents the number of lesions.

$$CS = \sum_{i=1}^{n} F_1 \times a_1 \tag{1}$$

In the calculation of CS, islands of pixels with an area of less than 1 mm^2 were not considered because it was established as such in the medical protocol [9].

2.2. Image Dataset

The dataset was integrated with 80 CTCS scans obtained in three hospitals that had different tomographic equipment. This implies that each scan has a different pixel area measurement that is obtained from the header of the DICOM file, and all images were reconstructed to 2.5 mm slice thickness. In the conformation of the database, 30 scans (Hospital 1: 15 scans, Hospital 2: 9 scans, Hospital 3: 6 scans) were chosen to have a representative sample of each cardiovascular event risk group: moderate ($10 < CS \leq 100$), moderate–high ($100 < CS \leq 400$), and high ($CS > 400$), the former due to the fact that they presented a greater number of lesions per scan, obtaining more information compared to the groups of very low ($CS = 0$) or low ($0 < CS \leq 10$) in which the number of pixel islands is minimal. To calculate the CS, the web application accesses the tags from the DICOM files (1) 0028,000A—columns, (2) 0028,0010—rows, (3) 0028,0030—pixel spacing, (4) 0028,0102—high bit, (5) 0028,1052—rescale intercept. No patient name or other information is necessary, so anonymous scans are possible to load.

2.3. Image Processing

In this stage, the Pydicom and OpenCV Python libraries are used. With Pydicom [42], DICOM files with information compatible to Python were integrated. With the OpenCV library [43], conversion, binarization and filtering operations were performed on the images obtained from Pydicom. To evaluate the CS, the lesions of each slice of the CTCS scan were selected; consequently, the image processing algorithm performs the following functions (Figure 3): (1) open the image set and navigate through the slices, (2) identify pixel areas greater than 130 HU, (3) select lesions of calcium in the arteries, adding labels according to the corresponding coronary artery (LAD, LM, CX, and RCA). The original image is represented in HU and is converted into a grayscale map, so that the user can easily identify the elements that comprise the CT image (Grayscale). Later, this image is represented in RGB format to obtain an image with color. With the original image (HU), two binary images are also generated. In the first, pixels with HU values greater than or equal to 130 HU are labeled with a "1", and in the second, pixels with HU values less than 130 HU are labeled "1". From the image with pixels $\geq$ 130 HU, an image (Labeling) with islands of labeled pixels is obtained that is used to obtain information that allows for finding the relationship between possible lesions and the corresponding coronary artery (Selected Calcifications). To obtain the image that is shown to the user (Final Image), areas greater than 130 HU are extracted from the RGB image, and the result is added to the Selected Calcifications image.

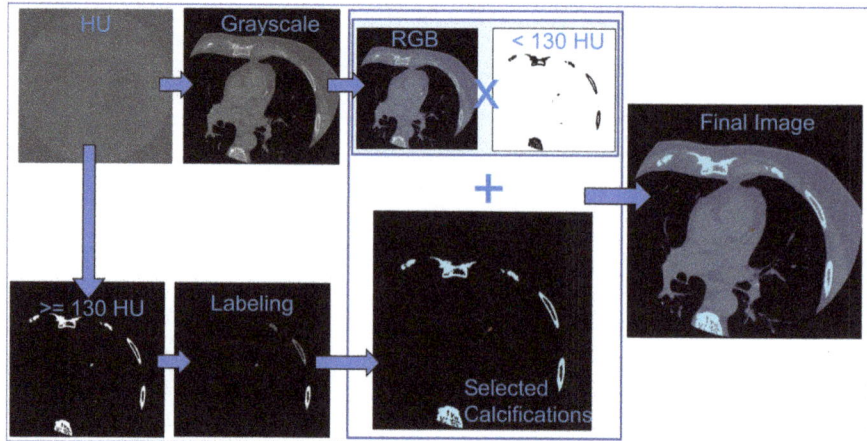

Figure 3. Digital processing of computed tomography images.

Each time the user points to a pixel island (Figure 4), it is labeled with the selected coronary artery (LAD, LM, CX and RCA), saving the relationship of each of the lesions in a Python list and changing the color of the island of pixels by that corresponding to the artery. The application calculates the area of the selected lesion. If the area is greater than or equal to 1 mm^2, the corresponding density score is calculated. Since there may be variations in the CTCS due to the size of the patient and the calibration of the tomographic equipment, increasing the final value of the CS [44], the application of two additional processing techniques for the attenuation of the variations was proposed, and three different density scores were calculated. The first density score (F1) corresponds to the selected island of pixels as proposed by Agatston [9]. The second proposed density score (F2) is calculated after the application of a Gaussian blur filter that was programmed with the GaussianBlur function that is included in the OpenCV library. The third proposed density score (F3) is calculated after applying a classification criterion that checks that the maximal intensity values. Maintaining a minimal mode, the algorithm separates the pixels into three groups according to their intensity level. The first group contains the pixels with an intensity greater than or equal to 400 HU (F = 4), the second group the pixels with an intensity greater than or equal to 300 HU (F = 3), and the third group the pixels with an intensity greater than or equal to 200 HU (F = 2). To obtain the resulting F, it is necessary to examine whether the number of pixels in each group maintains the minimal programmed mode; if more than one group meets the sufficient area, the highest density score is considered to be correct; if none of the groups meets the minimal pixel condition, then F = 1 (default value). Once the F values are obtained for each of the proposed methods (F1, F2, F3), a CS is calculated for each F of the selected lesion, and its value is added to the corresponding total CS as indicated in Equation (1).

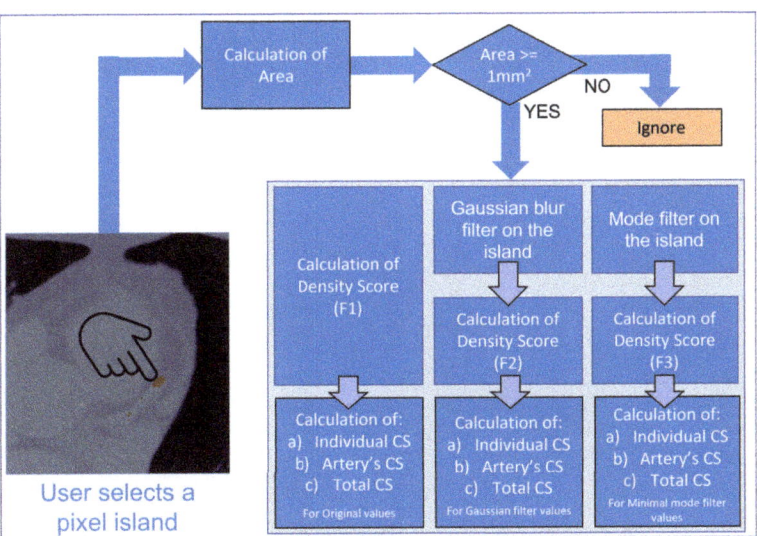

Figure 4. CS calculation flow.

2.4. Validation of Image Processing Calculation Results

To validate the CS calculation proposals, a medical specialist in cardiovascular imaging evaluated CS in each of the studies using the CS plugin of the OsiriX DICOM Viewer software, which is the application he uses daily, and then evaluated the studies selecting the same lesions using the developed image processing tool. The results obtained in the image processing tool are as follows: (1) before applying any processing (Original), (2) after applying the Gaussian filter (Gaussian) to the original image, (3) after applying the minimal mode algorithm (MinMode) to the original image. In this way, the CS results obtained for each density score were compared: (1) OsiriX vs. Original, (2) OsiriX vs. Gaussian, (3) OsiriX vs. MinMode.

2.5. Programming the Web Page and HTTP Requests

The web page was programmed using HTML, CSS, JavaScript, and the Python Flask library. Python is the programming language of the backend of the application, so the Flask instructions allow for transferring the results of image processing and CS calculation to the user interface (frontend) compiled with HTML code and Jinja2 (Used by Flask), in addition to performing traditional HTTP requests (GET or POST). The CSS language is used to define the styles of the page and JavaScript for the interaction and the request of HTTP requests (POST and GET). The requests were through AJAX functions and JSON codes which allows for the partial and asynchronous updating of the page, obtaining fluency in the interaction. The responses sent by the server are the image resulting from using some of the available functions and the results of the CS calculations. The responses are transferred back using JSON codes again; the resulting JPEG image is encoded with the base64 positional numbering system. The HTTP requests from the application (Figure 5) are the following: (a) increase and decrease the Z position of the set of images. This request helps in navigating through the different slices that the entire CTCS contains. The client performs one of the two GET requests (increase or decrease), and the server modifies the Z position and responds with the corresponding slice image. (b) Activate coronary artery This is a POST-type request where the client selects the label of the artery with which they want to indicate the lesions. The server receives the selected label and responds with a confirmation, which is reflected in the arteries menu on the web page. (c) Label the calcium lesion. The user can label the lesions by directly selecting the islands of pixels on the image, and the lesion is labeled according to the artery that is active at that moment. The server receives a POST-type request with the X, Y coordinates of the selected pixel, processes the image, performs the CS calculations, and responds to the client with the new image and the obtained results. In addition, a relational database was used for the administration of the users and the CTCS scans uploaded to the application by each of the users. The mysqlclient and SQLAlchemy Python libraries were used for the creation, migration, and updating of the database.

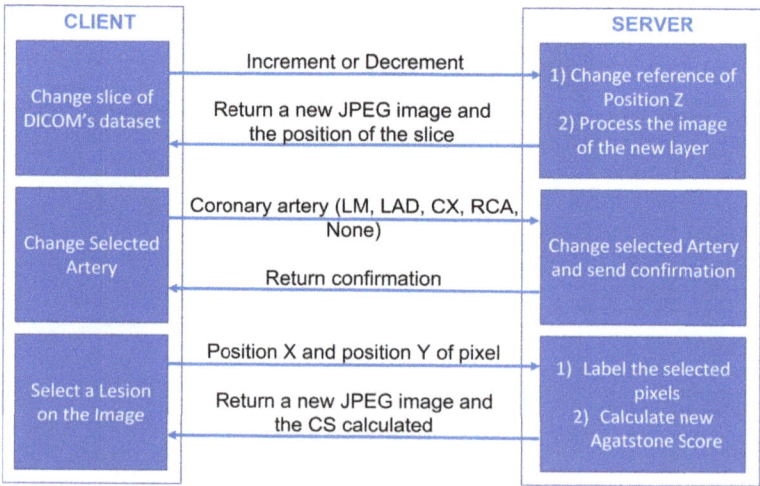

Figure 5. User functions in the web page.

2.6. Setting Up the Application on the Internet

The application was set up on a VPS with Ubuntu 20.04 operating system with NginX services to offer the web service and MariaDB for the database compatible with MySQL.

Using the Python Virtualenv library, a Python 3.8 virtual environment was created with the Pydicom, OpenCV, Flask, and Gunicorn libraries. The used VPS had 4 vCPU cores, 200 GB SSD, and 8 GB of RAM. A system service was activated for the application to have nonstop availability.

3. Results

3.1. CS Calculation and Validation

The diagnoses issued by the specialist were compared with the total CS value per scan for each of the density score calculation methods (Original, Gaussian, MinMode), and the average error was calculated between each of the comparisons, obtaining the following errors: (a) OsiriX vs. Original = 3.8%, (b) OsiriX vs. Gaussian= 4.7%, (c) Osirix vs. MinMode = 1.9%. Another characteristic that was compared was the risk of cardiovascular event corresponding to each of the studies according to the classification given by the CS. Of the 30 studies carried out with the OsiriX software, 7 belonged to the Moderate risk group, 10 to the Moderate–High group, and 13 to the High risk group. The Original function did not correctly classify 1 study as belonging to Moderate–High risk, while the functions with additional processing (Gaussian and MinMode) correctly classified all studies regarding to the results obtained with OsiriX. Figure 6 shows the results of the total CS of each one of the studies where the difference in the results of CS with each of the proposed methods is observed and the limits of the classification by risk of cardiovascular event are also observed.

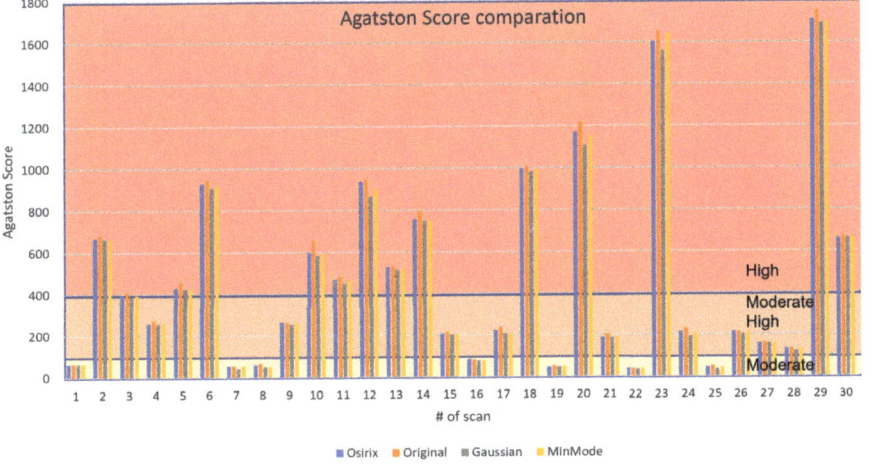

Figure 6. Total CS and risk category classification of the performed studies.

Subsequently, the Pearson's correlation coefficient (r) was calculated for each of the comparisons made, the OsiriX vs. Original comparison obtained r = 0.9996, the OsiriX vs. Gaussian comparison obtained the lowest coefficient with r = 0.9995, and the comparison of OsiriX vs. MinMode r = 0.9997, this being the one with the best correlation of the three.

According to the results obtained in the comparisons of the image processing and CS calculation methods, it is possible to observe that the MinMode technique is the one that most closely resembles the results obtained with the reference commercial software, so this proposal is the one selected to be used in the web application. Figure 7 shows an example on how the results were compared and validated using the same slice from a CTCS scan that had the same pixel area selected. Figure 7a shows the image that was analyzed with Osirix, and the image in Figure 7b was analyzed with the proposed web application.

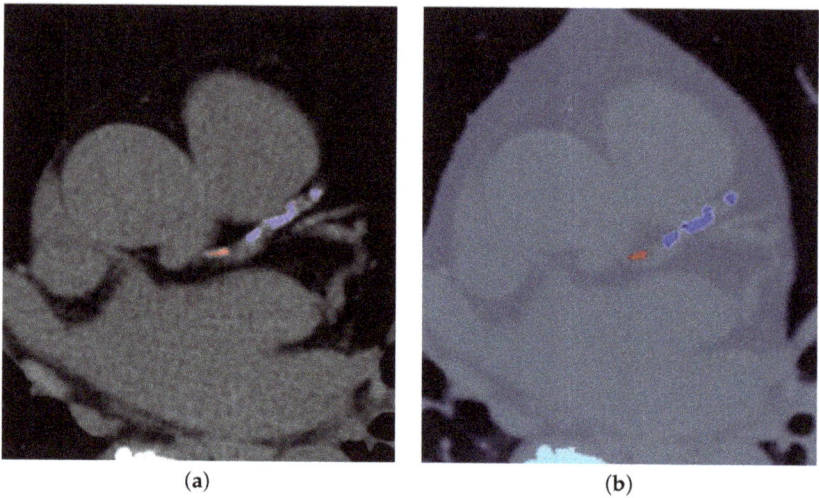

Figure 7. Comparison of the same slice from a CTCS scan. (**a**) Image in Osirix Dicom Viewer (**b**) Image in web application.

3.2. Access to the Web Application

The web application can be accessed from any device with an Internet connection to calculate the CS without the need to have specialized software installed. The proposed application is available to the general public and it has no cost. The application access link is the following: https://www.getcalciumscore.com, accessed on 7 October 2022.

The application has a registration page, as shown in Figure 8; username, e-mail, company, and password data are required. The form shown in Figure 9 is the one corresponding to the login for users who are already registered. Figures 8 and 9 show the main navigation header where the terms and conditions for the use of the application can be reviewed, and the "How to Use" link shows a video explaining the general operation of the web application.

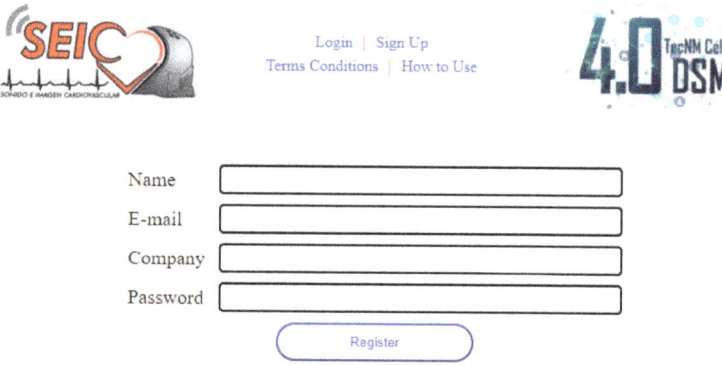

Figure 8. New user registration form.

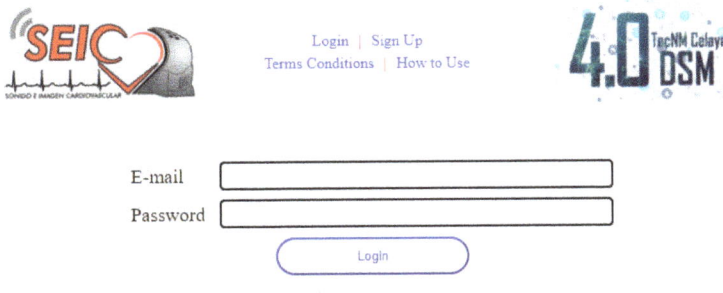

Figure 9. Registered user login form.

Once logged into the application, the user is redirected to the home page (Figure 10), where the option to upload scans is found using the "Upload a new Scan" section, a file in .zip containing a compressed folder with the set of .dcm files. In this section, if no scan is selected, a help image is displayed that indicates the location of each of the tools that the user can use. An exemplary scan is available to all users that does not allow for saving new results or to be eliminated, but it can load results from previously highlighted pixel areas.

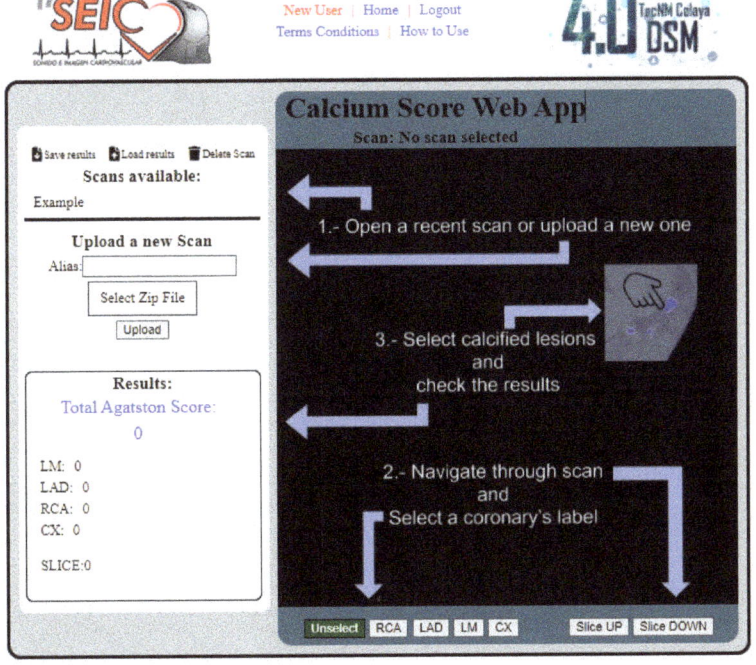

Figure 10. Home page with no scan selected.

The Slice UP and Slice DOWN buttons activate slice change requests and display the previous or next slice, respectively. The "Unselect", "RCA", "LAD", "LM" and "CX" buttons activate requests to change the coronary artery label, the selected label button remains green.

Figure 11 shows the example of the home page where the user has loaded two scans (Patients 1 and 2). Patient 2 is currently selected, and the lesions in the coronary arteries of the entire scan are selected, obtaining a CS of 425 as a result. In Slice 37 (shown in the example), three islands of pixels were selected as CAC lesions in the LAD, one in the LD and one in the CX. The results obtained with the selected islands are saved using the blue "Save results" icon next to the scan name. To load the previously saved results, the green "Load results" icon is used. The red "Delete Scan" icon is used when one wants to remove the scan from the web application; the deleted scans are deleted from the server and from the database. Each of the cyan islands represents the pixels that are above 130 HU (the majority are bones around the chest); they are displayed in this way to assist the user in identifying the ROIs.

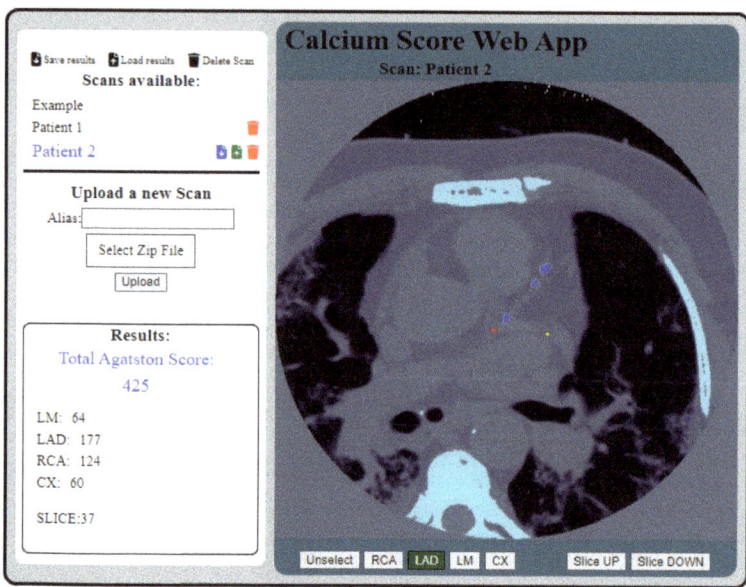

Figure 11. Example of home page with two scans loaded.

4. Discussion

Data comparisons indicate that the results obtained by the proposed web application are like the results obtained with OsiriX DICOM Viewer. The difference between the two tools is attributed to the fact that OsiriX software could use a low-pass filtering technique that is different from the one used in our proposal to reduce variations in the images. Pacsbin (Orion Medical Technologies, Baltimore, MD, pacsbin.com, accessed on 7 October 2022) is a picture archiving and communication system (PACS) that allows for viewing DICOM images; with support for the most common image manipulation tools, its main contribution is to bring a fully featured PACS environment to the web for teaching cases and research. Recent articles [45–47] mentioned the importance of Pacsbin in distance learning in the training of future radiologists, which is possible because it was developed as a web-based system. Although Pacsbin is an application with multiple image analysis tools, it does not allow for the measurement of calcium in coronary arteries like the web application proposed in this article.

Marco Aiello [48] provided a comparative table of the 10 DICOM viewers used in their study. The evaluated software can read and display DICOM images, and all are free-access or open-source; some paid software was included if a free trial version was available. Of the 10 listed programs, only two could be used from a web browser (Postdicom and Papaya Viewer), and two allow for calculating the CS (Horos Viewer, 3D slicer), but they do not meet both characteristics. In other web applications related to CS [49,50], statistical studies of patients with CAC were carried out, and calculators that estimate the percentage derived from the age, sex, ethnicity and CS of the patient were proposed, so the application suggested in this article complements this type of tools used by physicians.

5. Conclusions

In this study, a web application for the quantification of CS was implemented. Three measurements were proposed: (1) without using any additional processing for variations in the image, (2) using a Gaussian blur filter to attenuate the noise generated in the CTCS, and (3) using an algorithm that ensures a minimal number of pixels with the same density score. The data were compared against commercial software OsiriX DICOM Viewer where the third applied algorithm had a higher correlation ($r = 0.9997$). The average error that was obtained for the CS comparison in the proposal without filter was 3.8%, 4.7% for the proposal with Gaussian filter, and 1.9% for the minimal mode algorithm.

Of the studies, 96% for the original proposal and 100% using any of the proposed filtering algorithms were correctly classified in the corresponding risk group. The implementation of some additional processing to reduce noise in the image and thus have more stable HU values was considered to be important. This proposal offers a web application available from any device with Internet access and a web browser to perform the interpretation and calculation of the calcium score in the coronary arteries without the need for installing additional software. The medical specialist who supported the development of this application found it to be a notable and very useful tool that facilitates the calculation of the calcium score from any device and without the need for a specific DICOM viewer. He found that the application was not complicated in its operation, it was very intuitive, and that further it simplified the selection of calcified areas by having the high intensity areas marked before marking them. The clinical cardiologist would be able to elaborate, consult, and compare studies of their patients at any time. Lastly, it facilitates cardiologists or other medical specialists in interacting with one of the tools that is gaining the most acceptance worldwide in the prevention of cardiovascular risk.

Author Contributions: Conceptualization, J.A.-A. and S.O.-T.; methodology, J.A.-A. and J.M.-N.; software, J.A.-A. and J.P.-M.; validation, S.O.-T. and J.M.-N.; formal analysis, S.O.-T.; investigation, V.S.-O., M.B.-S. and J.P.-M.; resources, S.O.-T.; writing—review and editing, V.S.-O. and M.B.-S.; supervision, J.M.-N.; project administration, J.M.-N. All authors have read and agreed to the published version of the manuscript.

Funding: This research received no external funding.

Institutional Review Board Statement: Not applicable.

Informed Consent Statement: Not applicable.

Data Availability Statement: Not applicable.

Acknowledgments: This research did not receive any specific grant from funding agencies in the public, commercial, or not-for-profit sectors.

Conflicts of Interest: The authors declare no conflict of interest.

References

1. World Health Organization. Cardiovascular Diseases. Fact Sheet. 2021. Available online: https://www.who.int/news-room/fact-sheets/detail/cardiovascular-diseases-(cvds) (accessed on 10 July 2022).
2. Lusis, A.J. Atherosclerosis. *Nature* **2000**, *407*, 233–241. [CrossRef] [PubMed]
3. Patel, J.; Blaha, M.J.; McEvoy, J.W.; Qadir, S.; Tota-Maharaj, R.; Shaw, L.J.; Rumberger, J.A.; Callister, T.Q.; Berman, D.S.; Min, J.K.; et al. All-cause mortality in asymptomatic persons with extensive Agatston scores above 1000. *J. Cardiovasc. Comput. Tomogr.* **2014**, *8*, 26–32. [CrossRef] [PubMed]
4. Hecht, H.S. Coronary Artery Calcium and Prevention Guidelines. *JACC Cardiovasc. Imaging* **2020**, *13*, 1187–1190. [CrossRef] [PubMed]
5. Greenland, P.; LaBree, L.; Azen, S.P.; Doherty, T.M.; Detrano, R.C. Coronary Artery Calcium Score Combined With Framingham Score for Risk Prediction in Asymptomatic Individuals. *JAMA* **2004**, *291*, 210–215. [CrossRef] [PubMed]

6. Taylor, A.J.; Bindeman, J.; Feuerstein, I.; Cao, F.; Brazaitis, M.; O'Malley, P.G. Coronary Calcium Independently Predicts Incident Premature Coronary Heart Disease Over Measured Cardiovascular Risk Factors: Mean Three-Year Outcomes in the Prospective Army Coronary Calcium (PACC) Project. *J. Am. Coll. Cardiol.* **2005**, *46*, 807–814. [CrossRef]
7. Shaw, L.J.; Raggi, P.; Schisterman, E.; Berman, D.S.; Callister, T.Q. Prognostic Value of Cardiac Risk Factors and Coronary Artery Calcium Screening for All-Cause Mortality. *Radiology* **2003**, *228*, 826–833. [CrossRef]
8. Isgum, I.; Bartels-Rutten, A.; Prokop, M.; Ginneken, B. Detection of coronary calcifications from computed tomography scans for automated risk assessment of coronary artery disease. *Med. Phys.* **2007**, *34*, 1450–1461. [CrossRef]
9. Agatston, A.S.; Janowitz, W.R.; Hildner, F.J.; Zusmer, N.R.; Viamonte, M.; Detrano, R. Quantification of coronary artery calcium using ultrafast computed tomography. *J. Am. Coll. Cardiol.* **1990**, *15*, 827–832. [CrossRef]
10. Palomares, J.F.; Evangelista, A. Cuantificación del calcio aórtico y arteriosclerosis vascular en individuos asintomáticos: más allá de las arterias coronarias. *Rev. Esp. Cardiol.* **2016**, *69*, 813–816. [CrossRef]
11. Yoon, W.J.; Crisostomo, P.; Halandras, P.; Bechara, C.F.; Aulivola, B. The use of the Agatston calcium score in predicting carotid plaque vulnerability. *Ann. Vasc. Surg.* **2019**, *54*, 22–26. [CrossRef]
12. 3D Slicer Image Computing Platform. Available online: https://www.slicer.org/ (accessed on 10 July 2022).
13. Kay, F.U.; Abbara, S.; Joshi, P.H.; Garg, S.; Khera, A.; Peshock, R.M. Identification of high-risk left ventricular hypertrophy on calcium scoring cardiac computed tomography scans: validation in the DHS. *Circ.Cardiovasc. Imaging* **2020**, *13*, e009678 [CrossRef] [PubMed]
14. Foldyna, B.; Eslami, P.; Scholtz, J.E.; Baltrusaitis, K.; Lu, M.T.; Massaro, J.M.; D'Agostino, R.B.; Ferencik, M.; Aerts, H.J.; O'Donnell C.J.; et al. Density and morphology of coronary artery calcium for the prediction of cardiovascular events: insights from the Framingham Heart Study. *Eur. Radiol.* **2019**, *29*, 6140–6148. [CrossRef] [PubMed]
15. Dransfield, M.T.; Huang, F.; Nath, H.; Singh, S.P.; Bailey, W.C.; Washko, G.R. CT emphysema predicts thoracic aortic calcification in smokers with and without COPD. *COPD.* **2010**, *7*, 404–410. [CrossRef]
16. Image Processing and Analysis in Java. Available online: https://imagej.nih.gov/ij/index.html (accessed on 10 July 2022).
17. Sun, Z.; Ng, C.K. High calcium scores in coronary CT angiography: effects of image post-processing on visualization and measurement of coronary lumen diameter. *J. Med. Imaging. Health. Inform.* **2015**, *5*, 110–116. [CrossRef]
18. Phillips-Eakley, A.K.; McKenney-Drake, M.L.; Bahls, M.; Newcomer, S.C.; Radcliffe, J.S.; Wastney, M.E.; Van Alstine, W.G.; Jackson, G.; Alloosh, M.; Martin, B.R.; et al. Effect of high-calcium diet on coronary artery disease in Ossabaw miniature swine with metabolic syndrome. *J. Am. Heart. Assoc.* **2015**, *4*, e001620. [CrossRef]
19. Cahalane, R.M.; Broderick, S.P.; Kavanagh, E.G.; Moloney, M.A.; Mongrain, R.; Purtill, H.; Walsh, M.T.; O'Brien, J.M. Comparative analysis of calcification parameters with Agatston Score approximations for ex vivo atherosclerotic lesions. *J. Cardiovasc. Comput. Tomogr.* **2020**, *14*, 20–26. [CrossRef]
20. Bos, D.; Ikram, M.A.; Elias-Smale, S.E.; Krestin, G.P.; Hofman, A.; Witteman, J.C.; van der Lugt, A.; Vernooij, M.W. Calcification in major vessel beds relates to vascular brain disease. *Arterioscler. Thromb. Vasc. Biol.* **2011**, *31*, 2331–2337. [CrossRef]
21. OpenCV. Available online: https://opencv.org/ (accessed on 10 July 2022).
22. Durlak, F.; Wels, M.; Schwemmer, C.; Sühling, M.; Steidl, S.; Maier, A. Growing a random forest with fuzzy spatial features for fully automatic artery-specific coronary calcium scoring. In *International Workshop on Machine Learning in Medical Imaging*; Springer: Berlin/Heidelberg, Germany, 2017; pp. 27–35. [CrossRef]
23. Toji, B.; Ohmiya, J.; Kondo, S.; Ishikawa, K.; Yamamoto, M. Fully Automatic Extraction of Carotid Artery Contours from Ultrasound Images. *IEICE Trans. Inf. Syst.* **2014**, *97*, 2493–2500. [CrossRef]
24. Mirunalini, P.; Aravindan, C.; Nambi, A.T.; Poorvaja, S.; Priya, V.P. Segmentation of Coronary Arteries from CTA axial slices using Deep Learning techniques. In Proceedings of the TENCON 2019—2019 IEEE Region 10 Conference (TENCON), Kochi, India, 17–20 October 2019; pp. 2074–2080. [CrossRef]
25. de Vos, B.D.; Wolterink, J.M.; Leiner, T.; de Jong, P.A.; Lessmann, N.; Išgum, I. Direct automatic coronary calcium scoring in cardiac and chest CT. *IEEE Trans. Med. Imaging* **2019**, *38*, 2127–2138. [CrossRef]
26. Garousi, V.; Mesbah, A.; Betin-Can, A.; Mirshokraie, S. A systematic mapping study of web application testing. *Inf. Softw. Technol.* **2013**, *55*, 1374–1396. [CrossRef]
27. Verber, D.; Novak, D.; Borovič, M.; Dugonik, J.; Flisar, D. EQUIDopa: A responsive web application for the levodopa equivalent dose calculator. *Comput. Methods Programs Biomed.* **2020**, *196*, 105633. [CrossRef]
28. Al-Waisy, A.S.; Alruban, A.; Al-Fahdawi, S.; Qahwaji, R.; Ponirakis, G.; Malik, R.A.; Mohammed, M.A.; Kadry, S. CellsDeepNet: A Novel Deep Learning-Based Web Application for the Automated Morphometric Analysis of Corneal Endothelial Cells. *Mathematics* **2022**, *10*, 320. [CrossRef]
29. Pemmaraju, R.; Minahan, R.; Wang, E.; Schadl, K.; Daldrup-Link, H.; Habte, F. Web-Based Application for Biomedical Image Registry, Analysis, and Translation (BiRAT). *Tomography* **2022**, *8*, 1453–1462. [CrossRef]
30. Mora-Aguilera, G.; Martínez-Bustamante, V.; Acevedo-Sánchez, G.; Coria-Contreras, J.J.; Guzmán-Hernández, E.; Flores-Colorado, O.E.; Mendoza-Ramos, C.; Hernández-Nava, G.; Álvarez-Maya, I.; Gutiérrez-Espinosa, M.A.; et al. Surveillance web system and mouthwash-saliva qPCR for labor ambulatory SARS-CoV-2 detection and prevention. *Int. J. Environ. Res. Public Health* **2022**, *19*, 1271. [CrossRef]
31. Villavicencio, C.N.; Macrohon, J.J.; Inbaraj, X.A.; Jeng, J.H.; Hsieh, J.G. Development of a Machine Learning Based Web Application for Early Diagnosis of COVID-19 Based on Symptoms. *Diagnostics* **2022**, *12*, 821. [CrossRef]

2. Lanera, C.; Azzolina, D.; Pirotti, F.; Prosepe, I.; Lorenzoni, G.; Berchialla, P.; Gregori, D. A Web-Based Application to Monitor and Inform about the COVID-19 Outbreak in Italy: The {COVID-19ita} Initiative. *Healthcare* **2022**, *10*, 473. [CrossRef]
3. Nawi, N.A.M.M.; Sapiai, N.S.; Ghazali, S.A.M.; Rusok, N.H.M.; Zulkifli, F.Z.; Mazlan, F.M. Developing an E-College Monitoring System as a Web-Based Monitoring Tool Application. *Proceedings* **2022**, *82*, 25. [CrossRef]
4. Mejía, S.; Muñoz, I.C.; Serna, L.Y.; Sarmiento, C.A.; Bravo, C.L.; Hernández, A.M. Web Applications for Teaching the Respiratory System: Content Validation. *Appl. Sci.* **2022**, *12*, 4289. [CrossRef]
5. Udias, A.; Pistocchi, A.; Vigiak, O.; Grizzetti, B.; Bouraoui, F.; Alfaro, C. ESPRES: A web application for interactive analysis of multiple pressures in aquatic ecosystems. *Sci. Total Environ.* **2020**, *744*, 140792. [CrossRef] [PubMed]
6. Andreo-Martínez, P.; Ortiz-Martínez, V.M.; Muñoz, A.; Menchón-Sánchez, P.; Quesada-Medina, J. A web application to estimate the carbon footprint of constructed wetlands. *Environ. Model Softw.* **2021**, *135*, 104898. [CrossRef]
7. Cochard, T.; Branger, M.; Supply, P.; Sreevatsan, S.; Biet, F. MAC-INMV-SSR: a web application dedicated to genotyping members of Mycobacterium avium complex (MAC) including Mycobacterium avium subsp. paratuberculosis strains. *Infect. Genet. Evol.* **2020**, *77*, 104075. [CrossRef] [PubMed]
8. Karatzas, E.; Baltoumas, F.A.; Kasionis, I.; Sanoudou, D.; Eliopoulos, A.G.; Theodosiou, T.; Iliopoulos, I.; Pavlopoulos, G.A. Darling: A Web Application for Detecting Disease-Related Biomedical Entity Associations with Literature Mining. *Biomolecules* **2022**, *12*, 520. [CrossRef] [PubMed]
9. Bianchetti, G.; Abeltino, A.; Serantoni, C.; Ardito, F.; Malta, D.; De Spirito, M.; Maulucci, G. Personalized Self-Monitoring of Energy Balance through Integration in a Web-Application of Dietary, Anthropometric, and Physical Activity Data. *J. Pers. Med.* **2022**, *12*, 568. [CrossRef]
10. Cubillas, J.J.; Ramos, M.I.; Jurado, J.M.; Feito, F.R. A Machine Learning Model for Early Prediction of Crop Yield, Nested in a Web Application in the Cloud: A Case Study in an Olive Grove in Southern Spain. *Agriculture* **2022**, *12*, 1345. [CrossRef]
11. Paraschiv, L.S.; Acomi, N.; Serban, A.; Paraschiv, S. A web application for analysis of heat transfer through building walls and calculation of optimal insulation thickness. *Energy Rep.* **2020**, *6*, 343–353. [CrossRef]
12. Mason, D. SU-E-T-33: pydicom: An open source DICOM library. *Med. Phys.* **2011**, *38*, 3493–3493. [CrossRef]
13. Pulli, K.; Baksheev, A.; Kornyakov, K.; Eruhimov, V. Real-time computer vision with OpenCV. *Commun. ACM* **2012**, *55*, 61–69. [CrossRef]
14. Nelson, J.C.; Kronmal, R.A.; Carr, J.J.; McNitt-Gray, M.F.; Wong, N.D.; Loria, C.M.; Goldin, J.G.; Williams, O.D.; Detrano, R. Measuring coronary calcium on CT images adjusted for attenuation differences. *Radiology* **2005**, *235*, 403–414. [CrossRef]
15. McRoy, C.; Patel, L.; Gaddam, D.S.; Rothenberg, S.; Herring, A.; Hamm, J.; Chelala, L.; Weinstein, J.; Smith, E.; Awan, O. Radiology education in the time of COVID-19: a novel distance learning workstation experience for residents. *Acad. Radiol.* **2020**, *27*, 1467–1474. [CrossRef]
16. Awan, O.A.; Klein, J.S. Stepping Up to the Challenge: Overcoming Barriers to Radiology Training in the United States During COVID-19. *Can. Assoc. Radiol. J.* **2021**, *72*, 11–12. [CrossRef]
17. Sugi, M.D.; Kennedy, T.A.; Shah, V.; Hartung, M.P. Bridging the gap: interactive, case-based learning in radiology education. *Abdom. Radiol.* **2021**, *46*, 5503–5508. [CrossRef] [PubMed]
18. Aiello, M.; Esposito, G.; Pagliari, G.; Borrelli, P.; Brancato, V.; Salvatore, M. How does DICOM support big data management? Investigating its use in medical imaging community. *Insights Imaging* **2021**, *12*, 1–21. [CrossRef] [PubMed]
19. de Ronde, M.W.; Khoshiwal, A.; Planken, R.N.; Boekholdt, S.M.; Biemond, M.; Budoff, M.J.; Cooil, B.; Lotufo, P.A.; Bensenor, I.M.; Ohmoto-Sekine, Y.; et al. A pooled-analysis of age and sex based coronary artery calcium scores percentiles. *J. Cardiovasc. Comput. Tomogr.* **2020**, *14*, 414–420. [CrossRef] [PubMed]
20. McClelland, R.L.; Chung, H.; Detrano, R.; Post, W.; Kronmal, R.A. Distribution of coronary artery calcium by race, gender, and age: results from the Multi-Ethnic Study of Atherosclerosis (MESA). *Circulation* **2006**, *113*, 30–37. [CrossRef]

Article

EFCMF: A Multimodal Robustness Enhancement Framework for Fine-Grained Recognition

Rongping Zou [1,2,3], Bin Zhu [1,2,3,*], Yi Chen [1,2,3], Bo Xie [1,2,3] and Bin Shao [1,2,3]

1. College of Electronic Engineering, National University of Defense Technology, Hefei 230037, China
2. State Key Laboratory of Pulsed Power Laser Technology, Hefei 230037, China
3. Key Laboratory of Infrared and Low Temperature Plasma of Anhui Province, Hefei 230037, China
* Correspondence: zhubin@nudt.edu.cn

Abstract: Fine-grained recognition has many applications in many fields and aims to identify targets from subcategories. This is a highly challenging task due to the minor differences between subcategories. Both modal missing and adversarial sample attacks are easily encountered in fine-grained recognition tasks based on multimodal data. These situations can easily lead to the model needing to be fixed. An Enhanced Framework for the Complementarity of Multimodal Features (EFCMF) is proposed in this study to solve this problem. The model's learning of multimodal data complementarity is enhanced by randomly deactivating modal features in the constructed multimodal fine-grained recognition model. The results show that the model gains the ability to handle modal missing without additional training of the model and can achieve 91.14% and 99.31% accuracy on Birds and Flowers datasets. The average accuracy of EFCMF on the two datasets is 52.85%, which is 27.13% higher than that of Bi-modal PMA when facing four adversarial example attacks, namely FGSM, BIM, PGD and C&W. In the face of missing modal cases, the average accuracy of EFCMF is 76.33% on both datasets respectively, which is 32.63% higher than that of Bi-modal PMA Compared with existing methods, EFCMF is robust in the face of modal missing and adversarial example attacks in multimodal fine-grained recognition tasks. The source code is available at https://github.com/RPZ97/EFCMF (accessed on 8 January 2023).

Keywords: fine-grained recognition; multimodal; modal missing; adversarial examples

1. Introduction

The purpose of fine-grained recognition is to distinguish subordinate categories (like owls, albatrosses, and seagulls in birds) with subtle differences in the same primary category (such as birds [1], Flowers [2], dogs [3], cars [4], and fruits [5]). These are applied to real-world scenes in different fields, such as species identification, vehicle identification, product identification [6,7] and so on. Since subcategories are all similar to each other, different subcategories can only be distinguished by subtle and subtle differences, which makes fine-grained identification a challenging problem.

Many fine-grained recognition methods have been proposed, which can be divided into two categories on a single visual modality. (1) One is a strongly-supervised method based on a localization and classification subnetwork, and the other is a weakly-supervised method for end-to-end feature encoding [8]. In intensely supervised methods, techniques such as object detection [9–11] or segmentation [12,13], can be used to locate parts of objects with crucial fine-grained features and enhance the effect of recognition, such as the use of segmentation models for assisted classification of part-stacked [14], and part-based RCNN [15] with detection models. (2) The other is weakly-supervised methods. In weakly-supervised methods, most of the classical classification networks such as ResNet [15], DenseNet [16] and other backbone structures are used as feature extraction models, among which VggNet [17] is used to construct dual-stream branches and fuse

Citation: Zou, R.; Zhu, B.; Chen, Y.; Xie, B.; Shao, B. EFCMF: A Multimodal Robustness Enhancement Framework for Fine-Grained Recognition. *Appl. Sci.* 2023, 13, 1640. https://doi.org/10.3390/app13031640

Academic Editors: Jing Zhang, Jipeng Qiang and Cangqi Zhou

Received: 15 October 2022
Revised: 18 January 2023
Accepted: 19 January 2023
Published: 27 January 2023

Copyright: © 2023 by the authors. Licensee MDPI, Basel, Switzerland. This article is an open access article distributed under the terms and conditions of the Creative Commons Attribution (CC BY) license (https://creativecommons.org/licenses/by/4.0/).

them. The BCNN [18] and MOMN [19] methods are based on the BCNN method. These methods focus on improving the classification accuracy of the visual modality but are easily limited by a single visual modality.

Recently, some methods for fine-grained recognition based on multimodal data have been proposed. There are three data fusion methods in the data fusion modalities: vision and language, vision and speech, and vision and knowledge. Among them, the fusion method of vision and language is represented by CVL et al. [20–22]. In addition to using the two modalities of vision and language for fusion, Zhang et al. [23] also conducted corresponding research on vision and sound and fused the two modalities of vision and sound. In addition, related works introduce knowledge information [24–26] and fuse it with visual modalities. These methods effectively improve the accuracy of fine-grained recognition tasks by fusing data from multiple modalities. But its robustness in the face of modal missing and adversarial examples attacks is not well considered.

However, in practical fine-grained recognition tasks, modal missing and adversarial examples are often encountered, leading to the models based on multimodal data needing to be fixed. The reason for the modal missing is that in the data acquisition process, several modalities in a small part of the data need to be included due to factors such as instrument failure. Adversarial examples attacks refer to the unusual noise generated by the adversarial example method [27–32] that makes the model prone to fatal errors.

There are many application scenarios in which visual and language modalities exist in the actual usage process. For example, a product or a movie introduction often has visual modal information, such as pictures and videos, and language modality information, such as keywords and brief descriptions. The scenarios mentioned above are often prone to missing modalities. The standard solution is to train multiple models to cope with scenarios with only one modality, which is often more expensive. The EFCMF framework is proposed in this paper to utilize multimodal data better and reduce the cost.

This paper builds a multimodal fine-grained recognition framework EFCMF of visual language fusion with the same accuracy as the existing methods to solve the above problems. The framework adopts the technique of random modality deactivation for training while ensuring that original fusion accuracy remains unchanged. In this way, the model acquires the ability to cope with the modal missing and adversarial examples attacks, and dramatically improves its accuracy when attacked by adversarial examples.

The proposed framework's contributions are as follows: (1) The framework can deal with the modal missing problem without training additional single-modal fine-grained recognition models. (2) The framework can take advantage of multimodal data without adversarial training. The model accuracy is guaranteed to stay the same by using the modality that has not suffered from adversarial examples attacks. (3) Through a large number of experiments, hyperparameters to guide the use of random deactivation training methods are given.

2. Method

To address the problem of modal missing and adversarial example attacks in the multimodal fine-grained recognition task of vision and language fusion. The framework adopted in this study is shown in Figure 1, which consists of three parts: a visual feature extraction module, a language feature extraction module, and a feature fusion module.

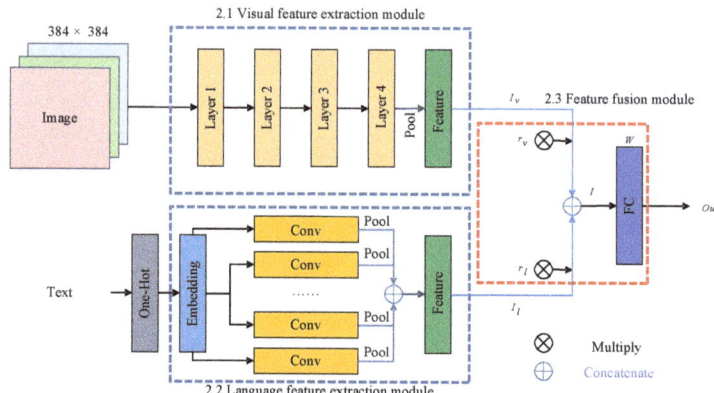

Figure 1. Structure of Enhanced Framework for Multimodal Feature Complementarity Based on the Modal Feature Random Deactivation Training Method.

2.1. Visual Feature Extraction Module

In the visual feature extraction module, the backbone network for feature extraction [33] is composed of four transformer layers. The input image is subjected to high-dimensional mapping of four feature extraction modules, and a high-dimensional vector I_v that can express the image features is obtained. The the input of the visual modality is represented as $\underset{3\times 384\times 384}{Img}$. The i-th layer of the network is denoted as $Layer_i$, and the number of channels of the output feature $\underset{c\times h\times w}{Feat_i}$ is c, and the size is $h \times w$. Then, the entire visual feature extraction module can be expressed as:

$$Layer_{1-4}(X) = Layer_4(Layer_3(Layer_2(Layer_1(X)))) \tag{1}$$

Its forward propagation process can be expressed as follows:

$$\underset{1536\times 144\times 1}{Feat_4} = Layer_{1-4}\left(\underset{3\times 384\times 384}{Img}\right) \tag{2}$$

After the image is subjected to high-dimensional mapping through four feature layers, a feature matrix with 1536 channels is obtained, and then the output features are globally pooled, and the pooled features are deformed to obtain a feature vector I_v with a length of 1536.

The backbone network of language modalities consists of several convolutional layers [34] (denoted as $Conv$). Its forward propagation process can be expressed as follows:

2.2. Language Feature Extraction Module

The input text (denoted as $Text = [Word_1, \ldots, Word_n]$) is a sequence of n words, and encodes words by constructing a dictionary to map words to the integer domain:

$$[num_1, \ldots, num_n] = [Encode(Word_1), \ldots, Encode(Word_n)] \tag{3}$$

Then, the one-hot encoding method is used to map from the integer domain to the sparse vector space, and the process is as follows:

$$\left[\underset{n\times 1}{Vec_1}, \ldots, \underset{n\times 1}{Vec_n}\right] = [OneHot(num_1), \ldots, OneHot(num_n)] \tag{4}$$

After that, take an embedding layer with weight $W_E_{50 \times n}$, map the sparse vector to a dense vector of 50 dimensions, and reshape it into a 3D embedding matrix $Mat_{1 \times n \times 50}$:

$$Mat_{1 \times n \times 50} = reshape\left(\left[W_E_{50 \times n} \times Vec_1_{n \times 1}, \ldots, W_E_{50 \times n} \times Vec_n_{n \times 1}\right]\right) \tag{5}$$

Next, feature extraction (represented as $Feat$) is performed by k convolution kernels with m convolutional layers of size $h \times w$ (the i-th convolutional layer is denoted as $Conv_i_{k_i \times w_i \times h_i}$), and the obtained features are pooled:

$$Feat_i_{k_i \times 1 \times 1} = Pool\left(Conv_i_{k_i \times w_i \times h_i}\left(Mat_{1 \times n \times 50}\right)\right) \tag{6}$$

2.3. Feature Fusion Module

Finally, all the features of the output are concatenated (represented as cat) and reshaped to obtain the features I_l for fusion:

$$Feat_{\sum_i^m k_i \times 1 \times 1} = cat\left(\left[Feat_1_{k_1 \times 1 \times 1} \ldots, Feat_m_{k_m \times 1 \times 1}\right]\right) \tag{7}$$

$$I_l = Feat_{\sum_i^m k_i} = reshape\left(Feat_{\sum_i^m k_i \times 1 \times 1}\right) \tag{8}$$

In the feature fusion module, the study adopts a feature-level fusion strategy to obtain new features by concatenating the features of the visual modality and language modality

$$\left[\frac{I_v}{I_l}\right] = cat(I_v, I_l) \tag{9}$$

The error is backpropagated through the classifier to jointly training the two feature extraction modules of the model.

The weight of the fully connected layer of the module is W, which can be regarded as the splicing of two weights using modal features for classification: $W = cat(W_v, W_l) = [W_v \mid W_l]$, and the matrix product with the feature to obtain the Out:

$$Out = W \times I = [\ W_v \mid W_l\ ] \times \left[\frac{I_v}{I_l}\right] \tag{10}$$

During training, in order to simulate modal missing to enhance the ability of the model to cope with modal missing and adversarial examples attacks, the input modal features are randomly deactivated. The random inactivation of features is a random event conforming to the Bernoulli distribution, and its Bernoulli random variable is $r_m \sim Bernoulli(p)$. When a modality is missing, the visual modality has a q probability of remaining intact, and the Bernoulli random variable for this event is $r_v \sim Bernoulli(q)$, and the language modality is $r_l = 1 - r_m r_v$. Then, the forward propagation process of the module is as follows:

$$I_v = r_v * I_v, I_l = r_l * I_l \tag{11}$$

$$I = cat(I_v, I_l) = \left[\frac{I_v}{I_l}\right] \tag{12}$$

The output of the model appears as follows:

$$\begin{aligned}
Out = W \times I &= \begin{bmatrix} W_v & | & W_l \end{bmatrix} \times \begin{bmatrix} I'_v \\ I'_l \end{bmatrix} \\
&= (1 - r_m(1 - r_v)) * W_v \times I'_v + r_l * W_l \times I'_l \\
&= (1 - r_m(1 - r_v)) * Out_v + r_l * Out_l \\
&= (1 - r_m(1 - r_v)) * Out_v + (1 - r_m r_v) * Out_l \\
&= (1 - r_m) * Out + r_m(r_v * Out_v + (1 - r_v) * Out_l)
\end{aligned} \tag{13}$$

The average expectation of the output is:

$$E(Out) = (1 - p) * Out + p * (q * Out_v + (1 - q) * Out_l) \tag{14}$$

At this time, the model can be considered as an ensemble model of three models with strong correlation. Out is a vector representing the confidence (denoted as $Conf_i$) of the classification result of the model for a total of k categories: $Out = [Conf_1, \ldots, Conf_i]$ Finally the output result is normalized by softmax to obtain the predicted value $Pred$, and the $Loss$ is calculated as follows:

$$Pred = \text{softmax}(Out) = \frac{1}{\sum_1^k e^{Conf_i}} \left[e^{Conf_1}, \ldots, e^{Conf_i} \right]$$
$$Loss = Label * \log(Pred) + (1 - Label) * \log(1 - Pred) \tag{15}$$

It can be inferred from the Formula (15) that when $p = 0$, the output expectation of the model is $E(Out) = q * Out_v + (1 - q) * Out_l$ At this time, if $q = 0.5$, it can be considered that Out is equal to the average of the outputs Out_v and Out_l of the visual modal classifier and the language modal classifier:

$$E(Out) = \frac{1}{2}(Out_v + Out_l) \tag{16}$$

Then, the model becomes a normal feature fusion model, and the average output of the model is expected

$$E(Out) = Out = W \times I \tag{17}$$

Since the error rate and correlation of the ensemble model are negatively correlated, we hope this method can weaken the correlation between submodels and improve the complementarity between modal features to improve the model's accuracy and robustness. this study performs related experiments in next Section to find the appropriate hyperparameters to optimize the model.

3. Experiment

3.1. Experimental setting

To verify the feasibility and universality of the method in this study, the experimental details are as follows:

The visual feature extraction module of the model has been pretrained on the ImageNet dataset [35], and the features output by the last layer of convolutions are pooled for feature-level fusion. The data of the visual modality adopt The Birds dataset [1] and Flowers dataset [2], the width and height of the image are scaled to 384 pixels, and some of the grayscale images are copied and synthesized into a three-channel image. Finally, the image is normalized using ImageNet data processing. The language modality adopts the text description extended by Reed et al. [36]. Because there are certain errors in the text description, the spelling correction operation is advanced on the text, and then lemmatizes words to form a new dictionary, Finally a 50-dimensional embedding layer is used for embedding.

The deep learning framework PyTorch [37] and the adversarial example toolbox torchattacks [38] are used in the experiments. The training parameters of each module of the model are shown in the Table 1.

Table 1. The training parameters of each module of the model.

	Optimizer	Learning Rate	Weight Decay	Dropout	Batch Size	Epoch
Vision	SGD	0.005	0.00001	0.5	8	50
Language	RAdam	0.01	0.0001	0.5	32	50
Fusion	SGD	0.005	0.00001	0.5	8	50

The parameters for generating adversarial examples are shown in the Table 2.

Table 2. Generating parameters for adversarial examples using torchattacks.

	Eps	Alpha	Steps	c	Kappa	lr	Random_Start
FGSM	0.014	/	/	/	/	/	/
BIM	0.01568	0.00392	0	/	/	/	/
PGD	0.03	0.00784	10	/	/	/	/
C&W	/	/	100	0.0001	0	0.1	True

3.2. Experiment Results

3.2.1. Analysis of the Robustness and Accuracy Performance of the Model

In this study, the robustness of the model is tested by attacking the model with adversarial examples and causing modal missing (deactivating the features of each modality of the model). The robustness results of the model are shown in Table 2. Accuracy represents the model's accuracy when adversarial examples do not attack it, and the modality is not missing. FGSM, BIM, PGD, and C&W are adversarial examples of attack methods. Vision Missing means visual modal features are missing (zeroing the input features of the visual modality), and Language Missing represents the absence of modal language features (zeroing out the input features of language modality).

The proposed method has excellent accuracy advantages compared with Bi-modal PMA. It can surpass the fine-grained recognition method of Bi-modal PMA in the Birds and the Flower datasets. At the same time, the method's robustness in this study is also excellent, and in the face of adversarial sample attacks, EFCMF can exceed Bi-modal PMA such as FGSM, BIM, PGD, and C&W in most cases. In the face of FGSM attacks, EFCMF's accuracy in the Birds dataset can exceed Bi-modal PMA by about 16% and on the Flowers dataset by about 70%. In addition, EFCMF performed well in the face of BIM attacks and PGD attacks, surpassing Bi-modal PMAs by about 9% on the Birds dataset and about 70% on the Flowers dataset. When attacking with powerful adversarial examples method PGD, the accuracy of Bi-model PMA on both datasets has been reduced to the lowest point, which is lower than that of random decider (0.0050). However, EFCMF is still able to exercise some judgment, still having an accuracy of 0.0642 on the Birds dataset and 38% accuracy on the Flowers data set. The case of C&W attacks is unique, and Bi-modal PMA has high accuracy on the Birds dataset. inactivation, which is a critical reason EFCMF can cope well with missing modality. In order to verify that random modal inactivation can effectively improve the model's ability to cope with modal loss, this study retrains Bi-modal PMA using this method. The model test results are shown in Table 3, and it can be seen that after random mode deactivation training, the model's ability to cope with modal loss can be effectively improved. After training with this method, Bi-modal PMA improved the model accuracy by 15% and 40% under the absence of visual modality in the Birds and Flowers datasets, respectively. At the same time, the accuracy of Bi-modal PMA in the face of FGSM and BIM counterattack attacks has also been improved. Random modality deactivation, which is a critical reason EFCMF can cope well with missing modality. In order to verify that random modal deactivation can effectively improve the model's ability to cope with modal loss, this study retrains Bi-modal PMA using this method. The model test results are shown in Table 4, and it can be seen that after random mode deactivation training, the model's ability to cope with modal loss can be effectively improved. After training with this method, Bi-modal PMA improved the model accuracy by 15% and 40% under the absence of visual modality in the Birds and Flowers datasets, respectively. At the same time, the accuracy of Bi-modal PMA in the face of FGSM and BIM counterattack attacks has also been improved.

Table 3. The model's accuracy in the face of adversarial example attacks and modalities is missing.

		Accuracy	FGSM	BIM	PGD	C&W	Vision Missing	Language Missing
Birds [1]	Bi-modal PMA	0.8870	0.2260	0.1350	0.0013	**0.7433**	0.0486	0.7899
	EFCMF ($p = 0.8$, $q = 0.4$)	**0.9114**	**0.3826**	**0.2231**	**0.0642**	0.5730	**0.5051**	**0.9099**
Flowers [2]	Bi-modal PMA	0.9700	0.1503	0.0488	0.0019	0.7509	0.0098	0.8999
	EFCMF ($p = 0.8$, $q = 0.4$)	**0.9931**	**0.8882**	**0.7656**	**0.3803**	**0.9509**	**0.6441**	**0.9941**

Table 4. Comparison of the accuracy of the Bi-modal PMA method trained by the random modality deactivation method.

		FGSM	BIM	PGD	C&W	Vision Missing	Language Missing
Birds	Bi-modal PMA	0.2260	0.1350	0.0013	**0.7433**	0.0486	**0.7899**
	Bi-modal PMA ($p = 0.8$, $q = 0.4$)	**0.3386**	**0.1824**	**0.0043**	0.7239	**0.2057**	0.7297
Flowers	Bi-modal PMA	0.1503	0.0048	**0.0019**	**0.7509**	0.0098	**0.8999**
	Bi-modal PMA ($p = 0.8$, $q = 0.4$)	**0.2109**	**0.0371**	0.0000	0.6582	**0.4362**	0.8735

EFCMF has more accuracy advantages than Bi-modal PMA and higher accuracy than other fine-grained recognition models. As shown in Table 5, it can be seen that the EFCMF method has higher accuracy than the multimodal fine-grained recognition models such as CVL, TA-FGVC, KERL, and KGRF. Furthermore, EFCMF has higher accuracy in single-modal fine-grained recognition methods such as Inception-v3 [39], ViT-B [40], and PART [41].

Table 5. Comparison of the accuracy of each method.

Method	Data Field	Birds [1]	Flowers [2]
CVL [21]	Vision+Language	0.8555	\
TA-FGVC [22]	Vision+Language	0.8810	\
KERL [25]	Vision+Knowledge	0.8700	\
KGRF [26]	Vision+Knowledge	0.8849	\
Bi-modal PMA [42]	Vision+Language	0.8870	0.9740
Inception-V3 [39]	Vision	0.8960	0.9737
ViT-B [40]	Vision	\	0.9850
PART [41]	Vision	0.9010	\
EFCMF (ours)	Vision+Language	**0.9114**	**0.9931**

3.2.2. Performance of the Model under Different Hyperparameters

In this study, the two hyperparameters p and q were performed 36 experiments on each dataset at intervals of 0.2 from 0 to 1. In order to investigate the effects of hyperparameters p and q on the model's robustness and accuracy, the experimental results are plotted in this study as heat maps shown in Figures 2–4.

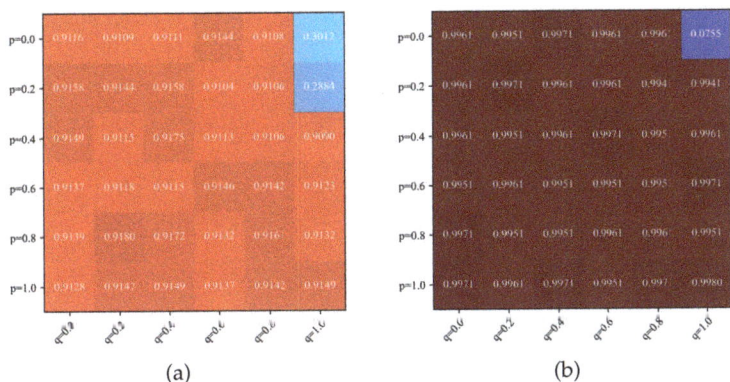

Figure 2. Heat map of model accuracy for different values of p and q. (**a**) Birds. (**b**) Flowers.

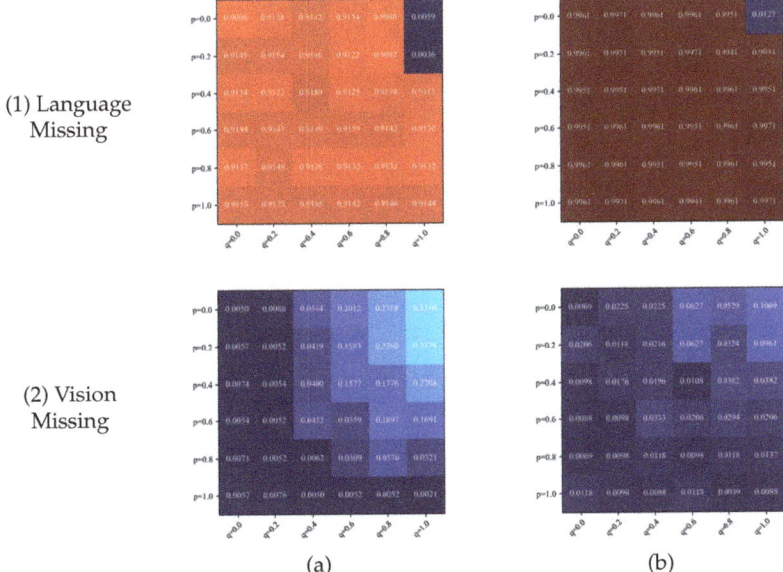

Figure 3. Heat map of accuracy of model facing modal missing for different values of p and q. (**a**) Birds. (**b**) Flowers.

Figure 2 shows the model's accuracy for different values of p and q. The most special cases are at $p = 1$, $q = 0$, and $q = 0.2$. The reason is that for $p = 1$, the model only has data from the visual or language modality for each input sample. When $q < 0.2$, the probability of missing data of visual modality is higher, and the model is mostly training the extraction module of language modality at this time. $q < 0.2$ makes the model use only the information of linguistic modality for fine-grained recognition, and therefore the accuracy is lower.

Figure 3 shows the heat map of the accuracy of the model in the face of the missing modality. It can be seen that the accuracy of the model increases with the increase of the modal deactivation probability p and the decrease of the visual modality integrity probability q and stays at a low level when facing the missing visual modality. The above phenomenon is related to the degree of training in the language modality feature extraction module. The higher the training degree of the linguistic modality feature extraction module, the better the model can face the visual modality missing.

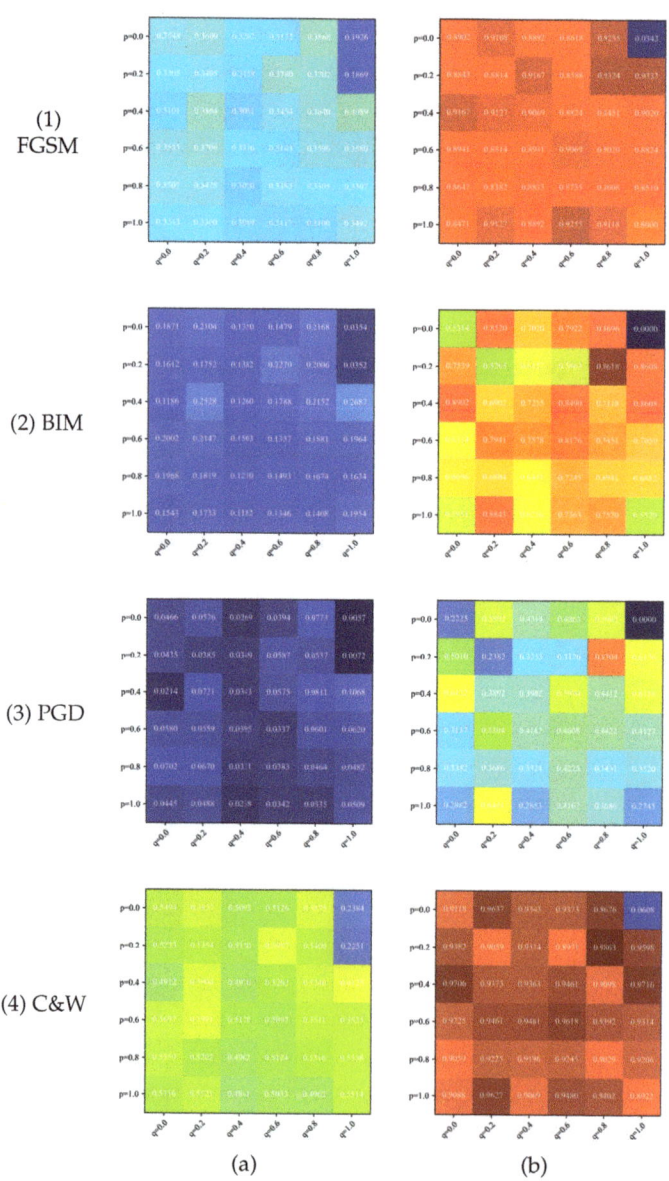

Figure 4. Heat map of the accuracy of the model against the adversarial examples attack with different values of p and q. (**a**) Birds. (**b**) Flowers.

Figure 4 shows the model's accuracy in the face of the adversarial example attack under different values of p and q. The p and q parameters not only have a particular influence on the model's ability to cope with the modal missing but also can impact the robustness of the adversarial sample attack. As shown in Figure 4b, with the appropriate selection of p and q parameters, the trained model has strong robustness and can maintain high accuracy against examples attacks.

In order to better demonstrate the effects of parameters p and q on the model, the data in Figures 2–4 are averaged on each axis to obtain the accuracy trend plots in Figures 5 and 6, respectively, and the results are given in the following.

(1) Analysis of the effect of the modality deactivation probability p on the model

Figure 5 shows the average model accuracy in various cases for the matrix data shown in Figures 2–4 for each p-value obtained by averaging over q-values. It can be seen that the impact of p-values in the face of adversarial sample attacks is similar for both datasets, with curves having extreme value points at $p = 0.2$ as well as $p = 0.8$ and a minimal value point at $p = 0.4$. The extreme value point implies that the random modal deactivation impacts the model's robustness relative to the case when $p = 0$ is not performed randomly and can enhance the model's ability to cope with counter-sample attacks at the appropriate value. Tables 6 and 7 correspond to the data in Figure 5a,b, respectively.

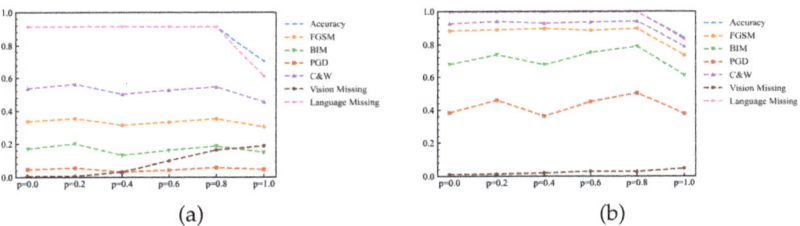

Figure 5. The accuracy trend of the probability of modality deactivation p. (**a**) Birds. (**b**) Flowers.

Table 6. Accuracy averages for different cases with different values of the modal deactivation probability p for the Birds data set.

	$p = 0.0$	$p = 0.2$	$p = 0.4$	$p = 0.6$	$p = 0.8$	$p = 1.0$
Accuracy	0.9142	0.9137	**0.9147**	0.9129	0.9128	0.7065
FGSM	0.3418	**0.3605**	0.3152	0.3341	0.3534	0.3044
BIM	0.1716	**0.2027**	0.1315	0.1622	0.1882	0.1491
PGD	0.0456	0.0557	0.0321	0.0436	**0.0587**	0.0468
C&W	0.5366	**0.5627**	0.5027	0.5272	0.5467	0.4558
Vision Missing	0.0070	0.0059	0.0321	0.0982	0.1630	**0.1872**
Language Missing	0.9137	0.9143	**0.9152**	0.9136	0.9120	0.6103

Table 7. Accuracy averages for different cases with different values of the modal deactivation probability p for the Flowers dataset

	$p = 0.0$	$p = 0.2$	$p = 0.4$	$p = 0.6$	$p = 0.8$	$p = 1.0$
Accuracy	**0.9962**	0.9958	0.9961	0.9959	0.9956	0.8426
FGSM	0.8828	0.8895	**0.8966**	0.8848	0.8962	0.7338
BIM	0.6786	0.7379	0.6773	0.7510	**0.7891**	0.6113
PGD	0.3843	0.4600	0.3636	0.4505	**0.5026**	0.3781
C&W	0.9263	0.9397	0.9291	0.9358	**0.9410**	0.7894
Vision Missing	0.0108	0.0136	0.0198	0.0297	0.0281	**0.0474**
Language Missing	0.9958	**0.9964**	0.9956	0.9956	0.9956	0.8317

Tables 6 and 7 show that the model's accuracy mostly stays the same when p is less than 0.8. The accuracy of the model drops substantially when $p = 1$. The reason is that with $p = 1$, the model only uses the data of the visual modality or the data of the linguistic modality to update the weights each time, especially in $q = 0$. The model only uses the features of the linguistic modality for training, and the model degenerates into a recognition model of the linguistic modality, so the accuracy drops considerably.

In the face of the adversarial example attack, the model can achieve the maximum number of accuracy maxima in the face of the adversarial sample attack at $p = 0.8$. This phenomenon is because a higher p-value can better ensure the independence between two features, whose standard features can represent more information in an integrated way and, therefore, can achieve higher accuracy. In contrast, at $p = 0$, the model is not trained with random modal deactivation. Its average accuracy will be lower than the two maximum value points and higher than the minimum points. The results show that the parameter p can improve in robustness only by using the correct value. Otherwise, it may not only fail to improve the robustness but may also decrease it.

In the face of modality missing, it shows that both $p = 0$ and $p = 1$ correspond to poor average accuracy. These extreme cases represent training only the verbal modal feature extraction module and the visual modal feature extraction module, respectively, leading to model failure.

(2) Analysis of the effect of the visual modal integrity probability parameter q on the model

By averaging Figures 2–4 on the vertical axis, we can obtain the average accuracy of the visual modal integrity probability q in each case, as shown in Figure 6. There is an maximum point at $q = 0.4$ for both datasets, achieving the highest accuracy under most adversarial sample attacks. Equation (14) shows the reason for this point. The parameter p controls the probability of training the model with visual modal data in the case of missing modality. A large or small probability p will result in one of the modality feature extraction modules that cannot be trained effectively. Therefore, the value $q = 0.4$ is suitable to meet the theoretical expectation.

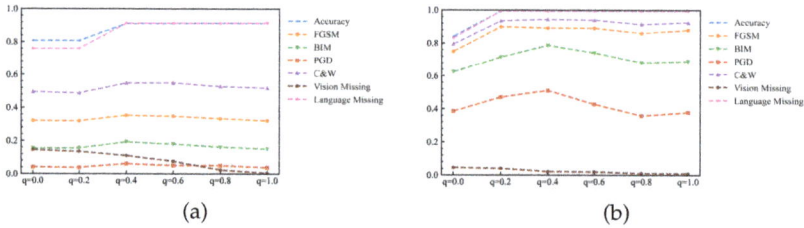

Figure 6. The accuracy trend of the visual modal integrity probability q. (**a**) Birds. (**b**) Flowers.

Table 8 and 9 shows the specific values of Figure 6. Tables show that the maximum number of maximum points for accuracy exists at $q = 0.4$ under the four adversarial examples attacks. The reason the accuracy maximum point appears at $q = 0.4$ when facing the adversarial example attack is that when the visual modality input data of the model is severely attacked, the unattacked linguistic modality features can describe the target better at this time. Lowering the p-value and making the model more biased to use the features of linguistic modality can improve some accuracy. Moreover, letting $q = 0$ and $q = 1$ both lead to a significant drop in the model's accuracy in the face of modal deficits, which suggests that when training with the random modal deactivation method, it is best not to have the model extremely biased towards training a single modality. A proper bias towards training linguistic modalities enables the model to learn better standard features.

Table 8. Accuracy averages for different cases with different values visual modal integrity probability parameter q for the Birds dataset.

	$q = 0.0$	$q = 0.2$	$q = 0.4$	$q = 0.6$	$q = 0.8$	$q = 1.0$
Accuracy	0.8100	0.8092	**0.9125**	0.9130	0.9153	0.9142
FGSM	0.3221	0.3203	**0.3538**	0.3486	0.3342	0.3223
BIM	0.1554	0.1562	**0.1934**	0.1809	0.1633	0.1528
PGD	0.0423	0.0394	0.0622	0.0515	**0.0505**	0.0393
C&W	0.4968	0.4888	0.5487	**0.5501**	0.5284	0.5198
Vision Missing	**0.1454**	0.1342	0.1098	0.0751	0.0232	0.0051
Language Missing	0.7606	0.7615	0.9136	0.9145	0.9135	**0.9154**

Table 9. Accuracy averages for different cases with different values of visual modal integrity probability parameter q for the Flowers dataset.

	$q = 0.0$	$q = 0.2$	$q = 0.4$	$q = 0.6$	$q = 0.8$	$q = 1.0$
Accuracy	0.8426	0.9956	**0.9959**	0.9956	0.9958	0.9967
FGSM	0.7520	**0.9011**	0.8943	0.8935	0.8619	0.8810
BIM	0.6245	0.7170	**0.7879**	0.7420	0.6835	0.6902
PGD	0.3866	0.4717	**0.5123**	0.4294	0.3595	0.3796
C&W	0.7959	0.9364	**0.9453**	0.9412	0.9160	0.9265
Vision Missing	**0.0458**	0.0408	0.0224	0.0204	0.0106	0.0093
Language Missing	0.8322	0.9954	0.9954	0.9959	0.9956	**0.9961**

(3) Analysis of the impact of pre-training on the model

The above experiments reveal that the model is more challenging to update the weights of the linguistic feature extraction module without the modal random deactivation method. After training with random modal deactivation, the model's accuracy in the face of language modality still needs to meet the requirements. For this reason, the number of training iterations required for each feature extraction module during the training of the multimodal model is not consistent. The feature extraction module of the visual modality is often already pre-trained on a large dataset, so the feature extraction module of the linguistic modality requires more iterations for training. Experiments were done with $p = 0.8$ and $q = 0.4$ to verify the above idea. Table 10 shows the experimental results, where pre-trained indicates that the language modality of the model has been pre-trained.

Table 10. The effect of pre-training of the language feature extraction module on various aspects of the model.

Dataset	p	q	Pretrained	Accuracy	FGSM	BIM	PGD	C&W	Vision Missing	Language Missing
Birds	0.8	0.4	False	0.9105	0.3639	0.2152	**0.0811**	0.3639	0.1775	**0.9138**
	0.8	0.4	True	**0.9114**	**0.3826**	**0.2231**	0.0642	**0.5730**	**0.5051**	0.9099
Flowers	0.8	0.4	False	**0.9951**	0.8451	0.7118	**0.4412**	0.9098	0.0382	**0.9961**
	0.8	0.4	True	0.9931	**0.8882**	**0.7656**	0.3803	**0.9509**	**0.6441**	0.9941

Table 10 shows that when the language feature extraction module is trained, the model's accuracy is substantially improved due to visual modality deficiency. At the same time, it can achieve some improvement in the face of the adversarial sample attacks of FGSM, BIM, and C&W. This indicates that the standard features of the multimodal fine-grained recognition model based on feature fusion are more likely to be biased to represent modal features that have been pre-trained. Therefore, it is desirable to pre-train each feature extraction module of the multimodal model to ensure that the standard features do not tend to represent a particular modality more often.

3.3. Discussion

The above experiments show that both EFCMF and Bi-modal PMA are multimodal fine-grained recognition methods based on feature fusion. However, the robustness of the two differs significantly because of the structural complexity between them. Bi-modal PMA transforms the features of the visual module into attention to linguistic modalities through the QRM eodule, a process that makes the model structure more complex. EFCMF, on the other hand, performs feature fusion using connections, which is a better way to reduce the complexity of multimodal fine-grained recognition models.

Bi-modal PMA and EFCMF without pre-training of the linguistic modality feature extraction module showed lower accuracy when faced with the missing of linguistic modality. The reason is that both models use a pre-trained visual modal feature extraction module, which requires far fewer iterations to train than the linguistic modal feature extraction module because it is pre-trained. At the same time, EFCMF is trained using random modal deactivation, which simulates the modal deficit and allows the model to cope with counter-sample attacks. The random deactivation train method and pre-training of the linguistic modal feature extraction module make EFCMF more capable of coping with the missing modality.

Although EFCMF is able to achieve 91.80% and 99.80% on Birds and Flowers datasets respectively, with specific parameters, the difference in accuracy of each parameter is not large, generally within 2%. Therefore, this study chooses to sacrifice some accuracy to improve the robustness of the model, which is also more beneficial to the application of the method in practical engineering.

In summary, it is because EFCMF employs various methods that facilitate the improvement of robustness that it has strong robustness in the face of modal deficiencies and against sample attacks.

4. Conclusions

In order to improve the ability of deep learning models to cope with modal missing and adversarial sample attacks, this study designs an enhanced framework for modal feature complementarity, EFCMF. The framework does not require additional expensive methods such as model distillation or adversarial training to train the models. The method effectively improves the models' robustness with appropriate parameter selection. Meanwhile, relevant experiments are conducted in the latest multimodal fine-grained classification methods using the training method of the framework, and the results show the validity of the findings. While ensuring the overall classification accuracy of the model and enhancing the ability of the model to extract features of each modality, the model gains the ability to cope with the lack of modality and some ability to cope with adversarial examples.

When facing the same level of adversarial sample attacks, EFCMF has a significant advantage over Bi-modal PMA in dealing with FGSM, PIM, and PGD adversarial sample attacks. It achieves a 15.56%, 8.81%, and 6.29% accuracy advantage on the Birds dataset and a 73.79%, 71.68%, and 37.84% accuracy advantage on the Flowers dataset, respectively. The average accuracy of EFCMF for both datasets is 52.85%, which is 27.13% higher than Bi-modal PMA when facing all four adversarial sample attacks. In the face of visual modal deficits, EFCMF achieves 45.65% and 63.43% higher accuracy on Birds and Flowers datasets, respectively. In the face of linguistic modal deficits, EFCMF achieved 12% and 9.42% higher accuracy on the Birds and Flowers datasets, respectively. The average precision of EFCMF for both datasets is 76.33%, which is 32.63% higher than that of Bi-modal PMA in the face of modal deficits. Regarding accuracy, EFCMF achieved 91.14% and 99.31% accuracy on the Birds and Flowers datasets. All these performances show that EFCMF has high accuracy and strong robustness.

Author Contributions: Conceptualization, R.Z., B.Z. and Y.C.; writing—original draft preparation, R.Z.; visualization, R.Z.; review and editing, Y.C., B.X. and B.S.; funding acquisition, B.Z. All authors have read and agreed to the published version of the manuscript.

Funding: This research was supported by the National Science Foundation of China (No. 61307025).

Institutional Review Board Statement: Not applicable.

Informed Consent Statement: Not applicable.

Data Availability Statement: The data presented in this study are available on request from the corresponding author.

Conflicts of Interest: The authors declare no conflict of interest.

References

1. Wah, C.; Branson, S.; Welinder, P.; Perona, P.; Belongie, S. *The Caltech-Ucsd Birds-200-2011 Dataset*; California Institute of Technology: Pasadena, CA, USA, 2011.
2. Nilsback, M.E.; Zisserman, A. Automated flower classification over a large number of classes. In Proceedings of the 2008 Sixth Indian Conference on Computer Vision, Graphics & Image Processing, Bhubaneswar, India, 16–19 December 2008; pp. 722–729. [CrossRef]
3. Khosla, A.; Jayadevaprakash, N.; Yao, B.; Li, F.F. Novel dataset for fine-grained image categorization: Stanford dogs. In *Proceedings of the CVPR Workshop on Fine-Grained Visual Categorization (FGVC)*; Citeseer: Princeton, NJ, USA, 2011; Volume 2.
4. Krause, J.; Stark, M.; Deng, J.; Fei-Fei, L. 3D Object Representations for Fine-Grained Categorization. In Proceedings of the IEEE International Conference on Computer Vision (ICCV) Workshops, Sydney, Australia, 1–8 December 2013.
5. Hou, S.; Feng, Y.; Wang, Z. Vegfru: A domain-specific dataset for fine-grained visual categorization. In Proceedings of the IEEE International Conference on Computer Vision, Venice, Italy, 22–29 October 2017; pp. 541–549.
6. Wei, X.S.; Cui, Q.; Yang, L.; Wang, P.; Liu, L. RPC: A large-scale retail product checkout dataset. *arXiv* **2019**, arXiv:1901.07249.
7. Peng, J.; Xiao, C.; Li, Y. RP2K: A large-scale retail product dataset for fine-grained image classification. *arXiv* **2020**, arXiv:2006.12634.
8. Wei, X.S.; Song, Y.Z.; Mac Aodha, O.; Wu, J.; Peng, Y.; Tang, J.; Yang, J.; Belongie, S. Fine-Grained Image Analysis with Deep Learning: A Survey. *IEEE Trans. Pattern Anal. Mach. Intell.* **2021**, *44*, 8927–8948. [CrossRef]
9. Ren, S.; He, K.; Girshick, R.; Sun, J. Faster R-CNN: Towards Real-Time Object Detection with Region Proposal Networks. In *Proceedings of the Advances in Neural Information Processing Systems*; Cortes, C., Lawrence, N., Lee, D., Sugiyama, M., Garnett, R., Eds.; Curran Associates, Inc.: Red Hook, NY, USA, 2015; Volume 28.
10. Carion, N.; Massa, F.; Synnaeve, G.; Usunier, N.; Kirillov, A.; Zagoruyko, S. End-to-end object detection with transformers. In Proceedings of the European Conference on Computer Vision, Glasgow, UK, 23–28 August 2020; pp. 213–229.
11. Redmon, J.; Farhadi, A. Yolov3: An incremental improvement. *arXiv* **2018**, arXiv:1804.02767.
12. Long, J.; Shelhamer, E.; Darrell, T. Fully convolutional networks for semantic segmentation. In Proceedings of the IEEE Conference on Computer Vision and Pattern Recognition, Boston, MA, USA, 7–12 June 2015; pp. 3431–3440.
13. Ronneberger, O.; Fischer, P.; Brox, T. U-net: Convolutional networks for biomedical image segmentation. In Proceedings of the International Conference on Medical image Computing and Computer-Assisted Intervention, Munich, Germany, 5–9 October 2015; pp. 234–241.
14. Huang, S.; Xu, Z.; Tao, D.; Zhang, Y. Part-stacked cnn for fine-grained visual categorization. In Proceedings of the IEEE Conference on Computer Vision and Pattern Recognition, Las Vegas, NV, USA, 27–30 June 2016.
15. Zhang, N.; Donahue, J.; Girshick, R.; Darrell, T. Part-based R-CNNs for fine-grained category detection. In *European Conference on Computer Vision*; Springer: Cham, Switzerland, 2014.
16. Huang, G.; Liu, Z.; Van Der Maaten, L.; Weinberger, K.Q. Densely connected convolutional networks. In Proceedings of the IEEE Conference on Computer Vision and Pattern Recognition, Honolulu, HI, USA, 21–26 July 2017; pp. 4700–4708.
17. Simonyan, K.; Zisserman, A. Very deep convolutional networks for large-scale image recognition. *arXiv* **2014**, arXiv:1409.1556.
18. Lin, T.Y.; RoyChowdhury, A.; Maji, S. Bilinear cnn models for fine-grained visual recognition. In Proceedings of the IEEE International Conference on Computer Vision, Santiago, Chile, 7–13 December 2015; pp. 1449–1457.
19. Min, S.; Yao, H.; Xie, H.; Zha, Z.J.; Zhang, Y. Multi-objective matrix normalization for fine-grained visual recognition. *IEEE Trans. Image Process.* **2020**, *29*, 4996–5009. [CrossRef] [PubMed]
20. Niu, L.; Veeraraghavan, A.; Sabharwal, A. Webly supervised learning meets zero-shot learning: A hybrid approach for fine-grained classification. In Proceedings of the IEEE Conference on Computer Vision and Pattern Recognition, Salt Lake City, UT, USA, 18–22 June 2018; pp. 7171–7180.
21. He, X.; Peng, Y. Fine-grained image classification via combining vision and language. In Proceedings of the IEEE Conference on Computer Vision and Pattern Recognition, Honolulu, HI, USA, 21–26 July 2017; pp. 5994–6002.
22. Li, J.; Zhu, L.; Huang, Z.; Lu, K.; Zhao, J. I Read, I Saw, I Tell: Texts Assisted Fine-Grained Visual Classification. In *Proceedings of the 26th ACM International Conference on Multimedia, MM '18*; Association for Computing Machinery: New York, NY, USA, 2018; pp. 663–671. [CrossRef]
23. Zhang, H.; Cao, X.; Wang, R. Audio Visual Attribute Discovery for Fine-Grained Object Recognition. In *Thirty-Second AAAI Conference on Artificial Intelligence and Thirtieth Innovative Applications of Artificial Intelligence Conference and Eighth AAAI Symposium on Educational Advances in Artificial Intelligence, AAAI'18/IAAI'18/EAAI'18*; AAAI Press: Washington, DC, USA, 2018.

24. Marino, K.; Salakhutdinov, R.; Gupta, A. The more you know: Using knowledge graphs for image classification. *arXiv* **2016**, arXiv:1612.04844.
25. Chen, T.; Lin, L.; Chen, R.; Wu, Y.; Luo, X. Knowledge-embedded representation learning for fine-grained image recognition. *arXiv* **2018**, arXiv:1807.00505.
26. He, Y.; Tian, L.; Zhang, L.; Zeng, X. Knowledge Graph Representation Fusion Framework for Fine-Grained Object Recognition in Smart Cities. *Complexity* **2021**, *2021*, 8041029. [CrossRef]
27. Szegedy, C.; Zaremba, W.; Sutskever, I.; Bruna, J.; Erhan, D.; Goodfellow, I.; Fergus, R. Intriguing properties of neural networks. *arXiv* **2013**, arXiv:1312.6199.
28. Goodfellow, I.J.; Shlens, J.; Szegedy, C. Explaining and harnessing adversarial examples. *arXiv* **2014**, arXiv:1412.6572.
29. Kurakin, A.; Goodfellow, I.J.; Bengio, S. Adversarial examples in the physical world. In *Artificial Intelligence Safety and Security*; Chapman and Hall/CRC: Boca Raton, FL, USA, 2018; pp. 99–112.
30. Madry, A.; Makelov, A.; Schmidt, L.; Tsipras, D.; Vladu, A. Towards deep learning models resistant to adversarial attacks. *arXiv* **2017**, arXiv:1706.06083.
31. Moosavi-Dezfooli, S.M.; Fawzi, A.; Frossard, P. Deepfool: A simple and accurate method to fool deep neural networks. In Proceedings of the IEEE Conference on Computer Vision and Pattern Recognition, Las Vegas, NV, USA, 27–30 June 2016; pp. 2574–2582.
32. Carlini, N.; Wagner, D. Towards evaluating the robustness of neural networks. In Proceedings of the 2017 IEEE Symposium on Security and Privacy, San Jose, CA, USA, 22–24 May 2017; pp. 39–57.
33. Liu, Z.; Lin, Y.; Cao, Y.; Hu, H.; Wei, Y.; Zhang, Z.; Lin, S.; Guo, B. Swin Transformer: Hierarchical Vision Transformer Using Shifted Windows. In Proceedings of the IEEE/CVF International Conference on Computer Vision (ICCV), Montreal, QC, Canada, 10–17 October 2021; pp. 10012–10022.
34. Zhang, Y.; Wallace, B. A sensitivity analysis of (and practitioners' guide to) convolutional neural networks for sentence classification. *arXiv* **2015**, arXiv:1510.03820.
35. Deng, J.; Dong, W.; Socher, R.; Li, L.J.; Li, K.; Fei-Fei, L. Imagenet: A large-scale hierarchical image database. In Proceedings of the 2009 IEEE Conference on Computer Vision and Pattern Recognition, Miami, FL, USA, 20–25 June 2009; pp. 248–255.
36. Reed, S.; Akata, Z.; Lee, H.; Schiele, B. Learning deep representations of fine-grained visual descriptions. In Proceedings of the IEEE Conference on Computer Vision and Pattern Recognition, Las Vegas, NV, USA, 27–30 June 2016; pp. 49–58.
37. Paszke, A.; Gross, S.; Massa, F.; Lerer, A.; Bradbury, J.; Chanan, G.; Killeen, T.; Lin, Z.; Gimelshein, N.; Antiga, L.; et al. PyTorch: An Imperative Style, High-Performance Deep Learning Library. In *Proceedings of the Advances in Neural Information Processing Systems*; Wallach, H., Larochelle, H., Beygelzimer, A., d'Alché-Buc, F., Fox, E., Garnett, R., Eds.; Curran Associates, Inc.: Red Hook, NY, USA, 2019; Volume 32.
38. Kim, H. Torchattacks: A pytorch repository for adversarial attacks. *arXiv* **2020**, arXiv:2010.01950.
39. Cui, Y.; Song, Y.; Sun, C.; Howard, A.; Belongie, S. Large scale fine-grained categorization and domain-specific transfer learning. In Proceedings of the IEEE Conference on Computer Vision and Pattern Recognition, Salt Lake City, UT, USA, 18–22 June 2018; pp. 4109–4118.
40. Touvron, H.; Cord, M.; El-Nouby, A.; Verbeek, J.; Jégou, H. Three things everyone should know about Vision Transformers. *arXiv* **2022**, arXiv:2203.09795.
41. Zhao, Y.; Li, J.; Chen, X.; Tian, Y. Part-Guided Relational Transformers for Fine-Grained Visual Recognition. *IEEE Trans. Image Process.* **2021**, *30*, 9470–9481. [CrossRef] [PubMed]
42. Song, K.; Wei, X.S.; Shu, X.; Song, R.J.; Lu, J. Bi-modal progressive mask attention for fine-grained recognition. *IEEE Trans. Image Process.* **2020**, *29*, 7006–7018. [CrossRef]

Disclaimer/Publisher's Note: The statements, opinions and data contained in all publications are solely those of the individual author(s) and contributor(s) and not of MDPI and/or the editor(s). MDPI and/or the editor(s) disclaim responsibility for any injury to people or property resulting from any ideas, methods, instructions or products referred to in the content.

Fuzzy MLKNN in Credit User Portrait [†]

Zhuangyi Zhang, Lu Han * and Muzi Chen

School of Management Science and Engineering, Central University of Finance and Economics, Beijing 100081, China
* Correspondence: hanluivy@126.com
† This paper is an extended version of a paper published in the proceedings of the 4th International Conference on Information Technology and Computer Communications, 23 August 2022, New York, United States.

Abstract: Aiming at the problems of subjective enhancement caused by the discretization of credit data and the lack of a multi-dimensional portrait of credit users in the current credit data research, this paper proposes an improved Fuzzy MLKNN multi-label learning algorithm based on MLKNN. On the one hand, the subjectivity of credit data after discretization is weakened by introducing intuitionistic fuzzy numbers. On the other hand, the algorithm is improved by using the corresponding fuzzy Euclidean distance to realize the multi-label portrait of credit users. The experimental results show that Fuzzy MLKNN performs significantly better than MLKNN on credit data and has the most significant improvement on *One Error*.

Keywords: Fuzzy MLKNN; multi-label learning; user portrait; Credit Reference Data

1. Introduction

The Credit Reference Database of the People's Bank in China is a fundamental credit database in which the basic information and credit information of legal persons and organizations are collected, sorted, preserved, and processed in accordance with the law, where credit data are generally divided into corporate credit data and personal credit data [1]. An enterprise's credit report data report generally includes the basic information of the enterprise, affiliated company information, financial statements, information summary, credit history, etc., while in a personal credit report, the content generally includes basic personal information, work, and residence. Information, individual credit card information, default information, etc. [2]. With the expansion of credit reporting, the credit reporting system is constantly being upgraded. The personal education and residence information of the first-generation system has been further improved, and the loan repayment record has been increased from two years to five years. It is known as "the most stringent credit investigation system in history" [3]. From a macro perspective, based on credit data, through database technology and the credit analysis system, it can help banks obtain various credit reports, thereby providing a reference for credit demanders to formulate plans and identify risks. At the same time, regularly publishing a blacklist of untrustworthy enterprises, introducing honest enterprises, and releasing relevant information to the public can play a role in monitoring bad business practices and encouraging honesty and trustworthiness. Therefore, credit data is the basic link to the operation of the social credit system, and it is of great significance for the realization of the functions of the social credit system. From a micro perspective, the revealing function of personal credit data can help individuals prove their credit status in a short period, thereby helping borrowers with good credit to obtain loans quickly. For lending institutions, they can also quickly learn about lenders to help judge and control credit risks and to assist them in credit management activities on this basis [4].

Categorized from the perspective of data processing, credit data mainly includes original survey data and processed data. From the perspective of data attributes, credit data is mainly divided into quantitative and qualitative data. Qualitative data is a record of some facts described in language form, and quantitative data can be directly used for quantitative analysis. Many qualitative data can be quantified, but credit data itself has the characteristics of many variables, a large amount of sample information, and is non intuitive [5]. Therefore, how to intuitively obtain the user's credit information from a large amount of data has become an urgent problem to be solved. In recent years, research on data mining has emerged. Some scholars have discussed the relationship between data mining and credit reporting systems, sorted out the basic framework of applying data mining in credit reporting systems, and applied traditional data mining methods to handling credit data [6]. According to the characteristics of credit data, some scholars use the method of feature selection and other basic machine learning algorithms to process personal credit data to study the personal credit status of users [7,8].

However, the limitation of past research is that, on the one hand, the discretization method used to process credit information data in the past process will weaken the objectivity of the data. On the other hand, the classification method of classical machine learning is used, along with a single label, such as portraits of users and "good" and "bad", which will bring about a lot of information loss. Therefore, developing a multi-label learning algorithm suitable for analyzing credit data is the key problem to solving the multi-dimensional portrait of credit users. Based on this, this paper first uses fuzzy Euclidean distance to improve the classical MLKNN multi-label learning algorithm based on fuzzing the data after the discretization of credit data. The improved algorithm is called Fuzzy MLKNN Then the processed data set is used to train the learner and implement multi-label portraits of credit reporting users during the testing process. Provide technical support for digging deeply into the characteristics of credit reporting user groups and interpreting credit reports. The innovations of this paper are as follows: On the one hand, it provides a new data processing method for the field of credit data mining and introduces an improved multi-label learning algorithm, which expands the breadth of machine learning in the field of credit data research. On the other hand, it creatively combines fuzzy set theory with a multi-label learning algorithm and conducts more in-depth research on improving the multi-label learning algorithm.

The structure of the rest of the paper is as follows. In Section 2, we summarize the related work of multi-label learning; in Section 3, we propose the Fuzzy MLKNN algorithm. Section 4 shows the experimental performance of Fuzzy MLKNN and traditional algorithms and the comparison of Fuzzy MLKNN and other classic multi-label learning algorithms; in Section 5 we use Fuzzy MLKNN to analyze the credit user portraits; in the final section we summarize the research conclusions and put forward suggestions for further study.

2. Literature Review
2.1. Multi-Label Learning

Multi-label learning is an important branch of machine learning, which is different from traditional single-label learning in that there are multiple labels corresponding to each predicted sample [9]. In recent years, multi-label learning has been widely used in text classification [10,11], sentiment analysis [12], image recognition, and other fields, and various multi-label classification algorithms have emerged one after another. The existing multi-label learning algorithms are mainly proposed from two perspectives: one is based on transformation, and the other is self-adaptation [13].

From the transformation, it is always based on converting to binary classification, typical methods directly convert multi-label problems into multiple single-label problems, and each label is judged by the presence or absence [14–16]. The three most commonly used problem transformation methods are Binary Correlation (BR) [17], Label Power Set (LP) [18], and Chain of Classifiers (CC) [19]. BR transforms the multi-label problem into a set of independent binary problems. Then, each binary problem is processed using a traditional classifier. LP treats each unique label set as a class identifier, transforming the original multi-label dataset into a multi-class dataset. After using it to train a regular classifier, the predicted classes are inverse transformed to label subsets. However, with the number of tags increasing, the number of binary codes tends to increase exponentially, affecting the algorithm's performance, so it does not have good generalization ability. CC is an extension of BR, which strings two classifiers into a chain for learning, considering the correlation between labels, but the algorithm's performance needs to be improved. Both BR and LP are the basis of many multi-label ensemble-based methods. CC addresses the BR limitation by considering the label association task. [20–22].

From the self-adaptation, it refers to the algorithms which can automatically adapt to the multi-label classification problem [23–25]. Typical adaptive multi-label classification algorithms are RankSVM, ML-DT, MLKNN, etc. RankSVM is an improvement to the traditional SVM, which modifies the loss in SVM to a ranking loss and optimizes the linear classifier to minimize the label ranking loss [26]. ML-DT is an improvement to the traditional decision tree. It draws on the idea of the decision tree to filter features according to the information gain to generate a classifier and uses the information gain to represent the feature's ability to discriminate all labels [27]. The MLKNN algorithm is a KNN-based multi-label classification algorithm [28–30]. The algorithm finds the K nearest neighbor samples. It performs statistical analysis on the labels of the K nearest neighbor samples to obtain the probability that the predicted sample contains each label. MLKNN outperforms some of the well-established multi-label learning algorithms mentioned above and is easy to understand and implement [31]. Furthermore, MLKNN is less restrictive in its use and is suitable for a wide variety of multi-label learning problems [28]. A summary of each algorithm, as well as the advantages and disadvantages, can be found in Table 1.

Table 1. Summary of advantages and disadvantages of multi-label learning algorithms.

Algorithm	Descriptions	Advantages	Disadvantages
Binary Correlation (BR)	Individual classifier for each label	Simple	Ignores label correlations
Label Power Set (LP)	Each unique label set as a class identifier	Simple	Not applicable to more labels
Chain of Classifiers (CC)	Extension of BR, String two classifiers into a chain for learning	Consider label correlations	Performance depends on the order of classifiers in the chain
RankSVM	Improvement to the traditional SVM	Performance improvement	Not suitable for dealing with high-dimensional samples
ML-DT	Improvement to the traditional DT	Performance improvement	Not suitable for processing continuous variables, large samples, and multi-class data
MLKNN	Improvement to the traditional KNN	Strong applicability, Performance improvement	Ignores label correlations

2.2. Application of Fuzzy Theory

Nowadays, fuzzy theory has also been used widely to measure uncertainty. It is a form of alternative mathematics suited for vagueness, especially for small quantities [32]. According to the characteristics of the multi-label problem, most of the multi-labels can be transformed into fuzzy numbers and then recognized and calculated through fuzzy rules using machine learning methods, such as clustering. The classic clustering algorithm is a fuzzy mean clustering algorithm. FCM is the most common way of introducing the membership function in fuzzy set theory into the calculation of distance to achieve better cluster division [33]. In recent years, scholars have not only improved fuzzy mean clustering on fuzzy computing rules [34–36] but also proposed a series of fuzzy clustering methods [37–39], such as Probabilistic Intuitionistic Fuzzy Hierarchical Clustering (PIFHC) [40]. PIFHC considers intuitionistic fuzzy sets to deal with the uncertainty present in the data. Instead of using traditional hamming distance or Euclidean distance measure to find the distance between the data points, PIFHC uses the probabilistic Euclidean distance measure to propose a hierarchical clustering approach. And from experiments with the real-world car dataset and the Listeria monocytogenes dataset, intuitionistic distance can improve by 1–3.5% in the clustering accuracy.

Based on the above research, MLKNN is a multi-label learning algorithm with excellent performance and strong applicability. At the same time, as an adaptive algorithm, it can process a large amount of data information quickly, and the operation efficiency is fast. Therefore, we select MLKNN as the learning algorithm, as the intuitionistic fuzzy number can express the discretized attribute variable value more objectively. Meanwhile, the distance calculation process existing in the MLKNN can be improved by a new fuzzy distance formula. We explore the intuitionistic fuzzy distance to improve the MLKNN algorithm, proposed as Fuzzy MLKNN.

3. Fuzzy MLKNN

This section will give a detailed introduction to Fuzzy MLKNN. Fuzzy MLKNN is an improvement based on classic MLKNN, mainly in finding K nearest neighbor samples in the traditional MLKNN algorithm. The distance between two sample points in high-dimensional space is changed from the traditional Euclidean measure improved to a fuzzy Euclidean one. Therefore, this part first defines the multi-label problem in Section 3.1, then introduces the related concepts of fuzzy sets and fuzzy distance measurement in Section 3.2, and finally introduces the specific process of Fuzzy MLKNN in Section 3.3.

3.1. Problem Definition

We define the problem to be studied in this paper as follows: Let $X = \{x_1, x_2, x_3 \ldots x_n\}$ denote the sample space, $L = \{l_1, l_2, l_3 \ldots l_m\}$ denote the label set, $Y = \{y_1, y_2, y_3 \ldots y_n\}$ represents the label space. For any item l_i in L ($1 \leq i \leq m$), there is $l_i \in \{0,1\}$, and when l_i takes 0, it means that the label is no related label, when l_i is 1, it means the label is a related label. Given training set D = $\{(x_i, l_i) \mid 1 \leq i \leq n, x_i \in X, l_i \in L\}$, the goal of multi-label learning-Fuzzy MLKNN is to train from a given training set D, A multi-label classifier Fuzzy MLKNN: $X \to 2^L$, obtained through a training label classifier to predict the set of labels contained in unknown samples.

3.2. Basic Concepts of Intuitionistic Fuzzy Sets

Fuzzy set theory was first proposed by Professor Zadeh in 1965 and was first used in fuzzy control [41]. It is an effective tool for dealing with uncertain information. Later, with the deepening of research, in 1986, the concept of the intuitionistic fuzzy set (IFS) was introduced into the traditional fuzzy sets [42]. Intuitionistic fuzzy sets can more accurately describe the nature of fuzziness in information from the two dimensions of membership and non-membership and have greater advantages and characteristics when dealing with uncertainty and ambiguity. It has attracted more attention in the application fields, such as pattern recognition, intelligent control, natural language processing, machine learning, etc. [43].

Definition 1. *Assuming that X is a non-empty set, $A = \{(x, \mu_A(x), v_A(x)) | x \in X\}$ is called an intuitionistic fuzzy set.*

Among them, $\mu_A(x) \in [0,1]$ and $v_A(x) \in [0,1]$ are the degree of membership and non-membership of element x belonging to A, respectively, $0 \leq \mu_A(x) + v_A(x) \leq 1\ \forall x \in X$. Also, $\pi_A(x) = 1 - \mu_A(x) - v_A(x)$ is called the degree of hesitation that the element x belongs to A. Generally, the intuitionistic fuzzy number is denoted as $\alpha = (\mu_\alpha, v_\alpha)$ [44]. The intuitionistic fuzzy set proposed by Atanassov is an extension of the traditional fuzzy set [32]. The introduction of the non-membership function enables the intuitionistic fuzzy set to express uncertain and fuzzy data more delicately and objectively.

Definition 2. *The Euclidean distance of any two intuitionistic fuzzy numbers $\alpha_1 = (\mu_{\alpha 1}, v_{\alpha 1})$ and $\alpha_2 = (\mu_{\alpha 2}, v_{\alpha 2})$ is defined as:*

$$d(\alpha_1, \alpha_2) = \sqrt{\frac{1}{2}(\mu_{\alpha 1} - \mu_{\alpha 2})^2 + (v_{\alpha 1} - v_{\alpha 2})^2} \tag{1}$$

3.3. Fuzzy MLKNN

The basic idea of the traditional MLKNN algorithm is to draw on the idea of the KNN algorithm to find K samples adjacent to the predicted sample, count the number of each label in the K samples, and then calculate the probability of the test sample containing each label through the maximum posterior probability [45]. The label whose predicted probability is greater than a certain threshold is the label of the predicted sample.

The improved MLKNN algorithm using the intuitionistic fuzzy distance is mainly the process of finding K nearest neighbor samples in the traditional MLKNN algorithm. The measure of the distance between two sample points in high-dimensional space is improved from the traditional Euclidean measure to the fuzzy Euclidean measure to find more accurate nearest neighbor sample points with reference significance for label prediction. The specific mathematical form and symbolic expression of the algorithm follow, and the basic notation is shown in Table 2.

Table 2. Notation.

Variables	Description
X	Samples space
Y	Labels space
x_i	Arbitrary i-th sample
α_i	Feature vector of x_i. The elements in α_i are composed of intuitionistic fuzzy numbers.
y_i	Label set of x_i
L	The label category vector
l	Arbitrary single category label $l \in L$
$N(x)$	The set of K nearest neighbors of x identified in the training set
$C_x(l)$	The number of sample with label l in neighbor set $N(x)$
H_1^l	the event that x has label l
H_0^l	The event that x has not label l
E_j^l	The event that, among the K nearest neighbors of x, there are exactly j instances with label l.

Suppose the training set is $X = \{x_1, x_2, x_3 \ldots x_n\}$, indicating that there are n training samples. The feature data in each training sample is represented by $\alpha = (\alpha_1, \alpha_2, \ldots \alpha_t)$. There are t features in total, and each feature data is represented by an intuitionistic fuzzy number. The label set of the training sample is $Y = \{y_1, y_2, y_3 \ldots y_n\}$, It represents the label set corresponding to each sample. $L = \{l_1, l_2, l_3 \ldots l_m\}$ represents the label category vector, and m represents the number of label types. It is known that the training sample is $x \in X$, and its corresponding label set is $y_x \subseteq Y$, If $y_x(l) = 1$, it means that the label l is included in the label set of the sample x, otherwise $y_x(l) = 0$, it means that the label set of sample x does not contain the label l. Furthermore, let $N(x)$ denote the set of K nearest neighbors of x identified in the training set, $C_x(l)$ refers to the number of samples with label l in the K nearest neighbors of x. H_1^l represents the event that sample x has the label l, H_0^l represents the event that sample x has not the label l. E_j^l represents the event that, among the K nearest neighbors of test sample x, there are exactly j samples with label l. At this time, the formula of MLKNN for multi-label classification obtained according to Bayes' theorem is as follows:

$$y_x(l) = \underset{b \in \{0,1\}}{\arg\max} \frac{P(H_b^l) P(E_q^l | H_b^l)}{P(E_q^l)} = \underset{b \in \{0,1\}}{\arg\max} P(H_b^l) P(E_q^l | H_b^l) \tag{2}$$

Among them, b takes 0 or 1. If we want to get whether the label l belongs to sample x, we only need to judge which value of b can maximize the value of the formula. If the formula value is the largest when $b = 1$, it is proved that $y_x(l) = 1$, that is, the sample x has the label l. On the contrary, if the value of the formula is the largest when $b = 0$, it is proved that $y_x(l) = 0$, that is, the sample does not have the label l. In calculating the K nearest neighbor samples, the distance calculation between samples is involved, so we use fuzzy Euclidean to measure the distance between fuzzy data. The specific measurement formula is shown in the above Equation (2).

For each label l in the equation, its corresponding prior probability $P(H_b^l)$ can be calculated by Equation (3). That is, divide the number of samples with label l in the training set by the total number of samples in the training set.

$$P(H_1^l) = (s + \sum_{i=1}^{n} y_x)/(s \times 2 + n)$$

$$P(H_0^l) = 1 - P(H_1^l) \tag{3}$$

Among them, s is a smoothing parameter controlling the strength of uniform prior. In this paper, s is set to be 1, which yields the Laplace smoothing, and $\sum_{i=1}^{n} y_x$ represents the total number of samples with label l in the n training samples.

The posterior probability can be calculated by Equations (4) and (5).

$$P(E_j^l | H_1^l) = (s + c[j])/(s \times (k+1) + \sum_{p=0}^{k} c[p]) \tag{4}$$

$$P(E_j^l | H_0^l) = (s + c'[j])/(s \times (k+1) + \sum_{p=0}^{k} c'[p]) \tag{5}$$

Among them, j represents the number of samples with label l in the K nearest neighbor samples of test sample x. $c[j]$ represents the number of samples in all training samples whose K neighbors have j samples with label l, and themselves also have label l. And $c'[j]$ means the number of samples in all training samples whose K neighbors have j samples with label l, but the samples themselves do not contain label l. Then, this paper calculates the probability that sample x contains label l by Equation (6).

$$P(l) = P(H_1^l)P(E_j^l|H_1^l)/P(H_1^l)P(E_j^l|H_1^l) + P(H_0^l)P(E_j^l|H_0^l) \tag{6}$$

The whole algorithm can be found in Appendix A.

4. Experiments

4.1. Evaluation Metrics

The general performance evaluation metrics of multi-label learning algorithms have been extensively studied and sorted out by researchers [46,47]. In this paper, we select the five most commonly used indicators to compare the performance of the algorithms. Among them, *HammingLoss* is considered from the perspective of samples. The other four indicators are considered from the perspective of label ranking. They include *Average_Precision*, *RankingLoss*, *OneError*, and *Coverage*. The specific calculation form of these indicators will be explained below.

HammingLoss refers to the average number of misclassifications of multiple labels on a single sample. The smaller the indicator, the better the performance of the algorithm.

$$HL = \frac{1}{t}\sum_{i=1}^{t}\frac{1}{m}|Z_i \Delta Y_i|$$

where t is the number of test samples, m is the number of labels, Z_i is the predicted label set, Y_i is the real label set, and | | represents the difference between the two sets, that is, the number of errors between the predicted labels and the true labels.

Average_Precision is different from Precision in single-label classification. It is not the average Precision of all training samples on each label but represents the average probability that the order of the predicted relevant labels is before the specific real relevant labels. The larger the index, the better the performance.

$$averagePrecision = \frac{1}{t}\sum_{i=1}^{t}\frac{1}{|Y_i|}\sum_{y \in Y_i}\frac{|\{y'|rank_f(x_i,y') \leq rank_f(x_i,y), y' \in Y_i\}|}{rank_f(x_i,y)}$$

RankingLoss indicates an incorrect ranking in the ranking sequence of the label set owned by the sample, that is, the number of times that the ranking of the relevant labels appears behind the irrelevant labels. The smaller the index, the better the performance of the algorithm.

$$RL = \frac{1}{t}\sum_{i=1}^{t}\frac{1}{|Y_i||\overline{Y_i}|}|\{(y',y'')|f(x_i,y') \leq f(x_i,y''), (y',y'') \in Y_i \times \overline{Y_i}\}|$$

where $\overline{Y_i}$ is the complementary set of Y_i to the total label set L.

OneError refers to the number of times that the first-ranked label in the predicted label of the sample does not belong to the sample-related label. The smaller the index, the better the performance of the algorithm.

$$oneError = \frac{1}{t}\sum_{i=1}^{t}(\underset{l_j \in L}{\operatorname{argmax}}f(x_i,l_j) \notin Y_i)$$

Coverage can be understood as the step size in the sorted sequence of predicted label sets that needs to be traversed to get all the true relevant label sets. Likewise, the smaller the metric, the better the algorithm performance.

$$coverage = \frac{1}{t}\sum_{i=1}^{t}\underset{y \in Y_i}{\operatorname{maxrank}}_f(x_i,y) - 1$$

where -1 ensures there is no limit case of misclassification; that is, the top-ranked predicted labels are their true labels.

4.2. Experiment Setting

The data in this experiment is the credit data of some users from 2008 to 2012 provided by the Credit Center of the People's Bank of China, including about 10,000 user records. The attributes involved in the data include three aspects: basic personal information, account opening information, and credit activity information. There are 37 attributes, including 6 binary attributes, 12 nominal attributes, and 19 numerical attributes. There are 8 pieces of corresponding label information, which are considered from three aspects: personal development and stability, frequency of credit activities, and attention to credit status. This part of the information is obtained from financial institutions. However, there is a lot of missing data and incomplete information in these data. Therefore, before conducting experiments, data cleaning and data preprocessing are required to ensure the quality of data used for model training.

First, after removing privacy variables, such as ID number, telephone number, address, etc., the correlation test of variables was carried out, and some variables with a correlation exceeding 0.7 were removed. A total of 11 attribute variables were selected from 37 attribute variables for the experiment (including 2 nominal attributes and 9 numerical attributes). The correlation matrices of some variables are shown in Table 3.

Then delete the missing and obviously unreasonable data in these attribute data and finally, select 1000 pieces of data with complete information for the experiments. The basic information of the data set used for the experiments is described in Table 4. Cardinality represents the average number of labels per sample; Density represents the label density, which is calculated by dividing Cardinality by the number of labels, and Proportion represents the specific label proportion of the samples.

Table 3. Correlation matrices of some variables.

Coefficient of Correlation	(1)	(2)	(3)	(4)	(5)	(6)	(7)	(8)	(9)	(10)
(1) year_income	1	0	0	0	0.01	0.01	0	0	0.04	0.03
(2) credit_over_amount	0	1	0.02	0.03	−0.02	−0.03	−0.02	−0.02	−0.01	−0.02
(3) loan_over_amount	0	0.02	1	1	−0.01	−0.01	−0.02	−0.02	0	−0.01
(4) total_over_amount	0	0.03	1	1	−0.01	−0.01	−0.02	−0.02	0	−0.01
(5) bank_legal_org_num	0.01	−0.02	−0.01	−0.01	1	0.99	0.94	0.94	0.58	0.64
(6) bank_org_num	0.01	−0.03	−0.01	−0.01	0.99	1	0.93	0.93	0.59	0.65
(7) credit_legal_org_num	0	−0.02	−0.02	−0.02	0.94	0.93	1	1	0.58	0.63
(8) credit_org_num	0	−0.02	−0.02	−0.02	0.94	0.93	1	1	0.58	0.63
(9) total_credit_amount	0.04	−0.01	0	0	0.58	0.59	0.58	0.58	1	0.52
(10) query	0.03	−0.02	−0.01	−0.01	0.64	0.65	0.63	0.63	0.52	1

Table 4. Original dataset information.

Examples		Features			Labels		
train	test	Nominal	Numeric	Numbers	Cardinality	Density	Proportion
700	300	2	9	8	3	0.375	0.018

Second, in the process of data preprocessing, since the original attribute data are different in nature and magnitude, this paper needs to uniformly convert nominal attributes and numerical attributes into discrete variables and perform segmentation processing. However, this process will cause the subjectivity of the real data to be amplified. Therefore, we intuitively fuzzify the discrete data to ensure the objectivity and accuracy of the original data as much as possible and to facilitate our calculations.

Therefore, we need to process the data in two stages. The first is discretization, and the second is fuzzification. According to the objective data interval distribution of the variables themselves after discretization, we assign corresponding fuzzy numbers to each group of variables using the cumulative probability distribution in probability statistics. For example, for the discrete variable distribution of annual income, we will count the probability of each discrete variable, such as "1", "2", "3", etc., and then calculate its cumulative distribution to determine the membership degree which belongs to the income set. In addition, for the convenience of calculation, the hesitation degree is set to 0, so the non-membership degree is 1 minus the membership degree. The specific processing processes are shown in Tables 5 and 6.

Table 5. Representative the credit variable data conversion process record.

Attribute Name	Data Conversion Process
education	Primary school = 1; Secondary technical school = 2; Junior high school = 3; Senior middle school =4; Junior college = 5; University = 6; Postgraduate = 7
year_income	1~10,000 RMB = 1; 10,001~50,000 RMB = 2; 50,001~100,000 RMB = 3; 100,001~500,000 RMB = 4; 500,001~1,000,000 RMB = 5; more than 1,000,000 RMB = 6
career	Soldier = 1; Heads of state agencies, party organizations, enterprises, and institutions = 2; Clerks and related personnel = 3; Production personnel in agriculture, forestry, animal husbandry, fishery, and water conservancy = 4; Commercial and service industry personnel = 5; Professional skill worker = 6; Production and transportation equipment operators and related personnel = 7
credit_account	1~5 = 1; 6~10 = 2; 11~20 = 3; 21~50 = 4; more than 50 = 5;

Table 5. *Cont.*

Attribute Name	Data Conversion Process
loan_strokecount	0~2 times = 1; 3~5 times = 2; 6~8 times = 3; 9~11 times = 4; more than 11 times = 5
total_credit_amount	1~10,000 RMB = 1; 10,001~50,000 RMB = 2; 50,001~100,000 RMB = 3; 100,001~500,000 RMB = 4; 500,001~1,000,000 RMB = 5; More than 1,000,000 RMB = 6
total_use_amount	1~10,000 RMB = 1; 10,001~50,000 RMB = 2; 50,001~100,000 RMB = 3; 100,001~500,000 RMB = 4; 500,001~1,000,000 RMB = 5; More than 1,000,000 RMB = 6
credit_amount_utilization_rate	0~0.3 = 1; 0.3~0.6 = 2; 0.6~0.9 = 3; 0.9~1 = 4
query	1~5 times = 1; 6~10 times = 2; 11~20 times = 3; 21~50 times = 4; 51~100 times = 5; more than 100 times = 6
credit_over_amount	No overdraft = 0; Overdraft = 1
total_over_amount	No overdue = 0; Overdue = 1

Table 6. Fuzzification process.

Attribute Name	Corresponding Intuitionistic Fuzzy Number
education	1:(0.01, 0.99); 2:(0.10, 0.90); 3:(0.17, 0.83); 4:(0.41, 0.59); 5:(0.79, 0.21); 6:(0.98, 0.02); 7(1, 0)
year_income	1:(0.01, 0.99); 2:(0.40, 0.60); 3:(0.73, 0.27); 4:(0.95, 0.05); 5:(0.98, 0.02); 6:(1, 0)
credit_amount_utilization_rate	1:(0.09, 0.91); 2:(0.20, 0.80); 3:(0.58, 0.42); 4:(0.97, 0.03); 5:(1, 0)

After the attributes are processed, the label information must be converted into numerical values. The label information is obtained from the experience data of financial institutions. The specific label information and serial numbers are shown in Table 7. In the process of experimental testing, any one of the 8 labels may exist in the label set of the predicted sample.

Table 7. Label information conversion process record.

Coding	1	2	3	4	5	6	7	8
Labels Name	Personal development stability	Personal development instability	Low frequency of credit activities	Medium frequency of credit activities	High frequency of credit activities	Low attention to credit status	Normal attention to credit status	High attention to credit status

In the experiment, we refer to the method of the paper [48], use the matrix to represent the situation between the sample and the label, establish an m*n matrix, let n be the number of samples, m the number of labels, let $m_i n_j = -1$ or 1, where =1 represents the jth sample and has the label i, otherwise meaning the sample does not have the label i.

The experimental environment in this research is MATLAB (R2019b). There are two parameters involved in the experiment. One is the selection of the K value; the other is the setting of smoothing parameters. Regarding the choice of K value, generally speaking, if the K value is too small, it is easily affected by abnormal points. The model is easy to overfit, while if the K value is too large, it is more likely to suffer from problems caused by unbalanced samples, resulting in under-fitting; such results can be seen in the work of [49]. Therefore, in this paper, K is changed from 2 to 40, and the traditional MLKNN algorithm and the improved MLKNN algorithm are compared. A total of 80 experiments are carried out to obtain the performance change effect chart, to determine the optimal K value under the two algorithms, and to compare the results. Regarding the smoothing parameter, we are consistent with the existing literature and are set to the default value of 1.

4.3. Comparison with Fuzzy MLKNN and Other Multi-Label Learning Algorithms

After determining the most suitable K value, this paper further compares the performance of the improved algorithm proposed with other commonly used multi-label learning algorithms on the credit data set. According to the classification of multi-label learning algorithms, this paper considers two types of multi-label learning algorithms. One is the multi-label algorithm based on problem transformation, including Binary Relevance and Classifier Chain, and the other is the adaptive algorithm Rank SVM. As a result, the performance of the algorithm is studied. The comparison results are shown in Table 8.

Table 8. Performance comparison between different multi-label algorithms.

	Binary Relevance	Classifier Chain	Rank SVM	Fuzzy MLKNN
HammingLoss	0.1947	0.2584	0.1688	0.0867
Average_Precision	0.8652	0.7542	0.8944	0.9436
RankingLoss	0.1281	0.2410	0.0900	0.0500
OneError	0.0852	0.2130	0.0667	0.0133
Coverage	3.0500	3.5200	2.9900	2.5267

By comparing the five indicators in the table, it is found that the improved Fuzzy MLKNN shows better and better performance in learning the credit data set. Among them, the two indicators of *HammingLoss* and *OneError* have the most obvious advantages. This paper finds that its learning time is relatively short. In addition, comparing the five indicators of other algorithms, it is found that the performance of Rank SVM is second, the performance of the *RankingLoss* indicator is relatively good, and the performance of Classifier Chain on the credit data set is the worst. Therefore, this paper further uses the improved MLKNN to predict the test set data.

4.4. Comparative Analysis of Fuzzy MLKNN with MLKNN

According to the above parameter settings, two sets of comparative experiments are carried out on the preprocessed data set to observe the performance under different K values and compare the advantages and disadvantages of the traditional algorithm and the improved algorithm. The results are shown in Figures 1–5.

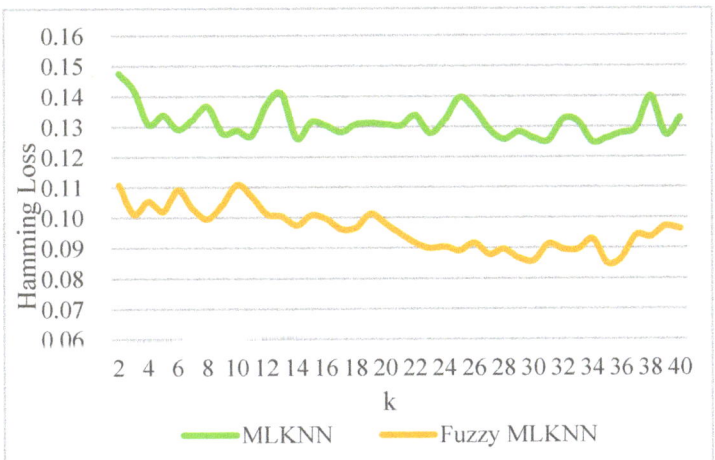

Figure 1. *HammingLoss* values under different K values.

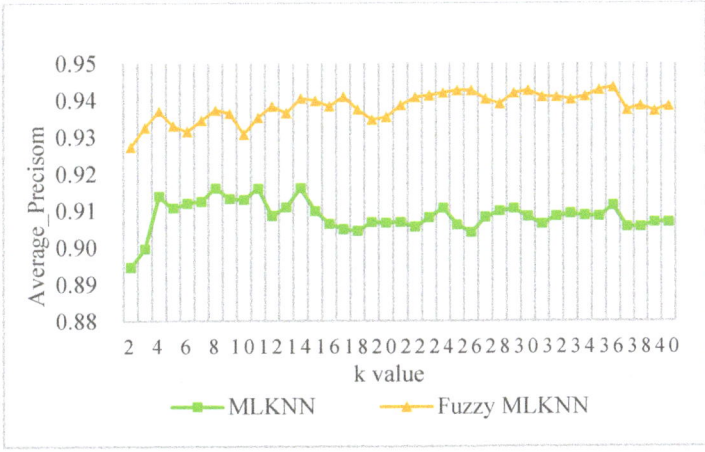

Figure 2. *Average_Precision* under different K values.

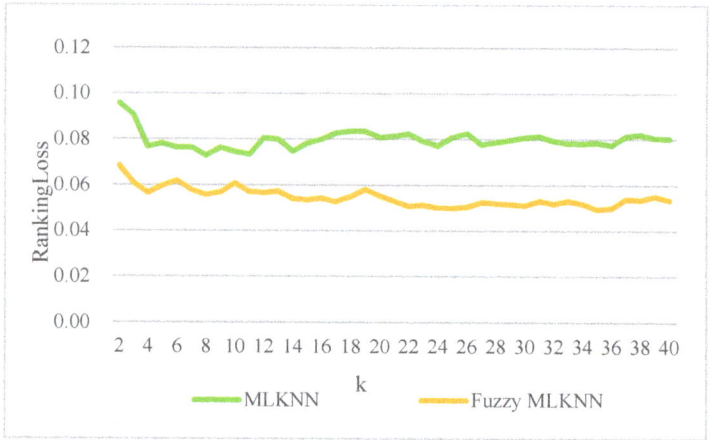

Figure 3. *RankingLoss* under different K values.

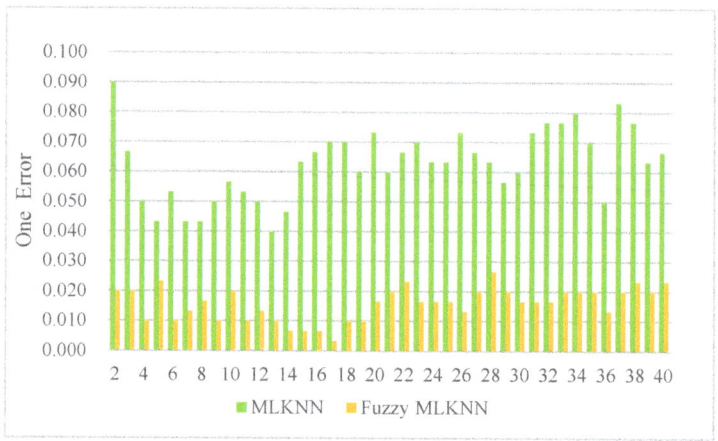

Figure 4. *One Error* under different K values.

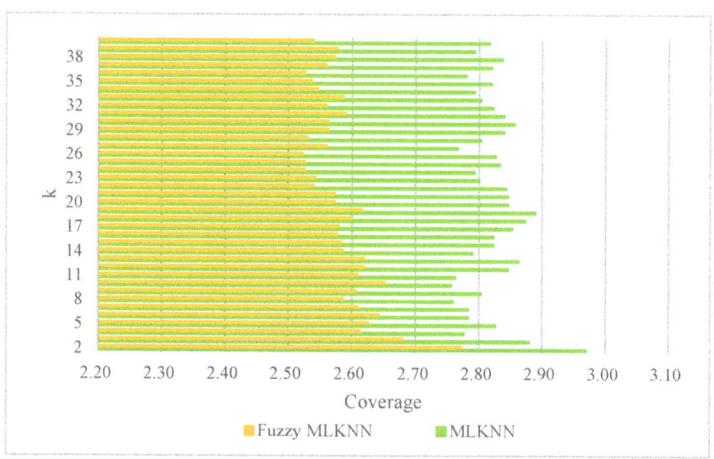

Figure 5. *Coverage* under different K values.

The smaller the *HammingLoss*, the smaller the average number of misclassifications, and therefore the better the performance. From Figure 1, it can be directly seen that the *HammingLoss* value of the improved algorithm has an overall improvement compared with the traditional algorithm. The *HammingLoss* value of the traditional algorithm is between 0.12 and 0.15, and the mean value is 0.132. The overall fluctuation is relatively stable, and the distribution of the smallest *HammingLoss* value is not obvious, which is obtained at K = 14, 28, 31, and 34, respectively. The *HammingLoss* value of the improved algorithm is between 0.08 and 0.11, with an average value of 0.096. During the change from K = 10 to 35, the overall trend decreases. The smallest *HammingLoss* value can be easily obtained from the figure at K = 35. At the same time, we can find that the algorithm's performance before and after the improvement in *HammingLoss* is not synchronous with the variation of the K value. From the perspective of *HammingLoss* only, the value of K selected for the optimal performance of the traditional algorithm and the improved algorithm is different.

The higher the *Average_Precision*, the better the performance of the multi-label learning algorithm. It can be observed from Figure 2 that the *Average_Precision* of the improved algorithm is significantly better than the traditional algorithm, and the gap between the two becomes more obvious with the increase of the K value. The value of *Average_Precision* of the traditional algorithm is between 0.89 and 0.92, with an average value of 0.909, and as the value of K increases, the overall trend decreases. The algorithm performs best when K = 14. The value of *Average_Precision* of the improved algorithm is between 0.92 and 0.95, with a mean value of 0.938, and with the increase of the K value, the overall trend is upward. When the value of K takes a value near 36, the performance is optimal, and when K = 36, the value of Average_Precision is at most 0.944.

Since *Rankingloss* and *OneError* are considered indicators based on the order of labels and are in the same order of magnitude, the smaller the two indicators are, the better the performance is. This paper considers these two indicators at the same time. In Figure 3, the blue line is the *RankingLoss* with MLKNN, and in Figure 4, the green columnar presents *OneError* values with MLKNN. Respectively, the red line in Figure 3 and the orange columnar in Figure 4 are the *RankingLoss* and *OneError* values of Fuzzy MLKNN.

First of all, from the value of *RankingLoss*, the improved algorithm is better than the traditional algorithm, and as the value of k increases, this advantage is gradually obvious. The average value of the traditional algorithm on *RankingLoss* is 0.08, and the low values are obtained at K = 8, 11, and 14. The mean *RankingLoss* of the improved algorithm is 0.055, and the minimum value is obtained at K= 36. Secondly, from the perspective of the *OneError* value, it can be seen from the figure that the *OneError* value of the traditional algorithm is significantly higher than that of the improved algorithm, and the former value fluctuates greatly. The average *OneError* value of the traditional algorithm is 0.063, while the average *OneError* value of the improved algorithm is 0.016. Based on the consideration of the *OneError* value, the optimal K value of the traditional algorithm is obtained when K = 14; the optimal K value of the improved algorithm is obtained when K = 17.

Figure 5 shows the performance of *Coverage* under different K values. *Coverage* is the step size required to traverse the correct label. The smaller the index, the better the performance. From the figure, we can see that the *Coverage* of the improved algorithm is also significantly lower than that of the traditional algorithm. The mean value of the improved algorithm on *Coverage* is 2.585, and the traditional algorithm is 2.822. The minimum *Coverage* values of the improved algorithm can be obtained at 24~26, 36, while the minimum *Coverage* values of the traditional algorithm are obtained at 10, 11, and 14.

Through the analysis of the above experimental results, we find that the improved algorithm is better than the traditional algorithm in all evaluation metrics, and the performance of the *OneError* value is the most significant, proving that the fuzzy distance measure is effective in the multi-label learning process of credit data. In addition, through the analysis of the optimal selection of the K value on different indicators, this paper finds that the traditional algorithm and the improved algorithm are not consistent in the selection of the optimal K value. The selection of the optimal K value of the traditional algorithm is significantly lower than the improved algorithm. From the comprehensive consideration of the performance of the above five indicators, it is more appropriate to take 14 for the optimal K value of the traditional algorithm. And the optimal K value of the improved algorithm is 36. Therefore, for these two results, we mainly use the improved algorithm with better performance in the following analysis process and select the K value of 36 to conduct further in-depth research on the data.

5. User Portrait

To make a portrait of users, we need to describe the distribution characteristics of labels. Referring to [50,51], we choose the best parameter with Fuzzy MLKNN, K = 36, and then conduct the algorithm with the whole dataset. The results are shown in Table 6 and Figure 6. Table 6 summarizes the proportion of one label, and Figure 6 describes user labels.

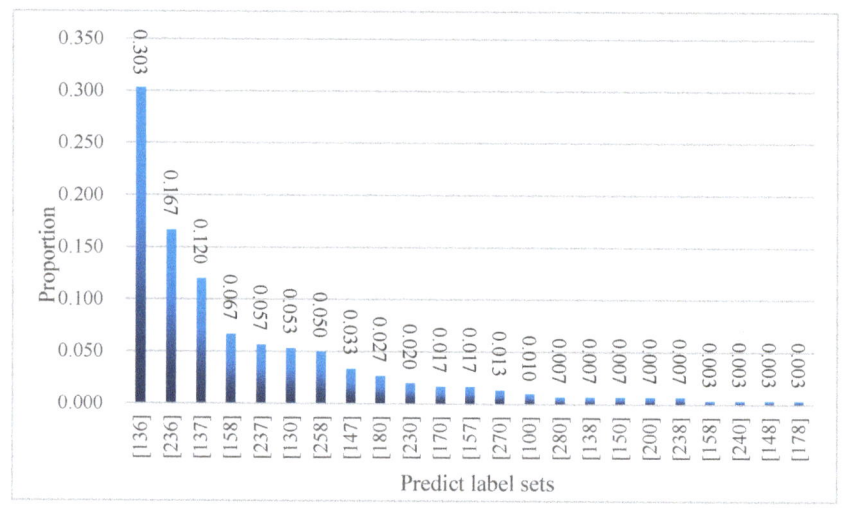

Figure 6. The distribution of user labels.

Firstly, from the learning results of one label in Table 9, users with low credit frequency account for the largest proportion, accounting for about 73%, followed by users with relatively stable personal development, accounting for about 67%, and the third is users with low credit concerns account for about 47%. It is more consistent with the actual situation. Most credit users have a low frequency of credit activities. The proportion of users with a medium frequency of credit activities is the least, indicating that the polarization of credit users is more serious in terms of credit activities.

Table 9. Proportion of one label.

Label Code	Labels Name	Proportion
1	Personal development stability	0.670
2	Personal development instability	0.330
3	Low frequency of credit activities	0.733
4	Medium frequency of credit activities	0.040
5	High frequency of credit activities	0.143
6	Low attention to credit status	0.470
7	Medium attention to credit status	0.260
8	High attention to credit status	0.173

Secondly, from the learning results of user labels, the proportion of credit users with predicted labels [136], [236], and [137] reached 59%, accounting for more than half of the total number of credit users, similar to the actual life situation. The user group represented by [136] has stable personal development, low credit frequency, and low credit concern. These users account for about 30% of the total number of users. [236] represents groups with unstable personal development, low credit frequency, and low credit concern, accounting for about 17% of the total users. From this, we can find that there is no significant correlation between the personal stability status and the credit status of credit reporting users to a certain extent. [137] represents groups with stable personal development, low credit frequency, and moderate credit concern, accounting for about 12% of the total population. The fourth and fifth place are [158] and [237], respectively, representing groups with stable personal development, high credit frequency, and high credit status concern, and individuals with unstable personal development, low credit frequency, and medium credit concern. This result also verifies the earlier conclusion that an individual's stability does not directly affect his credit status. In addition, we also found a relationship between the frequency of credit activities and attention to the credit situation. High credit frequency is accompanied by high credit attention, while low and medium credit frequency also pays less attention to credit status, which aligns with real life.

6. Conclusions

This paper proposes a systematic clustering algorithm–Fuzzy MLKNN, which uses intuitionistic fuzzy sets to conduct distance metrics, and then improves the MLKNN multi-label learning algorithm. From the experiments, we find it has three advantages over the classical algorithm. Firstly, by fuzzing the data, the subjectivity of the original data in the process of data discretization can be weakened, and the objectivity and authenticity of the experimental data can be enhanced simultaneously. Secondly, the classical algorithm is improved by using the Euclidean fuzzy distance formula; to a certain extent, the distance between sample points is more representative than the original distance. Third, the fuzzy-improved algorithm outperforms the classical algorithm in multiple performance indicators, among which the *OneError* indicator is the most obvious.

The limitation of this paper is that it only considers the advantages of the improved algorithm from an experimental point of view and has not yet obtained relevant theoretical proof. Therefore, some questions worthy of further study remain. Theoretical analysis concerning the effectiveness of Fuzzy MLKNN will need more discussion. Moreover, as with other multi-label algorithms, Fuzzy MLKNN may suffer from missing labels and noisy labels, which will need more data to test.

Author Contributions: Conceptualization, Z.Z. and L.H.; methodology, Z.Z.; software, Z.Z.; validation, Z.Z., L.H. and M.C.; formal analysis, L.H.; investigation, L.H.; resources, L.H.; data curation, L.H.; writing—original draft preparation, Z.Z.; writing—review and editing, Z.Z. and L.H.; visualization, M.C.; supervision, L.H.; project administration, L.H.; funding acquisition, L.H. All authors have read and agreed to the published version of the manuscript.

Funding: This research was funded by the National Natural Science Foundation of China (grant number: 72101279).

Data Availability Statement: The data will be open on Researchgate, the link is https://www.researchgate.net/profile/Lu-Han-57.

Acknowledgments: The work was supported by the National Natural Science Foundation of China (Grant No. 72101279).

Conflicts of Interest: The authors declare no conflict of interest.

Appendix A

function [Prior,PriorN,Cond,CondN]=MLKNN_train(train_data,train_target,Num,Smooth)

%MLKNN_train trains a multi-label k-nearest neighbor classifier
%
%   Syntax
%
%   [Prior,PriorN,Cond,CondN]=MLKNN_train(train_data,train_target,num_neighbor)
%
%   Description
%
%   KNNML_train takes,
%   train_data   - An MxN array, the ith instance of training instance is stored in train_data(i,:)
%   train_target - A QxM array, if the ith training instance belongs to the jth class, then train_target(j,i) equals +1 otherwise train_target(j,i) equals -1
%   Num   - Number of neighbors used in the k-nearest neighbor algorithm
%   Smooth   - Smoothing parameter
% and returns,
%   Prior   - A Qx1 array, for the ith class Ci, the prior probability of P(Ci) is stored in Prior(i,1)
%   PriorN   - A Qx1 array, for the ith class Ci, the prior probability of P(~Ci) is stored in PriorN(i,1)
%   Cond   - A Qx(Num+1) array, for the ith class Ci, the probability of P(k | Ci) (0<=k<=Num), i.e., k nearest neighbors of an instance in Ci will belong to Ci, is stored in Cond(i,k+1)
%   CondN   - A Qx(Num+1) array, for the ith class Ci, the probability of P(k | ~Ci) (0<=k<=Num), i.e., k nearest neighbors of an instance not in Ci will belong to Ci, is stored in CondN(i,k+1)

```
    [num_class,num_training]=size(train_target);

%Computing distance between training instances
    dist_matrix=diag(realmax*ones(1,num_training));
        for i=1:num_training-1
        if(mod(i,100)==0)
            disp(strcat('computing distance for instance:',num2str(i)));
        end
        vector1=train_data(i,:);
        for j=i+1:num_training
            vector2=train_data(j,:);
            dist_matrix(i,j)=sqrt(sum((vector1-vector2).^2));
            dist_matrix(j,i)=dist_matrix(i,j);
        end
    end

%Computing Prior and PriorN
    for i=1:num_class
        temp_Ci=sum(train_target(i,:)==ones(1,num_training));
        Prior(i,1)=(Smooth+temp_Ci)/(Smooth*2+num_training);
        PriorN(i,1)=1-Prior(i,1);
    end

%Computing Cond and CondN
    Neighbors=cell(num_training,1); %Neighbors{i,1} stores the Num neighbors of the ith training instance
    for i=1:num_training
        [temp,index]=sort(dist_matrix(i,:));
        Neighbors{i,1}=index(1:Num);
    end

    temp_Ci=zeros(num_class,Num+1);
        temp_NCi=zeros(num_class,Num+1);
```

```
    for i=1:num_training
        temp=zeros(1,num_class);
        neighbor_labels=[];
        for j=1:Num
            neighbor_labels=[neighbor_labels,train_target(:,Neighbors{i,1}(j))];
        end
        for j=1:num_class
            temp(1,j)=sum(neighbor_labels(j,:)==ones(1,Num));
        end
        for j=1:num_class
            if(train_target(j,i)==1)
                temp_Ci(j,temp(j)+1)=temp_Ci(j,temp(j)+1)+1;
            else
                temp_NCi(j,temp(j)+1)=temp_NCi(j,temp(j)+1)+1;
            end
        end
    end
    for i=1:num_class
        temp1=sum(temp_Ci(i,:));
        temp2=sum(temp_NCi(i,:));
        for j=1:Num+1
            Cond(i,j)=(Smooth+temp_Ci(i,j))/(Smooth*(Num+1)+temp1);
            CondN(i,j)=(Smooth+temp_NCi(i,j))/(Smooth*(Num+1)+temp2);
        end
    end
end

Function
[HammingLoss,RankingLoss,OneError,Coverage,Average_Precision,Outputs,Pre_Labels]=MLKNN_test(train_data,
train_target,test_data,test_target,Num,Prior,PriorN,Cond,CondN)
%MLKNN_test tests a multi-label k-nearest neighbor classifier.
%
%    Syntax
%
%
[HammingLoss,RankingLoss,OneError,Coverage,Average_Precision,Outputs,Pre_Labels]=MLKNN_test(train_data,train
_target,test_data,test_target,Num,Prior,PriorN,Cond,CondN)
%
%    Description
%
%       KNNML_test takes,
%           train_data       - An M1xN array, the ith instance of training instance is stored in train_data(i,:)
%           train_target     - A QxM1 array, if the ith training instance belongs to the jth class, then train_target(j,i)
equals +1, otherwise train_target(j,i) equals -1
%           test_data        - An M2xN array, the ith instance of testing instance is stored in test_data(i,:)
%           test_target      - A QxM2 array, if the ith testing instance belongs to the jth class, test_target(j,i) equals +1,
otherwise test_target(j,i) equals -1
%           Num              - Number of neighbors used in the k-nearest neighbor algorithm
%           Prior            - A Qx1 array, for the ith class Ci, the prior probability of P(Ci) is stored in Prior(i,1)
%           PriorN           - A Qx1 array, for the ith class Ci, the prior probability of P(~Ci) is stored in PriorN(i,1)
%           Cond             - A Qx(Num+1) array, for the ith class Ci, the probability of P(k|Ci) (0<=k<=Num), i.e., k
nearest neighbors of an instance in Ci will belong to Ci, is stored in Cond(i,k+1)
%           CondN            - A Qx(Num+1) array, for the ith class Ci, the probability of P(k|~Ci) (0<=k<=Num), i.e.,
k nearest neighbors of an instance not in Ci will belong to Ci, is stored in CondN(i,k+1)
%       and returns,
```

```
%           HammingLoss        - The hamming loss on testing data
%           RankingLoss        - The ranking loss on testing data
%           OneError           - The one-error on testing data as
%           Coverage           - The coverage on testing data as
%           Average_Precision- The average precision on testing data
%           Outputs            - A QxM2 array, the probability of the ith testing instance belonging to the jCth class is
stored in Outputs(j,i)
%           Pre_Labels         - A QxM2 array, if the ith testing instance belongs to the jth class, then Pre_Labels(j,i) is
+1, otherwise Pre_Labels(j,i) is -1

    [num_class,num_training]=size(train_target);
    [num_class,num_testing]=size(test_target);

%Computing distances between training instances and testing instances
    dist_matrix=zeros(num_testing,num_training);
    for i=1:num_testing
        if(mod(i,100)==0)
            disp(strcat('computing distance for instance:',num2str(i)));
        end
        vector1=test_data(i,:);
        for j=1:num_training
            vector2=train_data(j,:);
            dist_matrix(i,j)=sqrt(sum((vector1-vector2).^2));
        end
    end

%Find neighbors of each testing instance
    Neighbors=cell(num_testing,1); %Neighbors{i,1} stores the Num neighbors of the ith testing instance
    for i=1:num_testing
        [temp,index]=sort(dist_matrix(i,:));
        Neighbors{i,1}=index(1:Num);
    end

%Computing Outputs
    Outputs=zeros(num_class,num_testing);
    for i=1:num_testing
%       if(mod(i,100)==0)
%           disp(strcat('computing outputs for instance:',num2str(i)));
%       end
        temp=zeros(1,num_class); %The number of the Num nearest neighbors of the ith instance which belong to the
jth instance is stored in temp(1,j)
        neighbor_labels=[];
        for j=1:Num
            neighbor_labels=[neighbor_labels,train_target(:,Neighbors{i,1}(j))];
        end
        for j=1:num_class
            temp(1,j)=sum(neighbor_labels(j,:)==ones(1,Num));
        end
        for j=1:num_class
            Prob_in=Prior(j)*Cond(j,temp(1,j)+1);
            Prob_out=PriorN(j)*CondN(j,temp(1,j)+1);
            if(Prob_in+Prob_out==0)
                Outputs(j,i)=Prior(j);
            else
```

```
                Outputs(j,i)=Prob_in/(Prob_in+Prob_out);
            end
        end
    end

%Evaluation
    Pre_Labels=zeros(num_class,num_testing)
    for i=1:num_testing
        for j=1:num_class
            if(Outputs(j,i)>=0.5)
                Pre_Labels(j,i)=1;
            else
                Pre_Labels(j,i)=-1;
            end
        end
    end
    HammingLoss=Hamming_loss(Pre_Labels,test_target)
    RankingLoss=Ranking_loss(Outputs,test_target);
    OneError=One_error(Outputs,test_target);
    Coverage=coverage(Outputs,test_target);
    Average_Precision=Average_precision(Outputs,test_target);
```

References

1. Chen, X. Empirical Research on the Early Warning of Regional Financial Risk Based on the Credit Data of Central Bank. *Credit. Ref.* **2022**, *9*, 17–24.
2. Hou, S.Q.; Chen, X.J. Absence and Improvement of Legal Protection of Personal Credit Information Rights and Interests in the Era of Big Data. *Credit. Ref.* **2022**, *9*, 25–34.
3. Chen, Y.H.; Wang, J.Y. The Rule of Law Applicable to the 2nd Generation Credit Information System under the Background of the Social Credit System. *Credit. Ref.* **2020**, *38*, 51–55.
4. Li, Z. Research on the Development of Internet Credit Reference in China and the Supervision over It. *Credit. Ref.* **2015**, *33*, 9–15.
5. Tian, K. Constructing the Market-oriented Individual Credit Investigation Ecosystem. *China Financ.* **2022**, *8*, 90–92.
6. Han, L.; Su, Z.; Lin, J. A Hybrid KNN algorithm with Sugeno measure for the personal credit reference system in China. *J. Intell. Fuzzy Syst.* **2020**, *39*, 6993–7004. [CrossRef]
7. Lessmann, S.; Baesens, B.; Seow, H.; Thomas, L.C. Benchmarking state-of-the-art classification algorithms for credit scoring: An update of research. *Eur. J. Oper. Res.* **2015**, *247*, 124–136. [CrossRef]
8. Moscato, V.; Picariello, A.; Sperlí, G. A benchmark of machine learning approaches for credit score prediction. *Expert Syst. Appl.* **2021**, *165*, 113986. [CrossRef]
9. Tarekegn, A.N.; Giacobini, M.; Michalak, K. A review of methods for imbalanced multi-label classification. *Pattern Recognit.* **2021**, *118*, 107965. [CrossRef]
10. Song, D.; Vold, A.; Madan, K.; Schilder, F. Multi-label legal document classification: A deep learning-based approach with label-attention and domain-specific pre-training. *Inf. Syst.* **2022**, *106*, 101718. [CrossRef]
11. Tandon, K.; Chatterjee, N. Multi-label text classification with an ensemble feature space. *J. Intell. Fuzzy Syst.* **2022**, *42*, 4425–4436. [CrossRef]
12. Chen, D.; Rong, W.; Zhang, J.; Xiong, Z. Ranking based multi-label classification for sentiment analysis. *J. Intell. Fuzzy Syst.* **2020**, *39*, 2177–2188. [CrossRef]
13. Gibaja, E.L.; Ventura, S. A Tutorial on Multi-Label Learning. *Acm Comput. Surv.* **2015**, *47*, 1–38. [CrossRef]
14. Gui, X.; Lu, X.; Yu, G. Cost-effective Batch-mode Multi-label Active Learning. *Neurocomputing* **2021**, *463*, 355–367. [CrossRef]
15. Mishra, N.K.; Singh, P.K. Feature construction and smote-based imbalance handling for multi-label learning. *Inf. Sci.* **2021**, *563*, 342–357. [CrossRef]
16. Xu, X.; Shan, D.; Li, S.; Sun, T.; Xiao, P.; Fan, J. Multi-label learning method based on ML-RBF and laplacian ELM. *Neurocomputing* **2019**, *331*, 213–219.
17. Tsoumakas, G.; Katakis, I.; Vlahavas, I. Mining Multi-Label Data. In *Data Mining and Knowledge Discovery Handbook*; Springer: Boston, MA, USA, 2009; pp. 667–685.
18. Boutell, M.R.; Luo, J.; Shen, X. Learning multi-label scene classification. *Pattern Recognit.* **2004**, *37*, 1757–1771. [CrossRef]
19. Read, J.; Pfahringer, B.; Holmes, G. Classifier chains for multi-label classification. *Mach. Learn.* **2011**, *85*, 333–359.
20. Lango, M.; Stefanowski, J. What makes multi-class imbalanced problems difficult? An experimental study. *Expert Syst. Appl.* **2022**, *199*, 116962. [CrossRef]

21. Ruiz Alonso, D.; Zepeda Cortes, C.; Castillo Zacatelco, H.; Carballido Carranza, J.L.; Garcia Cue, J.L. Multi-label classification of feedbacks. *J. Intell. Fuzzy Syst.* **2022**, *42*, 4337–4343. [CrossRef]
22. Yapp, E.K.Y.; Li, X.; Lu, W.F.; Tan, P.S. Comparison of base classifiers for multi-label learning. *Neurocomputing* **2020**, *394*, 51–60. [CrossRef]
23. Lv, S.; Shi, S.; Wang, H.; Li, F. Semi-supervised multi-label feature selection with adaptive structure learning and manifold learning. *Knowl. Based Syst.* **2021**, *214*, 106757. [CrossRef]
24. Tan, A.; Liang, J.; Wu, W.; Zhang, J. Semi-supervised partial multi-label classification via consistency learning. *Pattern Recognit.* **2022**, *131*, 108839. [CrossRef]
25. Li, Q.; Peng, X.; Qiao, Y.; Hao, Q. Unsupervised person re-identification with multi-label learning guided self-paced clustering. *Pattern Recognit.* **2022**, *125*, 108521. [CrossRef]
26. Joachims, T. Optimizing search engines using clickthrough data. In Proceedings of the Eighth ACM SIGKDD International Conference on Knowledge Discovery and Data Mining KDD '02, Edmonton, AB, Canada, 23–26 July 2002; ACM: New York, NY, USA, 2002; pp. 133–142. [CrossRef]
27. Freund, Y.; Schapire, R.E. A Decision-Theoretic Generalization of On-Line Learning and an Application to Boosting. *J. Comput. Syst. Sci.* **1997**, *55*, 119–139. [CrossRef]
28. Zhang, M.; Zhou, Z. ML-KNN: A lazy learning approach to multi-label learning. *Pattern Recognit.* **2007**, *40*, 2038–2048. [CrossRef]
29. Zhu, D.; Zhu, H.; Liu, X.; Li, H.; Wang, F.; Li, H.; Feng, D. CREDO: Efficient and privacy-preserving multi-level medical pre-diagnosis based on ML-kNN. *Inf. Sci.* **2020**, *514*, 244–262. [CrossRef]
30. Zhu, X.; Ying, C.; Wang, J.; Li, J.; Lai, X.; Wang, G. Ensemble of ML-KNN for classification algorithm recommendation. *Knowl. Based Syst.* **2021**, *221*, 106933. [CrossRef]
31. Bogatinovski, J.; Todorovski, L.; Džeroski, S.; Kocev, D. Comprehensive comparative study of multi-label classification methods. *Expert Syst. Appl.* **2022**, *203*, 117215. [CrossRef]
32. Syropoulos, A.; Grammenos, T. *A Modern Introduction to Fuzzy Mathematics*; John Wiley & Sons, Ltd.: Hoboken, NJ, USA, 2020; pp. 39–69.
33. Dunn, J.C. A fuzzy relative of the ISODATA process and its use in detecting compact well-separated clusters. *J. Cybern.* **1973**, *3*, 32–57. [CrossRef]
34. Wu, C.; Wang, Z. A modified fuzzy dual-local information c-mean clustering algorithm using quadratic surface as prototype for image segmentation. *Expert Syst. Appl.* **2022**, *201*, 117019. [CrossRef]
35. Wu, Z.; Wang, B.; Li, C. A new robust fuzzy clustering framework considering different data weights in different clusters. *Expert Syst. Appl.* **2022**, *206*, 117728. [CrossRef]
36. Wei, H.; Chen, L.; Chen, C.P.; Duan, J.; Han, R.; Guo, L. Fuzzy clustering for multiview data by combining latent information. *Appl. Soft Comput.* **2022**, *126*, 109140. [CrossRef]
37. De Carvalho, F.D.A.T.; Lechevallier, Y.; de Melo, F.M. Relational partitioning fuzzy clustering algorithms based on multiple dissimilarity matrices. *Fuzzy Sets Syst.* **2013**, *215*, 1–28. [CrossRef]
38. Vluymans, S.; Cornelis, C.; Herrera, F.; Saeys, Y. Multi-label classification using a fuzzy rough neighborhood consensus. *Inf. Sci.* **2018**, *433–434*, 96–114. [CrossRef]
39. Zhao, X.; Nie, F.; Wang, R.; Li, X. Improving projected fuzzy K-means clustering via robust learning. *Neurocomputing* **2022**, *491*, 34–43. [CrossRef]
40. Varshney, A.K.; Muhuri, P.K.; Danish Lohani, Q.M. PIFHC: The Probabilistic Intuitionistic Fuzzy Hierarchical Clustering Algorithm. *Appl. Soft Comput.* **2022**, *120*, 108584. [CrossRef]
41. Zadeh, L.A. Fuzzy sets. *Inf. Control.* **1965**, *8*, 338–353. [CrossRef]
42. Atanassov, K. Intuitionistic fuzzy sets. *Fuzzy Sets Syst.* **1986**, *20*, 87–96. [CrossRef]
43. Li, G.Y.; Yang, B.R.; Liu, Y.H.; Cao, D.Y. Survey of data mining based on fuzzy set theory. *Comput. Eng. Des.* **2011**, *32*, 4064–4067+4264.
44. Xu, Z.S. Intuitionistic Fuzzy Aggregation Operators. *IEEE Trans. Fuzzy Syst.* **2007**, *15*, 1179–1187.
45. Zhang, Z.; Han, L.; Chen, M. Multi-label learning with user credit data in China based on MLKNN. In Proceedings of the 2nd International Conference on Information Technology and Cloud Computing (ITCC 2022), Qingdao, China, 20–22 May 2022; pp. 105–111.
46. Zhang, C.; Li, Z. Multi-label learning with label-specific features via weighting and label entropy guided clustering ensemble. *Neurocomputing* **2021**, *419*, 59–69. [CrossRef]
47. Hurtado, L.; Gonzalez, J.; Pla, F. Choosing the right loss function for multi-label Emotion Classification. *J. Intell. Fuzzy Syst.* **2019**, *36*, 4697–4708. [CrossRef]
48. Shu, S.; Lv, F.; Yan, Y.; Li, L.; He, S.; He, J. Incorporating multiple cluster centers for multi-label learning. *Inf. Sci.* **2022**, *590*, 60–73. [CrossRef]
49. Skryjomski, P.; Krawczyk, B.; Cano, A. Speeding up k-Nearest Neighbors classifier for large-scale multi-label learning on GPUs. *Neurocomputing* **2019**, *354*, 10–19. [CrossRef]
50. Liu, B.; Blekas, K.; Tsoumakas, G. Multi-label sampling based on local label imbalance. *Pattern Recognit.* **2022**, *122*, 108294. [CrossRef]

1. Lyu, G.; Feng, S.; Li, Y. Noisy label tolerance: A new perspective of Partial Multi-Label Learning. *Inf. Sci.* **2021**, *543*, 454–466. [CrossRef]

Article
Link Prediction with Hypergraphs via Network Embedding

Zijuan Zhao [1,†], Kai Yang [2,*,†] and Jinli Guo [1,*]

1. Business School, University of Shanghai for Science and Technology, Shanghai 200093, China
2. College of Information Engineering, Yangzhou University, Yangzhou 225127, China
* Correspondence: yangk@fudan.edu.cn (K.Y.); phd5816@163.com (J.G.)
† These authors contributed equally to this work.

Abstract: Network embedding is a promising field and is important for various network analysis tasks, such as link prediction, node classification, community detection and others. Most research studies on link prediction focus on simple networks and pay little attention to hypergraphs that provide a natural way to represent complex higher-order relationships. In this paper, we propose a link prediction method with hypergraphs using network embedding (HNE). HNE adapts a traditional network embedding method, Deepwalk, to link prediction in hypergraphs. Firstly, the hypergraph model is constructed based on heterogeneous library loan records of seven universities. With a network embedding method, the low-dimensional vectors are obtained to extract network structure features for the hypergraphs. Then, the link prediction is implemented on the hypergraphs as the classification task with machine learning. The experimental results on seven real networks show our approach has good performance for link prediction in hypergraphs. Our method will be helpful for human behavior dynamics.

Keywords: link prediction; hypergraph; network embedding; machine learning; heterogeneous network; library loan records; human behavior dynamics

1. Introduction

Link prediction [1–3] has been widely applied in many fields with extensive research studies, especially in society networks, such as community detection [4] and recommendation [5]. It aims to predict the potential links between nodes based on existing links, and has a wide range of applications in many fields, from bioinformatics [6,7] and social science [8] to computer science [9]. Existing traditional methods for link prediction [10–13] focus on simple graphs mostly and less on the interactions between pairs of nodes present in real-world systems, while research on high-order interactions is of great significance for modeling complex systems. For instance, in scientific collaboration networks, several researchers work together on a research project; in the brain network, a human behavior usually involves multiple neurons. Link prediction on high-order interactions leads to some challenges, while a hypergraph [14–16] provides a useful way to modeling such interactions. A hypergraph can reflect multiple nodes' relations with hyperlinks, and can be used in evaluating vital nodes [17], describing protein interaction [18] and so on. Hyperlink prediction on hypergraph has been investigated to predict higher-order links such as a user releasing a tweet containing a hashtag [19]. Hyperlink prediction [20] has also been helpful to predict multiactor collaborations [21]. By formulating various kinds of nodes and associations into a hypergraph, link prediction on heterogeneous networks has developed increasingly. Li Dong [19] modeled various types of objects and relations of networks as hypergraphs and used link proximities to construct a cost function to predict users' links. Maria [22] constructed relations between pairs of drugs into a hypergraph to predict multidrug interactions. Liu et al. [23] proposed a Metapath-aware HyperGraph Transformer (Meta-HGT) for node embedding to capture the high-order relations. Kang et al. [24] proposed dynamic hypergraph neural networks based on key hyperedges (DHKH) to consider

Citation: Zhao, Z.; Yang, K.; Guo, J. Link Prediction with Hypergraphs via Network Embedding. *Appl. Sci.* 2023, *13*, 523. https://doi.org/10.3390/app13010523

Academic Editors: Jing Zhang, Jipeng Qiang and Cangqi Zhou

Received: 9 October 2022
Revised: 21 December 2022
Accepted: 26 December 2022
Published: 30 December 2022

Copyright: © 2022 by the authors. Licensee MDPI, Basel, Switzerland. This article is an open access article distributed under the terms and conditions of the Creative Commons Attribution (CC BY) license (https://creativecommons.org/licenses/by/4.0/).

a dynamic hypergraph structure. Fan et al. [25] presented a method named heterogeneous hypergraph variational autoencoder (HeteHG-VAE) for link prediction in heterogeneous information networks (HINs) mapped to a heterogeneous hypergraph with a certain kind of semantics to capture both the high-order semantics and complex relations among nodes, while preserving the low-order pairwise topology information of the original HIN.

Network embedding [26,27] combining machine learning or deep learning with network science has made it possible to automatically learn and preserve network properties by representing nodes in a low-dimensional space. It is usually assumed that the distance between the representation vectors of nodes reflects the similarity of the nodes in networks [28]. Network embedding typically realizes a network representation through matrix factorization, random walk and neural network methods. The matrix factorization methods select an adjacency matrix, an incident matrix, a Laplacian matrix and their variant forms to factorize and obtain the embeddings, such as M-NMF [29] and Laplacian eigenmaps [30]. The random walk methods generate embeddings through a random walk of nodes on graphs and training node sequences in models; representative methods include the Deepwalk [31], Node2vec [32] and Graphwave models [33]. The methods based on a neural network realize an embedding by the nonlinear function of deep models to map the networks in a vector space, such as HeGan [34], VERSE [35] and SINE models [36]. Furthermore, deep-learning-based link prediction methods on hypergraphs have achieved rapid development. Yadati et al. [37] proposed a neural hyperlink predictor (NHP) adapting graph convolutional networks (GCNs) [38] for link prediction in hypergraphs. Node2vec [32] with a single-layer perceptron (Node2vec-SLP) was an improved version of Node2vec for hyperlink prediction, which employed a one-layer neural network to compute hyperlink scores [39].

Considering that hypergraphs can represent higher-order systems more conveniently, the interaction information of nodes is characterized into vectors with network embedding, so that the link prediction on hypergraphs can be converted into a classification problem. Therefore, we provide a novel idea of link prediction with hypergraphs with network embedding (HNE) in this paper. Our motivation is to predict the relationships of students based on the library loan records of universities, instead of higher-order relationships of students. Thus, we investigate the link prediction with hypergraphs. We use a hypergraph to model all types of objects and relations of the library loan record networks. Firstly, we construct different kinds of nodes associations in a heterogeneous network with a hypergraph according to the library loan records of seven universities. Secondly, a network embedding method, Deepwalk, is utilized to extract structural information and represent nodes by vectors. Thirdly, a machine learning model, a random forest [40], is applied as a classifier for the link prediction. The experiments are conducted on seven sizes of heterogeneous networks and compare several typical link prediction methods to verify the performance of the proposed approach and achieve the promising results on the seven datasets.

The innovations in this paper are as follows: We propose a link prediction method using hypergraphs based on network embedding. The representation of the features of library loan record associations are novel in the process of our overall algorithm for link prediction of the relationship of students, which means that learning technology is applied to human behavior dynamics networks, that is, network embedding technology is introduced into human behavior dynamics networks. Then, a vector of each student for library loan records is constructed as a training set. Our method achieves promising results on the seven different datasets.

2. Materials and Methods

Figure 1 shows the complete flow chart for HNE, the link prediction approach we propose based on hypergraphs with network embedding. First, the heterogeneous networks constructed from library loan records of seven universities are explored, which consists of two types of nodes (*Node I* represents students, *Node II* indicates the books borrowed by the students from libraries) and their interactions. The hypergraph is constructed according to these interactions; the hyperlinks represent *Node II* linked with *Node I*. The *Node I* network is constructed based on hypergraph properties. The incidence matrix denotes the relationships between *Node I* and hyperlinks. The adjacency matrix describes the links between *Node I*. Second, the embedding vectors of *Node I* are generated by the network embedding model. Then, the embedding vectors of links are generated by concatenating the vectors of pairwise nodes. Finally, the links vectors are divided into training data and testing data. The training data are put into the random forest classifier to train the model, then the testing data are used to predict potential links.

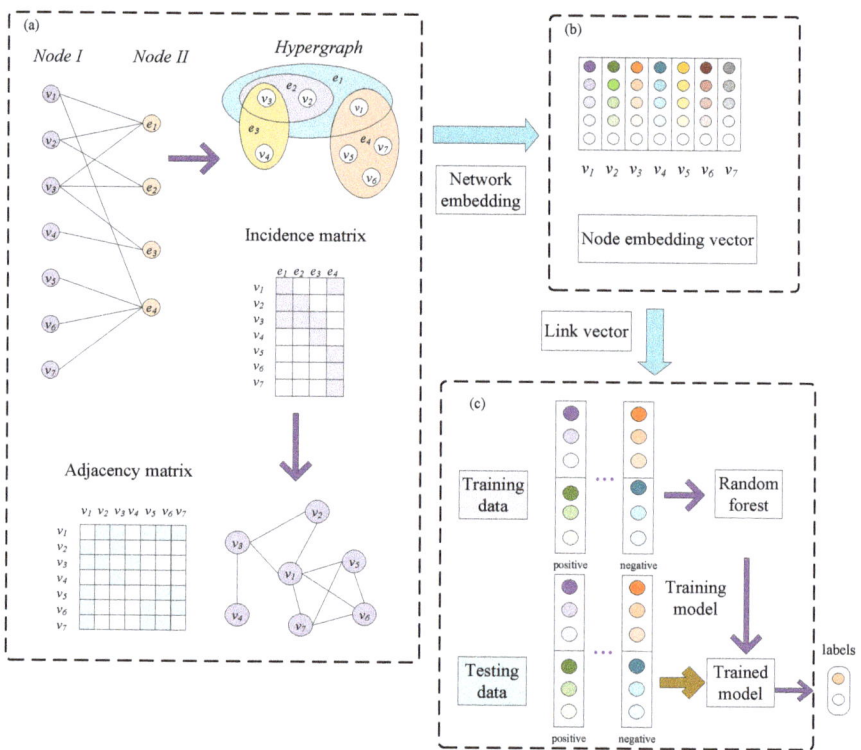

Figure 1. The framework of link prediction for hypergraphs via network embedding (HNE). (**a**) The heterogeneous network contains two types of nodes, *Nodes I* and *II*, with their interactions; it can be constructed by a hypergraph model. The incidence matrix represents the node–hyperlink interactions and the adjacency matrix describes node–node associations. (**b**) The Deepwalk model is applied to learn the node embedding vectors. (**c**) The random forest classifier is trained to predict link labels.

2.1. Hypergraph Construction

A hypergraph is defined as $H = (V, E)$ where $V = \{v_1, v_2, \ldots, v_n\}$ and $E = \{E_1, E_2, \ldots, E_m\}$ [41]. V is a set of n hypernodes and E is a set of m hyperlinks. The hyperlink $E_i = \{v_{i1}, v_{i2}, \ldots, v_{ij}\}$, $(i = 1, 2, \ldots, m; j = 1, 2, \ldots, n)$ contains j nodes, that is, the size of E_i is j. The $|V| \times |E|$ incidence matrix can be represented by H.

$$H(v,e) = \begin{cases} 1, & if\ v \in e \\ 0, & if\ v \notin e \end{cases} \quad (1)$$

Based on H, the node degree $d(v)$ of each node v meaning the number of neighbor nodes of node v is represented as

$$d(v) = \sum_{e \in E} H(v,e). \qquad (2)$$

The hyperdegree $d_H(v)$ of node v denotes the number of hyperlinks which the node v participates in. The degree $\delta(e)$ of hyperlink e is the total number of neighbor hyperlinks of hyperlink e as follows,

$$\delta(e) = \sum_{v \in V} H(v,e). \qquad (3)$$

The hyperdegree $\delta_H(e)$ of hyperlink e denotes the number of nodes of hyperlink e [42].

2.2. Learning Representations with Network Embedding

With the adjacency matrix from a hypergraph model, the representation learning vectors of nodes are obtained by a network embedding model. In this paper, we introduce the Deepwalk network embedding method which consists of two parts, that is, a random walk and Skip-gram. Firstly, some sequences of nodes with the same length t can be obtained by a random walk. Each node is the root of a walk sampling W_{v_i}; the root node v_i randomly selects one of the links connected to it and moves to the neighbor node to start the next walk until the walk length reaches t; the maximum length t denotes the size for a sequence of nodes. Secondly, a window of a specific length slides to sample the context for target node v_i in the sequence of nodes. Three layers are involved in the Skip-gram model: input, hidden and output layer. The initial representation of target node v_i is the input, the model parameters are trained and updated to maximize the probability of the neighbors of the target node v_i.

$$Pr(\{v_{i-w}, \ldots, v_{i+w}\} \setminus v_i \mid \Phi(v_i)) = \prod_{j=i-w, j \neq i}^{i+w} Pr(v_j \mid \Phi(v_i)) \qquad (4)$$

where $\Phi(v_i)$ denotes the current representation vector of node v_i, w is the size of the window in Skip-gram, $\{v_{i-w}, \ldots, v_{i+w}\} \setminus v_i$ is the context of node v_i, and the hierarchical softmax adopts a binary tree to reduce the complexity of calculating $Pr(v_j \mid \Phi(v_i))$. The problem turns into maximizing the probability of paths from the root node to the tree nodes.

2.3. Loss Function

Finally, the node embedding output from this model is applied to the specific node classification task of semi-supervised learning, and the loss function is calculated to minimize the cross-entropy loss value between the true label and the predicted value in the training set. The calculation process is shown in Equation (5):

$$\iota = -\sum_{l \in L} Y^l \ln(C \cdot Z^l) \qquad (5)$$

where C is the parameter of the classifier, L is the set of training set nodes, Y^l and Z^l represent the true labels corresponding to the training set data and the predicted values generated by the model, respectively. Based on the training set data, in this paper, we used the backpropagation method to train the parameters of the model for learning more accurate node embedding representations.

2.4. Datasets

In this paper, the real library loan records of seven universities in Shanghai, which were Shanghai University of Electric Power (SUEP), Shanghai Ocean University(SHOU), Shanghai University of Finance and Economics(SUFE), University of Shanghai for Science and Technology(USST), Shanghai International Studies University(SISU), Shanghai Normal University(SHNU) and Tongji University(TJU), were used to validate the performance of our approach. The datasets were collected from Huiyuan sharing [43]. We organized the data from 2017 to 2018 and took two columns of data, ISBN and PATRON_ID, as the different types of nodes to construct the hypergraphs. PATRON_ID represented $Node I$ and ISBN denoted the hyperlinks in Figure 1. The structural properties of the hypergraphs are analyzed in the Table 1. As shown in Table 1, n denotes the number of nodes, m_0 refers to the total number of links between nodes, $\langle k \rangle$ means the average degree of nodes, m is the number of hyperlinks, $\langle d_H(v) \rangle$ refers to the average hyperdegree of a node, $\langle \delta(e) \rangle$ means the average degree of hyperlink, and $\langle \delta_H(e) \rangle$ is the average hyperdegree of a hyperlink.

Table 1. The structural properties of the seven hypergraphs.

Datasets	n	m_0	m	Density	$\langle k \rangle$	$\langle d_H(v) \rangle$	$\langle \delta(e) \rangle$	$\langle \delta_H(e) \rangle$
SUEP	906	24,362	19,530	0.0297	27	29	47	1.3
SHOU	2680	222,126	64,958	0.0309	81	41	108	1.7
SUFE	1720	148,188	35,727	0.0501	86	33	62	1.6
USST	2733	230,597	54,437	0.0308	84	36	93	1.8
SISU	3089	478,953	72,100	0.0502	155	46	142	2
SHNU	3557	263,305	93,996	0.0208	74	43	120	1.6
TJU	6150	988,516	131,199	0.0261	161	42	134	1.9

3. Experiments

To evaluate the performance of HNE, we conducted experiments on the seven datasets Firstly, to train the model, we took the existing links as positive samples and then obtained random negative samples according to the number of positive samples. Given a test ratio (set as 30%) as input, the positive and negative samples were divided into a training set and a test set. Secondly, the embedding vectors of links were represented by concatenating the embedding vectors of the corresponding node pairs in the training set and test set for the unsupervised link prediction. After that, we input the embedding vectors of the samples in the training set into the random forest to learn the potential relationships among links and then input the embedding vectors of the samples in the test set into the trained random forest to predict possible links. Finally, the results of the link prediction were assessed with the AUC metric.

3.1. Compared Methods

In this paper, we compared the proposed HNE with three categories of baselines: similarity-based methods–CN [10], Jaccard coefficient [11], random-walk-based methods–Katz [12] and RWR [13], and deep-learning-based methods–Node2vec [32], GCN [38]. The existence probabilities of links were evaluated by the similarity between two nodes. Common neighbors (CN) is a link prediction method that is based on evaluating the overlap or similarity of two nodes by obtaining the number of common neighbors in a graph. The Jaccard coefficient is defined as the ratio of the common neighbor size of node i and node j to the size of all their neighbors. Katz centrality is an approach for summing all paths of nodes i and j, where the weight of paths decays exponentially according to their length, to evaluate how closely two nodes are related in the graph. Random walk with restart (RWR) provides a kind of random walk where node i moves to its neighbor with probability c or it jumps to the original node with probability $1 - c$. We set $c = 0.2$ in this paper. Node2vec learns a mapping of nodes to a low-dimensional space of features that maximizes the likelihood of preserving network neighborhoods of nodes. GCN is a classical graph neural network to learn the representation of nodes in graphs by convolutional networks. For the deep-learning-based methods, we set the embedding dimension as 64, and for all methods, we randomly ran them 10 times and reported the average results.

The training set data selected in this experiment were obtained by random sampling. In order to more comprehensively evaluate the accuracy and validity of the experimental results, in this paper, we used a weighted average processing to consider a training sample, the n classification problem was decomposed into two classification problems, and then the prediction results of the model were evaluated. Four evaluation indicators, AUC, precision, recall and F1-score were evaluated in the experimental results of the model to ensure the reliability and validity of the HNE method.

3.2. Results

To evaluate the performance of the four methods of link prediction, the experiment was implemented 10 times to compute the average AUC score and the results are shown in Figure 2. We observe that the AUC scores of HNE were 0.8247, 0.9077, 0.844, 0.8433, 0.8418, 0.8693 and 0.8120, respectively, on the seven datasets, which were better than those of the other methods on the seven datasets. The AUC scores improved by 26.9%, 16%, 19%, 32%, 1.67% and 7.38% at most compared with the scores of the CN, the Jaccard coefficient, the Katz centrality, the RWR, Node2vec and GCN, respectively. Based on the above analysis, a promising performance was achieved for the HNE method. Moreover, the performance of HNE was very stable on the seven datasets with different sizes.

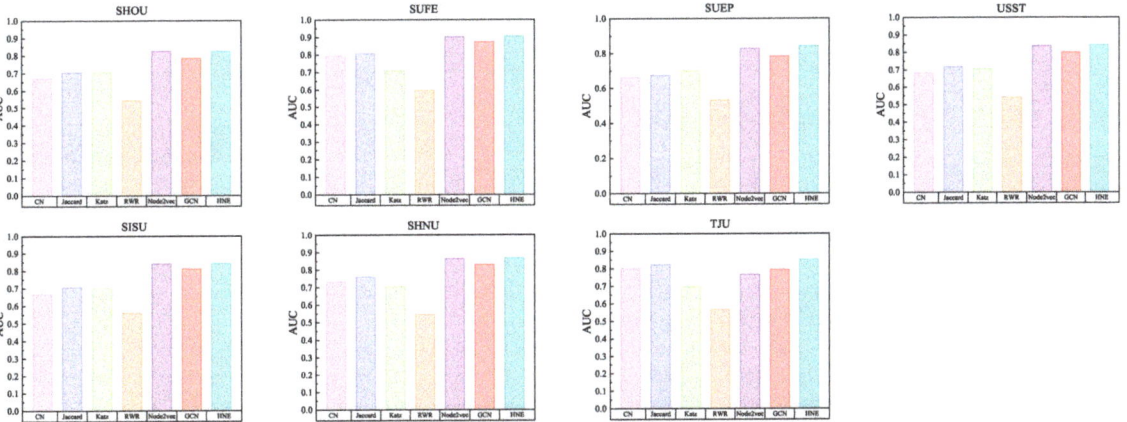

Figure 2. The AUC of CN, Jaccard, Katz, RWR, Node2vec, GCN and HNE on seven datasets.

We further evaluate the performance of our method with the precision, recall and F1-score on the seven datasets. As shown in Tables 2 and 3, the precision, recall and F1-score of our method achieved the best results on the seven datasets. Specifically, the precision of HNE was 0.9424 on the SUFE dataset, which was better than the other algorithms. For the recall and F1-score, our method improved by 2.2% and 28.7% and 7.7% and 19.2% compared to Node2vec and GCN, respectively. The F1-scores of HNE were superior to the other methods except on the TJU dataset. The experiment results show that our proposed method outperformed the CN, the Jaccard coefficient, the Katz centrality, the RWR, Node2vec and GCN on all datasets except the TJU dataset. Therefore, our algorithm showed a better performance and effectiveness for link prediction than traditional methods.

From the experiments, we can see that in the seven datasets, our method still maintained a relatively stable overall performance.

Table 2. The experimental results for the precision, recall and F1-Score on the SHOU, SUFE, SUEP.

	SHOU			SUFE			SUEP		
	Precision	Recall	F1-Score	Precision	Recall	F1-Score	Precision	Recall	F1-Score
CN	0.6971	0.6091	0.6499	0.8996	0.6654	0.7650	0.7063	0.5645	0.6275
Jaccard	0.7569	0.6034	0.6715	0.9034	0.6916	0.7834	0.7412	0.5424	0.6263
Katz	0.6705	0.8001	0.7333	0.6722	0.8121	0.7356	0.6663	0.8061	0.7296
RWR	0.5446	0.5456	0.5449	0.5929	0.6250	0.6083	0.5328	0.5366	0.5337
Node2vec	0.8317	0.8037	0.8223	0.9416	0.8566	0.898	0.8401	0.8154	0.8275
GCN	0.7959	0.7675	0.7814	0.9046	0.8372	0.8696	0.7934	0.7734	0.7832
HNE	0.8379	0.8052	0.8212	0.9424	0.8685	0.9040	0.8516	0.8331	0.8422

Table 3. The experimental results for the precision, recall and F1-score on the USST, SISU, SHNU and TJU.

	USST			SISU			SHNU			TJU		
	Precision	Recall	F1-Score	Precision	Recall	F1-Score	Precision	Recall	F1-Score	Precision	Recall	F1-Score
CN	0.6902	0.6663	0.678	0.6885	0.6161	0.8354	0.7594	0.6821	0.7187	0.8289	0.7467	0.7856
Jaccard	0.7685	0.6271	0.6906	0.7481	0.6246	0.6808	0.8107	0.6800	0.7396	0.8726	0.7596	0.8122
Katz	0.6711	0.8093	0.7337	0.6682	0.8022	0.7291	0.6706	0.8085	0.7331	0.6666	0.7925	0.7241
RWR	0.5438	0.5191	0.5306	0.5603	0.5455	0.5526	0.5457	0.5368	0.5411	0.5718	0.547	0.5588
Node2vec	0.8603	0.805	0.8317	0.866	0.8068	0.6502	0.8706	0.8582	0.8644	0.8668	0.8355	0.8512
GCN	0.8185	0.7738	0.7955	0.8328	0.7798	0.8054	0.8358	0.8229	0.7293	0.7848	0.7375	0.7604
HNE	0.8632	0.8160	0.8389	0.8657	0.8092	0.8365	0.8706	0.8674	0.8691	0.8365	0.7789	0.7972

4. Conclusions and Discussions

In this paper, a link prediction approach with network embedding was proposed for hypergraphs. The proposed HNE method applied the Deepwalk model to extract features of nodes according to the hypergraphs constructed from library loan records, then a classifier was trained to predict the potential links between nodes. The experiment results on seven datasets showed that our approach outperformed typical link prediction methods. The comparison of AUC, precision, recall and F1-score with six methods demonstrated the effectiveness of the proposed approach.

In the future, the idea of combining hypergraphs and network embedding can not only be applied to link prediction, but also implement more tasks, such as node importance, community detection and node classification. In addition, our proposed algorithm has wide practical applications, such as recommendations for online social networks, knowledge reasoning for knowledge hypergraph construction, drug-target prediction or drug-disease prediction in the field of bioinformatics and so on. In addition, as more graph neural network methods [44–47] are proposed, we can explore hyperlink prediction algorithms and other graph neural network models for preserving more structural and semantic information of hypergraphs to solve the fundamental problems in hypergraph analysis.

Author Contributions: Conceptualization, Z.Z. and K.Y.; methodology, K.Y.; software, Z.Z.; validation, Z.Z., K.Y. and J.G.; writing—original draft preparation, Z.Z.; writing—review and editing, Z.Z., K.Y. and J.G. All authors have read and agreed to the published version of the manuscript.

Funding: This research was funded by the National Natural Science Foundation of China (No. 71571119), and the Natural Science Foundation of the Jiangsu Higher Education Institutions of China (No. 22KJD120002).

Institutional Review Board Statement: Not applicable.

Data Availability Statement: Our datasets could be downloaded in http://hdl.handle.net/20.500.12291/10022 (accessed on 8 October 2022).

Conflicts of Interest: The authors declare no conflict of interest.

References

1. Lü, L.Y.; Zhou, T. Link prediction in complex networks: A survey. *Phys. A* **2011**, *6*, 1150–1170. [CrossRef]
2. Zhang, M.H.; Chen, Y.X. Link prediction based on graph neural networks. In Proceedings of the Annual Conference on Neural Information Processing Systems 2018, NeurIPS 2018, Montréal, QC, Canada, 3–8 December 2018; pp. 5171–5181.
3. Wang, H.W.; Zhang, F.Z.; Hou, M.; Xie, X.; Guo, M.Y.; Liu, Q. Shine: Signed heterogeneous information network embedding for sentiment link prediction. In Proceedings of the Eleventh ACM International Conference on Web Search and Data Mining, Marina del Rey, CA, USA, 5–9 February 2018; pp. 592–600.
4. Pulipati, S.; Somula, R.; Parvathala, B.R. Nature inspired link prediction and community detection algorithms for social networks: A survey. *Int. J. Syst. Assur. Eng. Manag.* **2021**, 1–18. [CrossRef]
5. Talasu, N.; Jonnalagadda, A.; Pillai, S.S.A.; Rahul, J. A link prediction based approach for recommendation systems. In Proceedings of the 2017 International Conference on Advances in Computing, Communications and Informatics (ICACCI), Manipal, India, 13–16 September 2017; pp. 2059–2062.
6. Patel, R.; Guo, Y.H.; Alhudhaif, A.; Alenezi, F.; Althubiti, S.A.; Polat, K. Graph-Based Link Prediction between Human Phenotypes and Genes. *Math. Probl. Eng.* **2021**, *2022*, 8. [CrossRef]
7. Yang, K.; Zhao, X.Z.; Waxman, D.; Zhao, X.M. Predicting drug-disease associations with heterogeneous network embedding. *Chaos* **2019**, *12*, 123109. [CrossRef]
8. Kushwah, A.K.S.; Manjhvar, A.K. A review on link prediction in social network. *Int. J. Grid Distrib. Comput.* **2016**, *2*, 43–50. [CrossRef]
9. Passino, F.S.; Turcotte, M.J.M.; Heard, N.A. Graph link prediction in computer networks using poisson matrix factorisation. *Ann. Appl. Stat.* **2022**, *3*, 1313–1332.
10. Zhou, T.; Kuscsik, Z.; Liu, J.-G.; Medo, M.; Wakeling, J.R.; Zhang, Y.-C. Solving the apparent diversity-accuracy dilemma of recommender systems. *Proc. Natl. Acad. Sci. USA* **2010**, *107*, 4511–4515. [CrossRef]
11. Real, R.; Vargas, J.M. The probabilistic basis of Jaccard's index of similarity. *Syst. Biol.* **1996**, *3*, 380–385. [CrossRef]
12. Katz, L. A new status index derived from sociometric analysis. *Psychometrika* **1953**, *1*, 39–43.
13. Tong, H.h.; Faloutsos, C.; Pan, J.Y. Fast random walk with restart and its applications. In Proceedings of the Sixth International Conference on Data Mining (ICDM'06), Hong Kong, China, 18–22 December 2006; pp. 613–622.
14. Gao, Y.; Zhang, Z.Z.; Lin, H.J.; Zhao, X.B.; Du, S.Y.; Zou, C.Q. Hypergraph learning: Methods and practices. *IEEE Trans. Pattern Anal. Mach. Intell.* **2020**, *44*, 2548–2566. [CrossRef]
15. Feng, Y.F.; You, H.X.; Zhang, Z.Z.; Ji, R.R.; Gao, Y. Hypergraph neural networks. In Proceedings of the AAAI Conference on Artificial Intelligence, Honolulu, HI, USA, 27 January–1 February 2019; pp. 3558–3565.
16. Bai, S.; Zhang, F.h.; Torr, P.H.S. Hypergraph convolution and hypergraph attention. *Pattern Recognit.* **2021**, *110*, 107637. [CrossRef]
17. Xiao, Q. Node importance measure for scientific research collaboration from hypernetwork perspective. *Teh. Vjesn.* **2016**, *2*, 397–404.
18. Gallagher, S.R.; Goldberg, D.S. Clustering coefficients in protein interaction hypernetworks. In Proceedings of the International Conference on Bioinformatics, Computational Biology and Biomedical Informatics, Wshington, DC, USA, 22–25 September 2013; pp. 552–560.
19. Li, D.; Xu, Z.; Li, S.; Sun, X. Link prediction in social networks based on hypergraph. In Proceedings of the 22nd International Conference on World Wide Web, Rio de Janeiro, Brazil, 13–17 May 2013; pp. 41–42.
20. Chen, C.; Liu, Y.Y. A survey on hyperlink prediction. *arXiv* **2022**, arXiv:2207.02911.
21. Sharma, A.; Srivastava, J.; Chandra, A. Predicting multi-actor collaborations using hypergraphs. *arXiv* **2014**, arXiv:1401.6404.
22. Vaida, M.; Purcell, K. Hypergraph link prediction: Learning drug interaction networks embeddings. In Proceedings of the 2019 18th IEEE International Conference on Machine Learning And Applications (ICMLA), Boca Raton, FL, USA, 16–19 December 2019; pp. 1860–1865.
23. Liu, J.; Song, L.; Wang, G.; Shang, X.Q. Meta-HGT: Metapath-aware HyperGraph Transformer for heterogeneous information network embedding. *Neural Netw.* **2023**, *157*, 65–76. [CrossRef]
24. Kang, X.; Li, X.; Yao, H.; Li, D.; Jiang, B.; Peng, X.; Wu, T.; Qi, S.H.; Dong, L.J. Dynamic hypergraph neural networks based on key hyperedges. *Inf. Sci.* **2022**, *616*, 37–51. [CrossRef]
25. Fan, H.; Zhang, F.; Wei, Y.; Li, Z.; Zou, C.; Gao, Y.; Dai, Q. Heterogeneous hypergraph variational autoencoder for link prediction. *IEEE Trans. Pattern Anal. Mach. Intell.* **2021**, *44*, 4125–4138. [CrossRef]
26. Cui, P.; Wang, X.; Pei, J.; Zhu, W.W. A survey on network embedding. *IEEE Trans. Knowl. Data Eng.* **2018**, *5*, 833–853. [CrossRef]
27. Chang, S.y.; Han, W.; Tang, J.L.; Qi, G.J.; Aggarwal, C.C.; Huang, T.S. Heterogeneous network embedding via deep architectures. In Proceedings of the 21th ACM SIGKDD International Conference on Knowledge Discovery and Data Mining, Sydney, Australia, 10–13 August 2015; pp. 119–128.
28. Arsov, N.; Mirceva, G. Network embedding: An overview. *arXiv* **2019**, arXiv:1911.11826.
29. Wang, X.; Cui, P.; Wang, J.; Pei, J.; Zhu, W.W.; Yang, S.Q. Community preserving network embedding. In Proceedings of the Thirty-First AAAI Conference on Artificial Intelligence, San Francisco, CA, USA, 4–9 February 2017.
30. Belkin, M.; Niyogi, P. Laplacian eigenmaps and spectral techniques for embedding and clustering. In Proceedings of the Advances in Neural Information Processing Systems, Vancouver, BC, Canada, 3–8 December 2001; p. 14.

31. Perozzi, B.; Al-Rfou, R.; Skiena, S. Deepwalk: Online learning of social representations. In Proceedings of the 20th ACM SIGKDD International Conference on Knowledge Discovery and Data Mining, New York, NY, USA, 24–27 August 2014; pp. 701–710.
32. Grover, A.; Leskovec, J. node2vec: Scalable feature learning for networks. In Proceedings of the 22nd ACM SIGKDD International Conference on Knowledge Discovery and Data Mining, San Francisco, CA, USA, 13–17 August 2016; pp. 855–864.
33. Donnat, C.; Zitnik, M.; Hallac, D.; Leskovec, J. Learning structural node embeddings via diffusion wavelets. In Proceedings of the 24th ACM SIGKDD International Conference on Knowledge Discovery & Data Mining, London, UK, 19–23 August 2018 pp. 1320–1329.
34. Hu, B.; Fang, Y.; Shi, C. Adversarial learning on heterogeneous information networks. In Proceedings of the 25th ACM SIGKDD International Conference on Knowledge Discovery & Data Mining, Anchorage AK, USA, 4–8 August 2019; pp. 120–129.
35. Tsitsulin, A.; Mottin, D.; Karras, P.; Müller, E. Verse: Versatile graph embeddings from similarity measures. In Proceedings of the 2018 World Wide Web Conference, Lyon, France, 23–27 April 2018; pp. 539–548.
36. Wang, S.H.; Tang, J.L.; Aggarwal, C.R.; Chang, Y.; Liu, H. Signed network embedding in social media. In Proceedings of the 2017 SIAM International Conference on Data Mining, Houston, TX, USA, 27–29 April 2017; pp. 327–335.
37. Yadati, N.; Nitin, V.; Nimishakavi, M.; Yadav, P.; Louis, A.; Talukdar, P. NHP: Neural hypergraph link prediction. In Proceedings of the 29th ACM International Conference on Information & Knowledge Management, Virtual Event, 19–23 October 2020; pp 1705–1714.
38. Kipf, T.N.; Welling, M. Semi-supervised classification with graph convolutional networks. *arXiv* **2016**, arXiv:1609.02907.
39. Yadati, N.; Nimishakavi, M.; Yadav, P.; Nitin, V.; Louis, A.; Talukdar, P.P. Hypergcn: A new method for training graph convolutional networks on hypergraphs. In Proceedings of the Annual Conference on Neural Information Processing Systems, Vancouver, BC, Canada, 8–14 December 2019; pp. 1509–1520.
40. Breiman, L. Random forests. *Mach. Learn.* **2001**, *45*, 5–32. [CrossRef]
41. Tu, K.; Cui, P.; Wang, X.; Wang, F.; Zhu, W.w. Structural deep embedding for hyper-networks. In Proceedings of the AAAI Conference on Artificial Intelligence, New Orleans, LA, USA, 2–7 February 2018; p. 1.
42. Ma, T.; Suo, Q. Review of Hypernetwork Based on Hypergraph. *Oper. Res. Manag. Sci.* **2021**, *2*, 232.
43. Service Centre of Huiyuan Sharing Academic Resources. University Library Dataset. Available online: http://hdl.handle.net/20.500.12291/10022 (accessed on 22 July 2021).
44. Zhang, C.X.; Song, D.j.; Huang, C.; Swami, A.; Chawla, N.V. Heterogeneous graph neural network. In Proceedings of the 25th ACM SIGKDD International Conference on Knowledge Discovery & Data Mining, Anchorage AK, USA, 4–8 August 2019; pp. 793–803.
45. Ding, Y.; Zhang, Z.L.; Zhao, X.F.; Cai, W.; He, F.; Cai, Y.M.; Cai, W.W. Deep hybrid: Multi-graph neural network collaboration for hyperspectral image classification. *Def. Technol.* **2022**, *in press*.
46. Wu, C.; Wu, F.; Cao, Y.; Huang, Y.; Xie, X. Fedgnn: Federated graph neural network for privacy-preserving recommendation. *arXiv* **2021**, arXiv:2102.04925.
47. Huang, C.; Xu, H.C.; Xu, Y.; Dai, P.; Xia, L.H.; Lu, M.Y.; Bo, L.F.; Xing, H.; Lai, X.P.; Ye, Y.F. Knowledge-aware coupled graph neural network for social recommendation. In Proceedings of the AAAI Conference on Artificial Intelligence, Virtually, 2–9 February 2021; pp. 4115–4122.

Disclaimer/Publisher's Note: The statements, opinions and data contained in all publications are solely those of the individual author(s) and contributor(s) and not of MDPI and/or the editor(s). MDPI and/or the editor(s) disclaim responsibility for any injury to people or property resulting from any ideas, methods, instructions or products referred to in the content.

Predicting Task Planning Ability for Learners Engaged in Searching as Learning Based on Tree-Structured Long Short-Term Memory Networks

Pengfei Li [1], Shaoyu Dong [2,*], Yin Zhang [3] and Bin Zhang [3]

[1] School of Computer Science and Engineering, Northeastern University, Shenyang 110167, China; leepengfei.neu@gmail.com
[2] School of Business Administration, Northeastern University, Shenyang 110167, China
[3] Software College, Northeastern University, Shenyang 110167, China; zhang-yin@mail.neu.edu.cn (Y.Z.); zhang-bin@mail.neu.edu.cn (B.Z.)
* Correspondence: sydong_91@163.com

Abstract: The growing utilization of web-based search engines for learning purposes has led to increased studies on searching as learning (SAL). In order to achieve the desired learning outcomes, web learners have to carefully plan their learning objectives. Previous SAL research has proposed the significant influence of task planning quality on learning outcomes. Therefore, accurately predicting web-based learners' task planning abilities, particularly in the context of SAL, is of paramount importance for both web-based search engines and recommendation systems. To solve this problem, this paper proposes a method for predicting the ability of task planning for web learners. Specifically, we first introduced a tree-based representation method to capture how learners plan their learning tasks. Subsequently, we proposed a method based on the deep learning technique to accurately predict the SAL task planning ability for web learners. Experimental results indicate that, compared to baseline approaches, our proposed method can provide a more effective representation of learners' task planning and deliver more accurate predictions of learners' task planning abilities in SAL.

Keywords: searching as learning; learning ability; HCDP; Tree-Structured Long Short-Term Memory Networks; user analysis; task planning

1. Introduction

In recent years, the advent of web-based search engines has revolutionized the way people access information. These ubiquitous tools are extensively employed, not only for informational queries but also increasingly for learning purposes [1,2]. Recognizing the potential of web-based search engines as valuable learning aids, researchers have focused on searching as learning (SAL), utilizing web-based search engines as a means to acquire knowledge and support learning processes and conceptualizing searching activities as learning activities [3,4].

Unlike the traditional field of information retrieval, which primarily views searching as a tool for information acquisition, studies on SAL place greater emphasis on the learning process that learners engage in through web-based searching. Building upon this perspective, research in the domain of SAL focuses on the role of search systems in directly facilitating human learning [5]. This area of study goes beyond mere information retrieval to emphasize examining the effects, implications, and results derived from utilizing search systems in the context of educational processes. From a perspective of information retrieval, SAL research shifts the focus from the relevance of individual search results to supporting the learning process itself [6]. From an educational perspective, SAL research concentrates on deeply understanding how learners use search engines to meet their learning needs and how optimization can enhance learning outcomes [2].

Studies have proposed that SAL combined with thoughtful task planning can lead to enhanced learning outcomes [7,8]. At the beginning of the SAL process, learners often only possess a vague understanding of the learning object, meaning their knowledge structures are insufficient to precisely articulate what they seek to learn. During the SAL process, learners are required to continually refine their learning tasks and retrieve relevant information from web-based search engine results, progressively constructing and refining their knowledge structures. This process involves the generation of queries, the evaluation of search results, and iterative adjustments and refinements of knowledge structures [5,9].

Understanding and predicting learners' task planning ability in SAL are crucial for web-based search engine providers, recommendation systems, and educators [6,10]. By comprehending learners' planning abilities, web-based search engines and recommendation systems can provide targeted guidance, suggest relevant learning resources, and optimize search results to facilitate effective learning [11]. Additionally, educators and instructional designers can utilize these insights to tailor instruction, provide appropriate scaffolding, and design interventions aimed at improving learners' planning skills, ultimately fostering metacognitive awareness and self-regulated learning [12].

To address the challenge of predicting learners' task planning ability, this paper proposes a novel method that leverages the Hierarchical Clustering Algorithm Based on Density Peaks (HCDP) model and the Tree-Structured Long Short-Term Memory Networks (Tree-LSTM) algorithm. The HCDP model is employed to capture and represent the hierarchical relationships among learning activities and learning subtasks. By modeling the learning process in this way, we can effectively capture the nuances of task planning in SAL. The Tree-LSTM algorithm is utilized to predict learners' SAL task planning ability based on the extracted features from the tree structure.

The experimental results demonstrate the efficacy of our proposed method in effectively predicting learners' task planning ability within the context of SAL. Furthermore, the key features extracted from the tree structure serve as reliable indicators of learners' planning ability, providing valuable insights for web-based search engines, recommendation systems, and instructional designers.

Overall, this paper contributes to the field of information retrieval and learning by offering a methodological approach to predict learners' task planning ability in the context of SAL. The findings hold implications for web-based search engine providers, recommendation systems, and educational practitioners. For search engine designers, our study aids in developing learner-focused search interfaces by understanding SAL task planning, leading to enhanced personalization and efficiency. For educational practice, our research informs educators about learner challenges in SAL, enabling more effective learning experience design and targeted support.

2. Related Works
2.1. Predictive Models for Learners' Abilities

The predictive modeling of learners' abilities has gained significant interest, especially due to its potential in customizing learning environments for individual learners, thereby optimizing the learning process.

Numerous models have been proposed that utilize Machine Learning (ML) and Artificial Intelligence (AI) algorithms to predict abilities. For example, Thai-Nghe et al. [13] introduced a method to predict student performance based on past interactions using collaborative filtering and matrix factorization techniques. Similarly, Márquez-Vera et al. [14] employed decision trees, Naive Bayes, and k-nearest neighbors to anticipate student dropouts in online courses. Liu et al. [15] propose a two-stage framework to predict the cognitive level of the learner. Agrawal et al. [16] pointed out that learning ability can be estimated by administering a test designed using modern practices such as those based on Item Response Theory (IRT). Bockmon et al. [17] conducted a comprehensive study on the predictive modeling of students' introductory programming abilities at the end of the semester. To achieve this, they employed a multinomial logistic regression approach, aiming to develop a robust model that could effectively forecast students' performance in programming tasks. This model's sophistication lies in its ability to handle multiple predictor variables and their interactions, offering a nuanced understanding of student performance. Furthermore, the research delved into the relationship between various factors, such as prior programming abilities, spatial skills, socioeconomic status, and students' attitudes toward computing, in order to determine their influence on the final programming outcomes. In sum, this comprehensive analysis provides a foundation for developing targeted educational strategies that can significantly improve student outcomes in programming and related technical disciplines.

The advancements in predictive modeling underscore the importance of understanding learners' abilities, which is a crucial aspect of Searching as Learning (SAL). This understanding aids in the development of more effective web-based learning tools and strategies.

2.2. Searching as Learning

The growing utilization of web-based search engines as tools for learning has attracted considerable attention from researchers. Studies have explored the impact of web-based search engine features, such as query formulation assistance, result evaluation techniques, and personalized recommendations, on learning outcomes [7,18]. These investigations highlight the significance of effective web-based search engine usage in supporting the learning process [19,20].

For instance, query formulation assistance helps learners in generating effective search queries, enabling them to retrieve relevant and accurate information [6,21,22]. Result evaluation techniques aid learners in critically assessing the credibility, relevance, and reliability of search results, enabling them to make informed decisions regarding the information they encounter during their learning process [23].

SAL studies use searching as a part of the learning process and aim to explore the integration of web-based search engine utilization and web learning to improve learning outcomes [6,24,25]. Similar SAL studies conceptualize searching as an integral component of the learning process and underscore the significance of search in enhancing learning outcomes [6,26,27]. These studies emphasize the importance of task planning quality, including query formulation and result evaluation, in achieving desired learning outcomes.

3. Data Collection and Labeling

In this section, we discuss the dataset employed in our experiments that was procured from the University Writing Program (UWP) courses at Northeastern University. Further, we discuss how we achieved capability labeling for task planning in the SAL context.

3.1. Data Collection

In this section, we begin by detailing the SAL dataset utilized in this study, collected from learners enrolled in the UWP course at Northeastern University. The data collection methodology has been described in our previous work [6]. Here, we briefly outline the types of SAL data captured for each learner:

(1) Search logs. We recorded learners' search activities with web-based search engines by developing a Firefox browser plug-in. Specifically, for a learner, we recorded searching activities such as their issued search queries, clicking on URLs, and reading duration times.
(2) Search results. We recorded search results after each issued search query.
(3) Learning outcomes. We recorded programming snapshots for each learner during compilation.

In the initial five weeks of our study, we systematically introduced tasks with an incrementally increasing number of subtasks. The distribution of these subtasks within the assignments is illustrated in Figure 1. Research conducted in the domain of SAL has suggested that the act of searching within SAL can be perceived as a sequence of activities with the purpose of learning [28]. Although we cannot directly observe, we can predict their learning state by analyzing their search activities and learning outcomes.

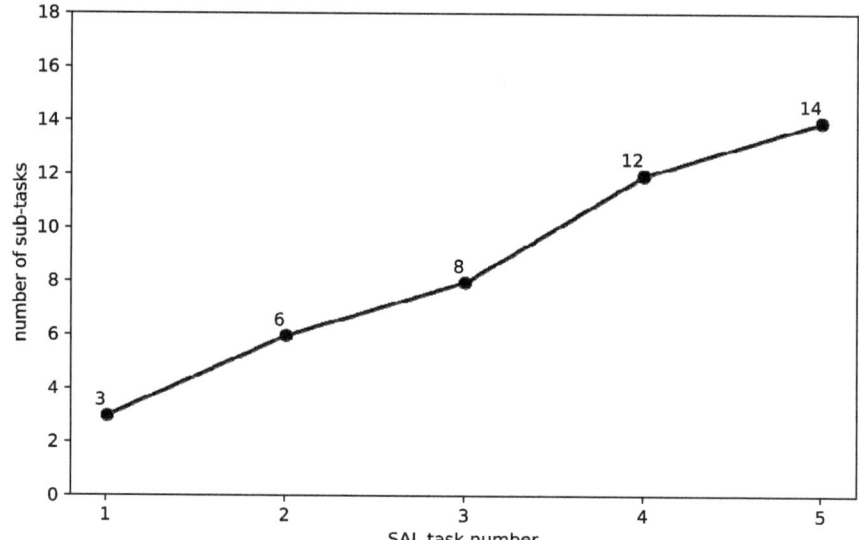

Figure 1. The distribution of subtasks in the learning assignments.

3.2. Data Labeling

In this study, six researchers specializing in the field of SAL from Northeastern University participated in the labeling process. These experts included two associate professors, two doctoral candidates, and two master's degree learners. Each participant was tasked with evaluating the SAL abilities of learners based on the dataset we collected. This evaluation involved reviewing the collected data in conjunction with the scores of corresponding assignments within the course curriculum. The average scores from five distinct assignments were ultimately employed as the annotated indicators for gauging the SAL abilities of the learners.

To facilitate the labeling of SAL task planning abilities, it is first necessary for each participant to analyze the learning process of learners in order to understand how these learners decompose their learning tasks. To ensure the validity of manual annotations, we required participants to answer specific questions given different types of interaction behaviors. This ensures a comprehensive understanding of the learner's learning process during analysis, as illustrated in Table 1. Additionally, participants can also refer to the learner's phased learning outcomes and final grades for labeling.

The statistical outcomes of the capability labeling for task planning in the SAL context is illustrated in Figure 2. For the purpose of this research, the manually annotated SAL task planning abilities are classified into five distinct levels, ranging from 1 to 5. A score of 1 represents the lowest level of capability, while a score of 5 signifies the highest level of proficiency in SAL task planning.

Table 1. Questions that need to be answered for different types of SAL behavior.

Issuing queries
1. Why did the learner issue this query? 2. Is this query related to the previously submitted queries? 3. What is the relationship between the results returned by this query and the results returned by previous queries?
Clicked on URLs
1. What learning object is the learner interested in? 2. Was this click event triggered by the most recent query? 3. Is the learner's learning objective the same as or related to the learning objective of the previously submitted queries?
Programming
1. Through which queries did the learner acquire his/her learning outcomes? 2. To achieve the learning outcomes, did the learner experience struggles or study unrelated content?

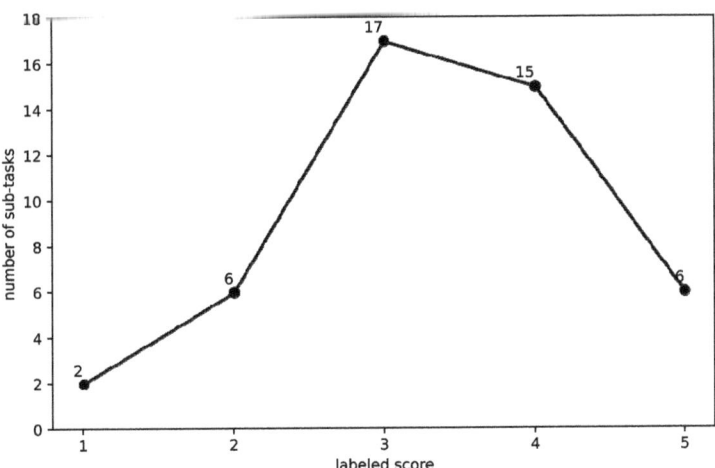

Figure 2. Results of SAL Task planning Capability Labeling.

4. Proposed Methodology

In this section, we will accomplish two primary objectives. First, we innovatively employ the HCDP method for constructing tree-like structures, effectively enabling the hierarchical representation of SAL task planning. Second, we introduce the use of the Tee-LSTM approach to facilitate the prediction of SAL task planning abilities.

4.1. Representation of Task Planning in Searching as Learning

In this section, we focus on the construction of a structured representation for task planning in SAL. While linear structures have been extensively employed for representing task planning, recent research has indicated that learning processes are often intricate search activities requiring learners to navigate among varying learning objectives and tasks [29]. Consequently, a linear structure proves insufficient for capturing the complexity inherent in a learner's task planning strategies.

Mehrotra et al. [30] substantiated the advantages of tree-structured representations in modeling search task planning. Moreover, current research has indicated that hierarchical clustering algorithms can effectively capture the subtask structure of learners' search tasks [6]. Accordingly, in the present study, we adopt a tree-structured approach to provide a more nuanced and effective representation of task planning in SAL.

To fully leverage the unique context-specific features of SAL and to provide a more accurate representation of a learner's task-based structural divisions, we introduce a novel method for SAL task partitioning based on HCDP. This advanced hierarchical clustering algorithm allows for capturing the intricacies of searching and learning interactions in SAL [31].

To accurately model the structure of a learner's task planning, we consolidate his/her SAL-related interactive activities prior to initiating the modeling process. We complete this based on the observation that learning activities are triggered by issuing search queries. Furthermore, what learners acquire is contingent upon the queries they submit. Hence, in constructing the structural representation of a learner's task planning, we employ queries as the nodes of the structure. While these nodes are represented by queries, it should be noted that they encapsulate not only the search queries themselves but also the subsequent learning that occurs as a result.

In traditional HCDP, the algorithmic framework is fundamentally structured around three core procedures: the computation of local densities, the construction of a hierarchical representation of the data, and the extraction of optimal clusters [32–34]. Given that our research objective specifically aims to establish a hierarchical architecture for task partitioning in SAL, our study focuses only on executing the initial two procedures.

HCDP employs k-nearest neighbors for the computation of local densities. The HCDP model computes the local density as follows [34]:

$$\rho_i = \max_{j \in knn(i)} dist(i,j) \quad (1)$$

where ρ_i is the $Node_i$'s k-nearest density, $dist(i,j)$ denotes the distance between $Node_i$ and $Node_j$.

For each $Node_i$, SAL establishes a connection to its nearest neighbor with higher density using edge weight φ. The computation for φ is as follows.

$$\varphi_i = \min_{j:\rho_i > \rho_j} dist(i,j) \quad (2)$$

Therefore, in our task of hierarchical representation for task planning, the focus is on being able to calculate $dist(i,j)$ by integrating features from SAL. To achieve this goal, we calculate $dist(i,j)$ from three dimensions: search, learning, and the connection between search and learning. We list the SAL features for calculat $dist(\cdot)$ that we employed in Table 2. The hierarchical clustering visualization of partial SAL data for a learner in the UWP dataset is shown in Figure 3.

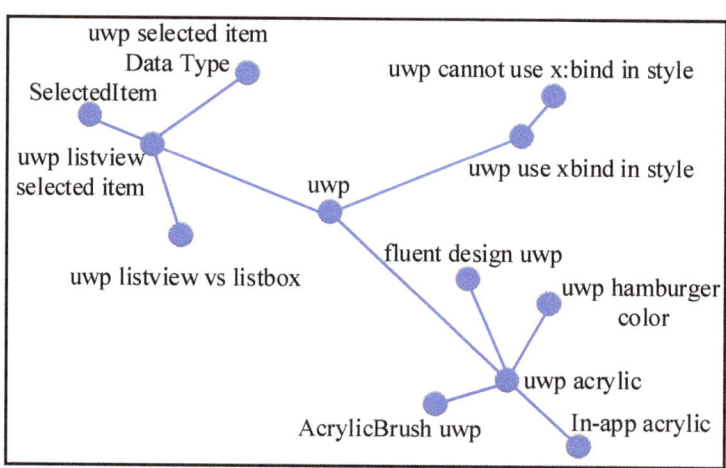

Figure 3. The hierarchical clustering visualization of partial SAL data for a learner.

Table 2. The SAL features for calculating $dist(\cdot)$.

Search-related features
1. Cosine distance between two sets of query terms.
2. Edit distance between two sets of query terms.
3. Jaccard distance between two sets of query terms.
4. The proportion of identical terms in two search queries.
5. Semantics distance between queries.
Features of the relationship between searching and learning
1. The average cosine distance between the web page links clicked after queries.
2. The average edit distance between the web page links clicked after queries.
3. Cosine distance between the sets of UWP terms contained in clicked links after two queries.
4. Cosine distance between the sets of UWP terms contained in the search results after two queries.
Learning-related features
1. Cosine distance between the sets of UWP classes contained in programming snapshots after two queries.
2. Edit distance between the sets of UWP classes contained in programming snapshots after two queries.
3. Semantic distance between two programming snapshots.

4.2. SAL Task Planning Ability Predicted Based on the Tree-LSTM Model

In this paper, we address the challenge by employing the Tree-LSTM model. A Tree-LSTM is a neural network architecture that extends the standard Long Short-Term Memory (LSTM) framework [35]. While standard LSTM models are designed to process sequential data, Tree-LSTM models are adapted to handle tree-structured data. This makes them particularly useful for tasks that involve hierarchical or nested structures, such as natural language sentences, computer programs, or chemical molecules [31]. Therefore, the Tree-LSTM model serves as an instrumental methodology, enabling a more nuanced understanding of hierarchical dependencies and thereby predicting task planning ability from tree hierarchical representation.

The key advantage of Tree-LSTMs lies in their ability to capture the hierarchical dependencies within tree-structured data [35,36]. This is particularly beneficial in educational contexts where learning tasks often involve layered concepts or stepwise procedures. For instance, in the realm of programming education, the Tree-LSTM model can effectively represent and analyze the structure of code, discerning the underlying logic and predicting potential errors or areas of improvement in student submissions [37,38].

In the context of our research framework, the Tree-LSTM model ingests a tree-structured representation encapsulating the complexities of the learning task as its input. The tree-structured data input represents the hierarchical organization of a learning task, capturing various elements such as the sequence of steps, dependencies among concepts, and the progression of learning objectives. The Tree-LSTM model then processes this input to generate an output in the form of a predictive assessment, quantifying a learner's abilities in task planning. Analogous to the conventional LSTM model, each unit in a Tree-LSTM architecture is equipped with input gates denoted as i_m, output gates symbolized by o_m, along with a memory cell c_m and a hidden state h_m. Unique to the Tree-LSTM model, the updating mechanism for these gate vectors and memory cells is conditioned upon the aggregated states of multiple child units, if present. Moreover, each Tree-LSTM unit is endowed with specialized forget gates $f_{m,k}$ for each child unit k [39,40]. This design intricacy enables the Tree-LSTM to serve as a robust framework for modeling hierarchical relationships, particularly valuable for tree-structure presentation of learning tasks.

Let $S(m)$ denote the subtree of m, and the transition equations of the Tree-LSTM model are as follows [41]:

$$\widetilde{h_m} = \sum_{n \in S(j)} h_n \qquad (3)$$

$$i_m = \sigma\left(W^{(i)} x_m + U^{(i)} h_m + b^{(i)}\right) \quad (4)$$

$$f_{m,k} = \sigma\left(W^{(f)} x_m + U^{(f)} h_m + b^{(f)}\right) \quad (5)$$

$$o_m = \sigma\left(W^{(o)} x_m + U^{(o)} h_m + b^{(o)}\right) \quad (6)$$

$$u_m = \tanh\left(W^{(u)} x_m + U^{(u)} h_m + b^{(u)}\right) \quad (7)$$

$$c_m = i_m \circ u_m + \sum_{k \in S(m)} f_{m,k} \circ c_k \quad (8)$$

$$h_m = o_m \circ \tanh(c_m) \quad (9)$$

where $\sigma(\cdot)$ denotes the logistic sigmoid function, and $\circ$ denote the element-wise multiplication. In the Tree-LSTM model, the state of the composite nodes is derived from the states of the nodes, as illustrated in Figure 4.

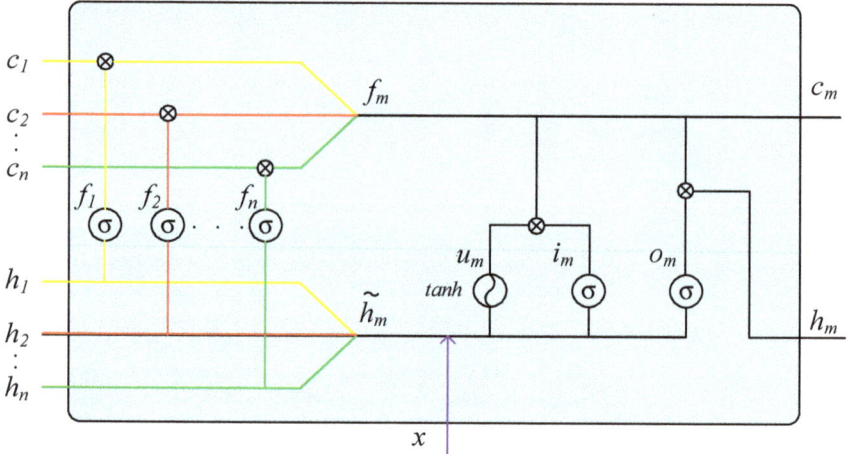

Figure 4. Tree-LSTM model for task planning ability prediction.

The inclusion of these additional gates and the unique updating mechanism enables the Tree-LSTM model to effectively capture and analyze the intricacies of hierarchical data, making it a powerful tool for modeling the dynamic nature of learning tasks. This advanced functionality positions the Tree-LSTM as an ideal framework for tasks that require an understanding of nested or sequential dependencies, such as predicting a learner's ability to plan and execute complex learning tasks.

5. Experiments

To assess the efficacy of our proposed methodology in forecasting learners' abilities in task planning within the SAL, we executed an array of experiments utilizing the Northeastern University UWP dataset as our empirical foundation. This section commences by detailing the experimental setup. Subsequently, we substantiate the merits of our approach by juxtaposing its performance metrics against those of established baseline algorithms.

5.1. Experimental Setup

To verify the performance of our proposed method, we commence by delineating the experimental setup. The design of our experiments employed the dataset gathered from the UWP course at Northeastern University (China), and the manually labeled task planning abilities that we discussed in Section 3.2. To ensure the reliability of our findings, we employed stratified ten-fold cross-validation for dataset partitioning into training and testing subsets. The rationale behind utilizing stratified ten-fold cross-validation lies in its capacity to mitigate the introduction of potential biases and anomalous results, which may stem from imbalanced or skewed data distributions.

For comparative model analysis, our methodology underwent a two-phase evaluation. Initially, we compared our proposed method with state-of-the-art (SOAT) hierarchical clustering algorithms, thereby establishing the performance efficiency of the HCDP algorithm in the hierarchical representation within the SAL task planning. Subsequently, our framework was benchmarked against baseline predictive models for assessing the model's predictive accuracy.

5.2. Comparison with SOAT Hierarchical Clustering Methods Based on the UWP Dataset

In this section, we evaluate the advanced nature of our proposed methodology in the domain of learning task-structured representation through comparative experiments with SOAT methods. Selected methods for comparison include hierarchical clustering methods like Bayesian Hierarchical Clustering (BHC) [42], Min-Min-Roughness (MMR) [43], and Bayesian Rose Tree (BRT) [30]. A commonality between these methods and our proposed approach is their capability to construct hierarchical representations for learning task-planning. To ensure fairness and validity in the comparative analysis, all methods utilize SAL features consistent with those presented in Table 3 wherever possible. During the prediction phase, all of these hierarchical clustering methodologies employ the same Tree-LSTM model and undergo parameter optimization through identical procedures.

Table 3. The experimental results with hierarchical clustering methods.

Method	Precision	Recall	F1
BHC	0.717	0.701	0.709
MMR	0.782	0.73	0.755
BRT	0.82	0.805	0.812
Our method	0.889	0.825	0.856

As illustrated in Table 3, it is evident that the methodology proposed in this study demonstrates a superior performance over the baseline methods across multiple evaluation metrics. Specifically, the proposed approach surpasses the best-performing baseline method by approximately 7.1% in terms of average prediction accuracy for the UWP dataset. Notably, our method's performance exceeds that of the original BRT model, thereby substantiating the efficacy of the proposed model in the learning process. Moreover, among all methods, the BHC method exhibits the weakest predictive performance. This can be attributed to the fact that the binary tree structure is not congruent with the structural nuances of the learning process. In Table 4, the confusion matrix corresponding to the method we have proposed is delineated. This matrix effectively illustrates the performance of our methodology in terms of true positives, false positives, true negatives, and false negatives. Through this representation, we aim to provide a clear and comprehensive understanding of the accuracy, precision, recall, and specificity of our approach.

Table 4. The confusion matrix our method.

Method	TP	FP	TN	FN
Our method	104	13	91	22

Further, we conducted a comparative analysis of various algorithms' predictive capabilities across learning tasks with varying numbers of subtasks. As illustrated in Figure 5 (where the X-axis represents the number of subtasks in a learning task), with an increase in the number of subtasks, the prediction accuracy of the method proposed in this paper declines less compared to that of other baseline methods. When the number of tasks reaches 14 (which corresponds to the assignment with the most subtasks in this course), the difference in prediction accuracy between our proposed method and the best-performing baseline algorithm is at its maximum. In summary, as the number of subtasks increases the performance advantage of our proposed algorithm becomes increasingly evident.

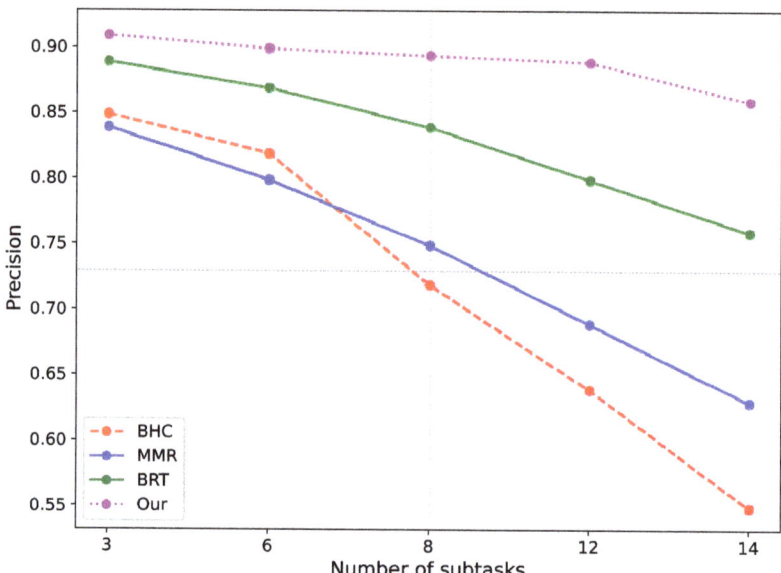

Figure 5. Comparison results for different numbers of subtasks.

5.3. Comparison with Predicative Methods

In this section, we evaluate the efficacy of our proposed methodology in the realm of task planning capability prediction by contrasting it with baseline approaches. The selected comparative methodologies include fundamental ML algorithms like Graph Neural Networks (GNNs) [44] and Recursive Neural Networks (RecNNs) [45]. These models were chosen for their capacity to accommodate tree-structured input data, thereby ensuring a level playing field for comparative analysis. The input to all of the models was constructed using HCDP, a preprocessing technique suited for SAL. During the training phase, parameter optimization was performed across all models to ensure performance.

Table 5 showcases a comprehensive evaluation of various algorithms, including our proposed methodology. The results elucidated in this table are a testament to the effectiveness of our technique. It is evident from the empirical data that our approach has a definitive edge over the baseline methodologies.

Table 5. The experimental results with baseline predicative methods.

Method	Precision	Recall	F1
GNN	0.843	0.824	0.833
RecNN	0.835	0.817	0.826
Our method	0.889	0.825	0.856

In the field of SAL, the precision and accuracy of predictions hold paramount significance. Given the complexities inherent to SAL, it is imperative for algorithms to adeptly predict and optimize task planning. As delineated in Table 5, our methodology distinctly excels in this dimension. It not only assures enhanced accuracy but also emphasizes the salience of context-aware predictions within SAL. Multiple elements bolster the preeminence of our approach. Primarily, the strategy we introduced is congruent with the task planning architecture intrinsic to learners. Subsequently, the Tree-LSTM exhibits remarkable efficacy in modeling and predicting tree-structured data.

6. Conclusions

This research innovatively introduces a novel method for the accurate prediction of task planning abilities in the context of SAL. By utilizing the HCDP algorithm, we offer a hierarchical representation of the task planning for learners engaged in SAL. Leveraging the Tree-LSTM algorithm, we subsequently achieve precise predictive abilities for assessing task planning in SAL. Empirical validation, based on the UWP dataset, corroborates the effectiveness of our proposed approach.

For search engine designers, our research will assist web-based search engine designers in constructing learner profiles and in understanding how learners progressively complete their tasks in the context of SAL. Additionally, our findings will guide designers in creating more personalized and efficient search interfaces tailored for educational purposes. Moreover, our research can inform the optimization of query suggestions and the customization of result filtering based on learners' task planning abilities in SAL.

For educational practice, our research will significantly aid educational practitioners in designing more effective learning experiences. Specifically, it will help practitioners promptly identify and address the challenges and struggles learners may encounter, offering robust support in instructional design. Furthermore, this understanding will enable practitioners to provide targeted guidance and support, particularly for learners who struggle with planning and organizing learning tasks.

Future research avenues may encompass the analysis and understanding of various other abilities demonstrated by learners throughout the learning process. Additionally, the role of metacognition in influencing learning trajectories within SAL contexts warrants further investigation.

Author Contributions: Conceptualization, P.L. and B.Z.; Data curation, P.L., S.D. and Y.Z.; Formal analysis, P.L., B.Z. and Y.Z.; Funding acquisition, B.Z.; Investigation, P.L. and S.D.; Methodology, P.L. and Y.Z.; Resources, P.L. and S.D.; Software, P.L.; Validation, P.L., S.D., B.Z. and Y.Z.; Writing—original draft, P.L.; Writing—review & editing, P.L. All authors have read and agreed to the published version of the manuscript.

Funding: This research was funded by the key project of the national natural science foundation of China: U1908212.

Institutional Review Board Statement: Not applicable.

Informed Consent Statement: Informed consent was obtained from all subjects involved in the study.

Data Availability Statement: Data are contained within the article.

Conflicts of Interest: The authors declare no conflict of interest.

References

1. Rahman, M.M.; Abdullah, N.A. A Personalized Group-Based Recommendation Approach for Web Search in E-Learning. *IEEE Access* **2018**, *6*, 34166–34178. [CrossRef]
2. Von Hoyer, J.; Hoppe, A.; Kammerer, Y.; Otto, C.; Pardi, G.; Rokicki, M.; Yu, R.; Dietze, S.; Ewerth, R.; Holtz, P. The Search as Learning Spaceship: Toward a Comprehensive Model of Psychological and Technological Facets of Search as Learning. *Front. Psychol.* **2022**, *13*, 827748. [CrossRef]
3. Zhang, P.; Soergel, D. Process patterns and conceptual changes in knowledge representations during information seeking and sensemaking: A qualitative user study. *J. Inf. Sci.* **2016**, *42*, 59–78. [CrossRef]
4. Su, Y.-S.; Huang, C.S.; Ding, T.-J. Examining the Effects of MOOCs Learners' Social Searching Results on Learning Behaviors and Learning Outcomes. *Eurasia J. Math. Sci. Technol. Educ.* **2016**, *12*, 2517–2529. [CrossRef]
5. Hansen, P.; Rieh, S.Y. Editorial: Recent advances on searching as learning: An introduction to the special issue. *J. Inf. Sci.* **2016**, *42*, 3–6. [CrossRef]
6. Rieh, S.Y.; Collins-Thompson, K.; Hansen, P.; Lee, H.-J. Towards searching as a learning process: A review of current perspectives and future directions. *J. Inf. Sci.* **2016**, *42*, 19–34. [CrossRef]

7. Piech, C.; Sahami, M.; Koller, D.; Cooper, S.; Blikstein, P. Modeling how students learn to program. In Proceedings of the 43rd ACM Technical Symposium on Computer Science Education (SIGCSE '12), Raleigh, NC, USA, 29 February–3 March 2012; Association for Computing Machinery: New York, NY, USA, 2012; pp. 153–160. [CrossRef]
8. Li, P.; Zhang, B.; Zhang, Y. Extracting Searching as Learning Tasks Based on IBRT Approach. *Appl. Sci.* **2022**, *12*, 5879. [CrossRef]
9. Vakkari, P. Searching as learning: A systematization based on literature. *J. Inf. Sci.* **2016**, *42*, 7–18. [CrossRef]
10. Bhattacharya, N. LongSAL: A Longitudinal Search as Learning Study with University Students. In Proceedings of the Extended Abstracts of the 2023 CHI Conference on Human Factors in Computing Systems (CHI EA '23), Hamburg, Germany, 23–28 April 2023; Association for Computing Machinery: New York, NY, USA, 2023; p. 570. [CrossRef]
11. Liu, J. Deconstructing search tasks in interactive information retrieval: A systematic review of task dimensions and predictors. *Inf. Process. Manag.* **2021**, *58*, 3. [CrossRef]
12. Reynolds, R.B. Relationships among tasks, collaborative inquiry processes, inquiry resolutions, and knowledge outcomes in adolescents during guided discovery-based game design in school. *J. Inf. Sci.* **2016**, *42*, 35–58. [CrossRef]
13. Thai-Nghe, N.; Drumond, L.; Horváth, T.; Krohn-Grimberghe, A.; Nanopoulos, A.; Schmidt-Thieme, L. Factorization techniques for predicting student performance. In *Educational Recommender Systems and Technologies: Practices and Challenges*; Santos, O.C. Boticario, J.G., Eds.; IGI Global: Hershey, PA, USA, 2012; pp. 129–153.
14. Marquez-Vera, C.; Morales, C.R.; Soto, S.V. Predicting School Failure and Dropout by Using Data Mining Techniques. *IEEE Rev. Iberoam. Tecnol. Aprendiz.* **2013**, *8*, 7–14. [CrossRef]
15. Liu, Y.; Liu, Q.; Wu, R.; Chen, E.; Su, Y.; Chen, Z.; Hu, G. Collaborative Learning Team Formation: A Cognitive Modeling Perspective. In *Database Systems for Advanced Applications, Proceedings of the 21st International Conference, DASFAA 2016, Dallas, TX, USA, 16–19 April 2016*; Navathe, S., Wu, W., Shekhar, S., Du, X., Wang, S., Xiong, H., Eds.; Lecture Notes in Computer Science; Springer: Cham, Switzerland, 2016; Volume 9643. [CrossRef]
16. Agrawal, R.; Golshan, B.; Terzi, E. Grouping students in educational settings. In Proceedings of the 20th ACM SIGKDD International Conference on Knowledge Discovery and Data Mining (KDD '14), New York, NY, USA, 24–27 August 2014; Association for Computing Machinery: New York, NY, USA, 2014; pp. 1017–1026. [CrossRef]
17. Bockmon, R.; Cooper, S.; Gratch, J.; Zhang, J.; Dorodchi, M. Can Students' Spatial Skills Predict Their Programming Abilities? In Proceedings of the 2020 ACM Conference on Innovation and Technology in Computer Science Education (ITiCSE '20), Trondheim, Norway, 15–19 June 2020; Association for Computing Machinery: New York, NY, USA, 2020; pp. 446–451. [CrossRef]
18. Pardi, G.; von Hoyer, J.; Holtz, P.; Kammerer, Y. The Role of Cognitive Abilities and Time Spent on Texts and Videos in a Multimodal Searching as Learning Task. In Proceedings of the 2020 Conference on Human Information Interaction and Retrieval (CHIIR '20), Vancouver, BC, Canada, 14–18 March 2020; Association for Computing Machinery: New York, NY, USA, 2020; pp. 378–382. [CrossRef]
19. Ghosh, S.; Rath, M.; Shah, C. Searching as Learning: Exploring Search Behavior and Learning Outcomes in Learning-related Tasks. In Proceedings of the CHIIR '18: Conference on Human Information Interaction and Retrieval, New Brunswick, NJ, USA, 11–15 March 2018; pp. 22–31. [CrossRef]
20. Demaree, D.; Jarodzka, H.; Brand-Gruwel, S.; Kammerer, Y. The Influence of Device Type on Querying Behavior and Learning Outcomes in a Searching as Learning Task with a Laptop or Smartphone. In Proceedings of the 2020 Conference on Human Information Interaction and Retrieval (CHIIR '20), Vancouver, BC, Canada, 14–18 March 2020; Association for Computing Machinery: New York, NY, USA, 2020; pp. 373–377. [CrossRef]
21. Syed, R.; Collins-Thompson, K. Retrieval Algorithms Optimized for Human Learning. In Proceedings of the 40th International ACM SIGIR Conference on Research and Development in Information Retrieval (SIGIR '17), Tokyo, Japan, 7–11 August 2017; Association for Computing Machinery: New York, NY, USA, 2017; pp. 555–564. [CrossRef]
22. Syed, R.; Collins-Thompson, K.; Bennett, P.N.; Teng, M.; Williams, S.; Tay, W.W.; Iqbal, S. Improving Learning Outcomes with Gaze Tracking and Automatic Question Generation. In Proceedings of the Web Conference 2020 (WWW '20), Taipei, Taiwan, 20–24 April 2020; Association for Computing Machinery: New York, NY, USA, 2020; pp. 1693–1703. [CrossRef]
23. Roy, N.; Torre, M.V.; Gadiraju, U.; Maxwell, D.; Hauff, C. Note the Highlight: Incorporating Active Reading Tools in a Search as Learning Environment. In Proceedings of the 2021 Conference on Human Information Interaction and Retrieval (CHIIR '21), Canberra, Australia, 14–19 March 202; Association for Computing Machinery: New York, NY, USA, 2021; pp. 229–238. [CrossRef]
24. Mao, J.; Liu, Y.; Kando, N.; Zhang, M.; Ma, S. How Does Domain Expertise Affect Users' Search Interaction and Outcome in Exploratory Search? *ACM Trans. Inf. Syst.* **2018**, *36*, 42. [CrossRef]
25. El Zein, D.; Câmara, A.; Da Costa Pereira, C.; Tettamanzi, A. RULKNE: Representing User Knowledge State in Search-as-Learning with Named Entities. In Proceedings of the 2023 Conference on Human Information Interaction and Retrieval (CHIIR '23), Austin, TX, USA, 19–23 March 2023; Association for Computing Machinery: New York, NY, USA, 2023; pp. 388–393. [CrossRef]
26. Liu, J.; Jung, Y.J. Interest Development, Knowledge Learning, and Interactive IR: Toward a State-based Approach to Search as Learning. In Proceedings of the 2021 Conference on Human Information Interaction and Retrieval (CHIIR '21), Canberra, Australia, 14–19 March 2021; Association for Computing Machinery: New York, NY, USA, 2021; pp. 239–248. [CrossRef]
27. Collins-Thompson, K.; Rieh, S.Y.; Haynes, C.C.; Syed, R. Assessing Learning Outcomes in Web Search: A Comparison of Tasks and Query Strategies. In Proceedings of the 2016 ACM on Conference on Human Information Interaction and Retrieval (CHIIR '16), Canberra, Australia, 14–19 March 2021; Association for Computing Machinery: New York, NY, USA, 2016; pp. 163–172. [CrossRef]

8. Zhu, H.; Tian, F.; Wu, K.; Shah, N.; Chen, Y.; Ni, Y.; Zhang, X.; Chao, K.-M.; Zheng, Q. A multi-constraint learning path recommendation algorithm based on knowledge map. *Knowl. Based Syst.* **2018**, *143*, 102–114. [CrossRef]
9. Zhou, X.; Chen, J.; Jin, Q. Discovery of Action Patterns in Task-Oriented Learning Processes. In *Advances in Web-Based Learning—ICWL 2013, Proceedings of the 12th International Conference, Kenting, Taiwan, 6–9 October 2013*; Wang, J.F., Lau, R., Eds.; Lecture Notes in Computer Science; Springer: Berlin/Heidelberg, Germany, 2013; Volume 8167. [CrossRef]
10. Mehrotra, R.; Yilmaz, E. Extracting Hierarchies of Search Tasks & Subtasks via a Bayesian Nonparametric Approach. In Proceedings of the 40th International ACM SIGIR Conference on Research and Development in Information Retrieval (SIGIR '17), Tokyo, Japan, 7–11 August 2017; Association for Computing Machinery: New York, NY, USA, 2017; pp. 285–294. [CrossRef]
11. Hastuti, R.P.; Suyanto, Y.; Sari, A.K. Q-Learning for Shift-Reduce Parsing in Indonesian Tree-LSTM-Based Text Generation. *ACM Trans. Asian Low-Resour. Lang. Inf. Process.* **2022**, *21*, 64. [CrossRef]
12. Lin, J.-L.; Kuo, J.-C.; Chuang, H.-W. Improving Density Peak Clustering by Automatic Peak Selection and Single Linkage Clustering. *Symmetry* **2020**, *12*, 1168. [CrossRef]
13. Min, X.; Huang, Y.; Sheng, Y. Automatic Determination of Clustering Centers for "Clustering by Fast Search and Find of Density Peaks". *Math. Probl. Eng.* **2020**, *2020*, 4724150. [CrossRef]
14. Yang, Q.-F.; Gao, W.-Y.; Han, G.; Li, Z.-Y.; Tian, M.; Zhu, S.-H.; Deng, Y.-H. HCDC: A novel hierarchical clustering algorithm based on density-distance cores for data sets with varying density. *Inf. Syst.* **2023**, *114*, 102159. [CrossRef]
15. Ahmed, M.; Samee, M.; Mercer, R. Improving Tree-LSTM with Tree Attention. In Proceedings of the 2019 IEEE 13th International Conference on Semantic Computing (ICSC), Newport Beach, CA, USA, 30 January–1 February 2019; pp. 247–254. [CrossRef]
16. Shido, Y.; Kobayashi, Y.; Yamamoto, A.; Miyamoto, A.; Matsumura, T. Automatic Source Code Summarization with Extended Tree-LSTM. In Proceedings of the 2019 International Joint Conference on Neural Networks (IJCNN), Budapest, Hungary, 14–19 July 2019; pp. 1–8. [CrossRef]
17. Yu, X.; Li, G.; Chai, C.; Tang, N. Reinforcement Learning with Tree-LSTM for Join Order Selection. In Proceedings of the 2020 IEEE 36th International Conference on Data Engineering (ICDE), Dallas, TX, USA, 20–24 April 2020; pp. 1297–1308. [CrossRef]
18. Yu, Y.; Si, X.; Hu, C.; Zhang, J. A Review of Recurrent Neural Networks: LSTM Cells and Network Architectures. *Neural Comput.* **2019**, *31*, 1235–1270. [CrossRef]
19. Su, C.; Huang, H.; Shi, S.; Jian, P.; Shi, X. Neural machine translation with Gumbel Tree-LSTM based encoder. *J. Vis. Commun. Image Represent.* **2020**, *1*, 102811. [CrossRef]
20. Lindemann, B.; Müller, T.; Vietz, H.; Jazdi, N.; Weyrich, M. A survey on long short-term memory networks for time series prediction. *Procedia CIRP* **2021**, *99*, 650–655. [CrossRef]
21. Tai, K.S.; Socher, R.; Manning, C.D. Improved Semantic Representations From Tree-Structured Long Short-Term Memory Networks. In Proceedings of the 53rd Annual Meeting of the Association for Computational Linguistics and the 7th International Joint Conference on Natural Language Processing, Beijing, China, 26–31 July 2015; Volume 1, pp. 1556–1566. [CrossRef]
22. Blundell, C.; Teh, Y.W. Bayesian hierarchical community discovery. In Proceedings of the 26th International Conference on Neural Information Processing Systems (NIPS '13); Curran Associates Inc.: Red Hook, NY, USA, 2013; Volume 1, pp. 1601–1609.
23. Parmar, D.; Wu, T.; Blackhurst, J. MMR: An algorithm for clustering categorical data using Rough Set Theory. *Data Knowl. Eng.* **2007**, *63*, 879–893. [CrossRef]
24. Jin, W. Graph Mining with Graph Neural Networks. In Proceedings of the 14th ACM International Conference on Web Search and Data Mining (WSDM '21); Association for Computing Machinery: New York, NY, USA, 2021; pp. 1119–1120. [CrossRef]
25. Ma, J.; Gao, W.; Joty, S.; Wong, K.-F. An Attention-based Rumor Detection Model with Tree-structured Recursive Neural Networks. *ACM Trans. Intell. Syst. Technol.* **2020**, *11*, 42. [CrossRef]

Disclaimer/Publisher's Note: The statements, opinions and data contained in all publications are solely those of the individual author(s) and contributor(s) and not of MDPI and/or the editor(s). MDPI and/or the editor(s) disclaim responsibility for any injury to people or property resulting from any ideas, methods, instructions or products referred to in the content.

Article

Prompt Tuning for Multi-Label Text Classification: How to Link Exercises to Knowledge Concepts?

Liting Wei [1,2], Yun Li [1,*], Yi Zhu [1], Bin Li [1] and Lejun Zhang [1]

[1] School of Information Engineering, Yangzhou University, Yangzhou 225012, China
[2] Jiangsu Provincial Key Constructive Laboratory for Big Data of Psychology and Cognitive Science, Yancheng Teachers University, Yancheng 224002, China
* Correspondence: liyun@yzu.edu.cn; Tel.: +86-13852785198

Abstract: Exercises refer to the evaluation metric of whether students have mastered specific knowledge concepts. Linking exercises to knowledge concepts is an important foundation in multiple disciplines such as intelligent education, which represents the multi-label text classification problem in essence. However, most existing methods do not take the automatic linking of exercises to knowledge concepts into consideration. In addition, most of the widely used approaches in multi-label text classification require large amounts of training data for model optimization, which is usually time-consuming and labour-intensive in real-world scenarios. To address these problems, we propose a prompt tuning method for multi-label text classification, which can address the problem of the number of labelled exercises being small due to the lack of specialized expertise. Specifically, the relevance scores of exercise content and knowledge concepts are learned by a prompt tuning model with a unified template, and then the multiple associated knowledge concepts are selected with a threshold. An Exercises-Concepts dataset of the Data Structure course is constructed to verify the effectiveness of our proposed method. Extensive experimental results confirm our proposed method outperforms other state-of-the-art baselines by up to 35.53% and 41.78% in Micro and Macro F1, respectively.

Keywords: linking exercises to concepts; multi-label text classification; prompt tuning; few-shot

1. Introduction

In recent decades, personalized learning has become a mainstream solution to enhance students' learning interest, and experience in intelligent education systems [1–3]. One of the fundamental and key tasks in personalized learning is knowledge tracing [4,5], which aims to evaluate the students' learning state of knowledge concepts.

Exercises have played an important role in the knowledge tracing tasks, which is one of the evaluation metrics of whether students have mastered specific knowledge concepts [6,7]. Students in intelligent education systems choose the right exercises according to their own needs and acquire specific knowledge concepts during exercise. In turn, we can track changes in students' acquisition of knowledge concepts during their exercising process. From this perspective, knowledge tracing should consist of a students–exercises–knowledge concepts hierarchy [8]. However, most existing methods of knowledge tracing approaches [9–11] are partially modeled among the hierarchy (i.e., students–exercises or students–concepts). This is because, in some intelligent systems, there is a lack of connection between exercises and knowledge concepts. To this end, we take the automatic linking of exercises to knowledge concepts into consideration for knowledge tracing tasks.

In essence, linking exercises to knowledge concepts is a multi-label text classification (MLTC) problem. As shown in Figure 1, the relationship between exercises and knowledge concepts is one-to-one or one-to-many, which aims to assign one or more concepts to each input exercise in the dataset. Moreover, Figure 1 shows that the semantics between exercises and knowledge concepts are highly correlated.

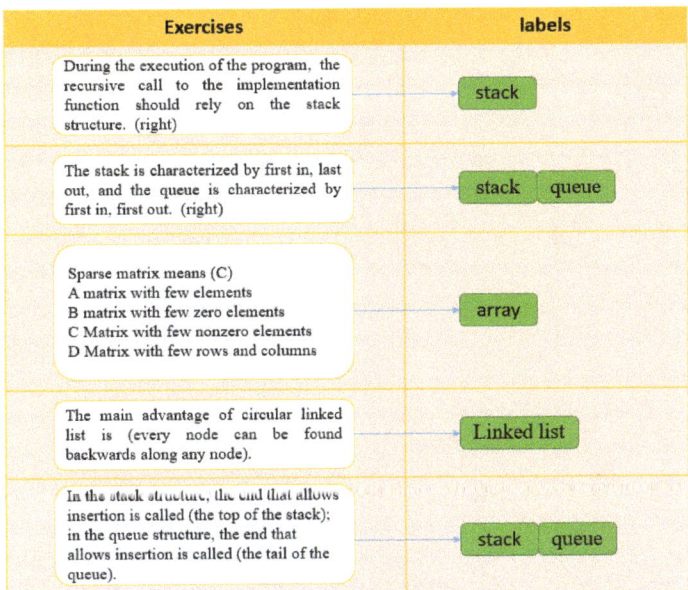

Figure 1. Examples of exercises linking to knowledge concepts from dataset.

Recently, deep-learning-based methods have achieved fairly good performance in MLTC for the superiority of feature representation learning. For example, Liu et al. [12] utilized the strengths of the existing convolutional neural network and took multi-label co-occurrence patterns into account in the optimization objective to produce good results in MLTC. Pal et al. [13] proposed a graph attention network-based model to capture the attentive dependency structure among the labels. Chang et al. [14] fine-tuned the BERT language model [15] to capture the contextual relations between input text and the induced label clusters. However, these deep-learning-based methods in MLTC tasks require large amounts of training data for model optimization, which is usually time-consuming and labour-intensive in real-world scenarios. Unfortunately, linking exercises to knowledge concepts usually lacks training data because some knowledge concepts corresponding to a few exercises or new courses may contain a paucity of labelled data.

To address these problems, we propose a Prompt Tuning method for Multi-Label Text classification (PTMLTC for short). First, the prompt tuning model with a unified template predicts the relevance scores of exercises and knowledge concepts. Then, the multiple associated knowledge concepts are picked with a threshold. In order to verify the effectiveness of our proposed method, an Exercises–Concepts dataset of the Data Structure course is constructed. Extensive experimental results confirm our method outperforms other state-of-the-art methods by up to 32.53% and 41.78% in Micro and Macro F1, respectively.

The contribution of our paper can be summarized as follows:

(1) To the best of our knowledge, this is the first attempt to automatically link exercises to knowledge concepts. We built an Exercises–Concepts dataset of the Data Structure course and reconstructed the few-shot dataset.

(2) We propose a prompt tuning method for multi-label text classification to link exercises to knowledge concepts. Large amounts of labelled or unlabeled training data are not required.

(3) Extensive experimental results confirm that our proposed method outperforms other state-of-the-art deep-learning-based methods.

2. Related Work

In this section, firstly, we introduce the deep-learning-based multi-label text classification methods. Then, the prompt tuning learning methods used in our models will be presented.

2.1. Multi-Label Text Classification

The goal of MLTC is to associate one or more relevant labels for each input text instance. The traditional MLTC methods include one-vs-all methods [16,17], tree-based methods [18,19] and embedding-based methods [20,21]. For example, Babbar et al. [16] proposed a distributed learning mechanism for MLTC, which can use doubly parallel training to reduce the expensive computational cost of one-vs-all methods. Prabhu et al. [22] presented a method called FastXML by optimizing an nDCG-based ranking loss function to further reduce expensive computational costs. Tagami [21] proposed a graph embedding method, which learns partition data points by the k-nearest neighbour graph (KNNG) and uses an approximate k-nearest neighbour to predict results by exploring KNNG in the embedding space.

In recent years, due to the powerful ability of feature representations learning [23,24], deep models have gained much attention and achieved superior performances over traditional methods. The focus of existing deep-learning-based methods on MLTC is learning enhanced text representation for improving performance. For example, Liu et al. [12] utilized the strengths of the existing convolutional neural network (CNN) and dynamic pooling to model the text representation for MLTC. Xiao et al. [25] employed an attention mechanism to explore highlight important context representation in MLTC tasks. Ma et al. [26] utilized the bidirectional Gated Recurrent Unit network and hybrid embedding for learning the representation of the text level-by-level. Chang et al. [14] proposed to fine-tune the BERT language model [15] in order to capture the contextual relations between input text for MLTC.

In addition, recently, the dependencies or correlations among labels have demonstrated the ability to improve performance in most MLTC tasks. Along this line, many deep-learning-based methods have been proposed to model label dependencies. For example, Chen et al. [27] explored labels' correlations through Recurrent Neural Networks, which were used to predict labels one-by-one sequentially. Pal et al. [13] proposed a graph-attention network-based model to capture the attentive dependency structure among the labels. Yang et al. [28] treated MLTC tasks as a sequence generation problem and proposed a decoder structure to capture the dependencies between labels that selected the most informative words automatically while predicting different labels. Xun et al. [29] learned label correlation by introducing an extra CorNet module that is applied to a deep model at the prediction layer to enhance raw label predictions with correlation knowledge.

However, most existing deep-based MLTC methods require a large amount of labelled or unlabeled training data for model optimization, which is often time-consuming and labour-intensive. Therefore, designing methods that can achieve promising results in the few-shot scenario remain a huge challenge in real-world MLTC tasks.

2.2. Prompt Tuning

Prompt-based learning [30–32] is regarded as a new paradigm in natural language processing and has drawn great attention from multiple disciplines, which promotes the downstream tasks by using the pre-training knowledge as much as possible. Starting from the GPT-3 [33], Prompt tuning has demonstrated unique strengths in a variety of tasks, which contain text classification [32,34], relation extraction [35], event extraction [36] and so on. Prompt-based learning directly models the probability of text on top of language models. It is different from traditional supervised learning, which trains a model to predict the output y as $P(x \mid y)$ with the input x. Specifically, in the prediction task, firstly, a template is added to the original input x to form a new textual string prompt x' with [MASK]. Then, the reconstructed $\hat{x}$ is learned with the language model to probabilistically fill the unfilled information. For example, Cui et al. [37] employed closed prompts filled by a candidate named entity span as the target sequence in named entity recognition tasks. Li et al. [38] proposed Prefix-tuning that uses continuous templates to improve performance than discrete prompts. There has already been some recent effort in devoting external knowledge to prompt design. For example, Hu et al. [34] proposed a knowledgeable prompt-tuning by expanding the label word space of the verbalizer with external knowledge bases. Chen et al. [35] proposed a knowledge-aware prompt-tuning approach, which introduced relation labels knowledge into prompt construction. In addition, many works [34,39] have demonstrated that prompt-based learning greatly improves model performance in few-shot scenarios. Hambardzumyan et al. [40] proposed an automatic prompt generation method to transfer knowledge from large Pre-trained Language Models, which achieved excellent performance in a few-shot setting. Gu et al. [41] proposed to add soft prompts into the pre-training stage and pre-train soft prompts in the form of unified classification tasks, which can reach or even outperform in few-shot settings. However, in the knowledge tracing tasks, we are not aware of existing prompt-learning-based approaches that automatically link exercises to knowledge concepts. To this end, we propose a prompt tuning method for multi-label text classification to link exercises to knowledge concepts.

3. Prompt Tuning Method for Multi-Label Text Classification

In this section, the details of our proposed PTMLTC are given, and the general framework is shown in Figure 2.

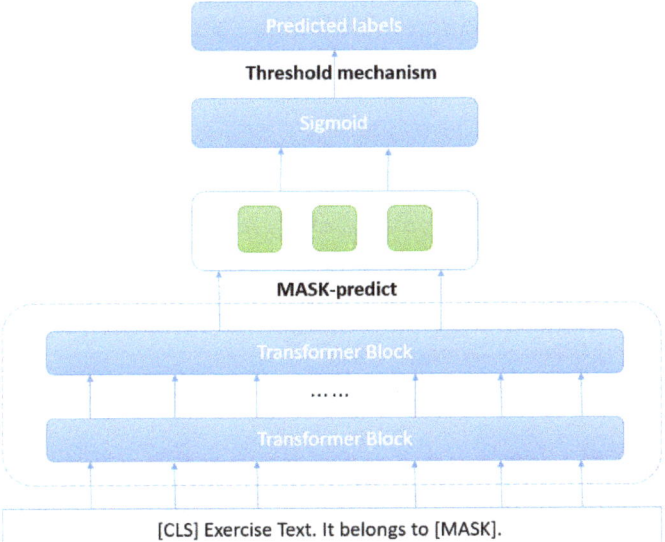

Figure 2. The general framework of our PTMLTC. Exercise Text sequence is connected with united template as the input of prefix Language Model. It will then predict the probability of filling the token [MASK] with each word of knowledge concepts. $Sigmoid()$ function is used to obtain the probability of exercise texts linking to knowledge concept labels. Finally, a threshold mechanism is adopted to predict all the possible knowledge concept labels.

3.1. Problem Formalization

In this paper, we aim to use few exercises with labeled concepts to predict one or more related concepts for each input exercise text. Given $C = \{c_1, c_2, \cdots c_N\}$ is the label space with N concepts, the goal is to learn a function $h(\cdot) : E \rightarrow 2^C$ from the support set $S = \{(E_i, C_i)\}_i^{N_S}$, where E denotes the exercise-instance space, S usually contains K exercise-instances (K-shot) of N concept-labels (N-way), N_S is the size of the support set.

For each learning instance (E_i, C_i), $E_i \subseteq E$ is l-dimensional input and $C_i \subseteq C$ is the related concepts set. For an unseen instance e in the query set, the classifier predicts a set of concepts $P = h(e) \subseteq C$.

3.2. Prompt Tuning Method for Multi-Label Text Classification

As is shown in Figure 2, our methods adopt a threshold-based strategy [42,43] to achieve multi-label text classification. Firstly, the relevance scores of exercise content and knowledge concepts are transformed into a masked language model by prompt tuning methods. Specifically, a prompt template is defined as $V_{prompt} = $ "It belongs to [MASK]" and combine the exercise text $x = \{x_0, x_1, x_2, \cdots, x_n\}$ to form the final input for prompt tuning input e_{prompt}, which can be shown as Equation (1):

$$e_{prompt} = [CLS]x, \text{It belongs to } [MASK]. \tag{1}$$

Suppose that M is a large corpus of Pre-trained Language Models (PLMs in short), the probability of filling the token [MASK] for each word of concept c in the knowledge concepts set C can be denoted as $P_M([MASK] = c \mid e_{prompt})$. Here, we need a map function $Sigmoid()$ to predict the probability of each concept independently. The relevance scores can be represented as (2):

$$P(c \mid e_{Prompt}) = Sigmoid(P_M([MASK] = c \mid e_{prompt})) \tag{2}$$

Finally, we add an additional threshold mechanism to determine knowledge concepts corresponding to exercises, which can be formulated as (3):

$$P(e) = \{c \mid P(c \mid e_{Prompt}) > t, c \in C\} \tag{3}$$

where t is the threshold.

To better introduce our method, we take an example shown in Figure 3. The exercise text "The stack is characterized by first in, last out, and the queue is characterized by first in, first out. (right)" is wrapped with template as the input. PLM is adopted to predict the predict the probability of filling the token [MASK] with knowledge concepts word set array, stack, queue, linked list. Then, $Sigmoid()$ function is used to obtain the probability of exercise text linking to labels $\{array, stack, queue, linked list\}$. Due to the probability of exercise text linking to stack, queue greater than threshold, exercise text is regarded as linking to $\{stack, queue\}$.

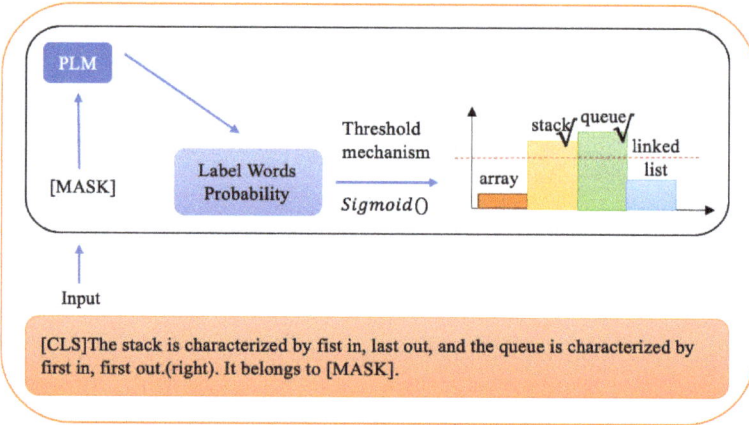

Figure 3. An example of our proposed method.

It has been proven that binary cross-entropy loss (BCE) over sigmoid activation is more suited for multi-label problems and outperforms cross-entropy loss [12]. Therefore, in our paper, the BCE loss function is chosen to learn parameters in the tasks, which can be formulated as (4):

$$\min_{\Theta} -\frac{1}{K}\sum_{i=1}^{K}\sum_{j=1}^{N}[y_{ij}\log(\sigma(\hat{p}_{ij})) + (1-y_{ij})\log(1-\sigma(\hat{p}_{ij}))] \qquad (4)$$

where $\hat{p}_{ij}$ represents the predicted value of exercise i belongs to concept j. y_{ij} represents the value of exercise i belongs to concept j, and σ is the sigmoid function $\sigma(x) = \frac{1}{1+e^{-x}}$.

4. Experiment

In this section, we conduct extensive experiments on the constructed Exercises–Concepts dataset of the Data Structure course to verify the effectiveness of our proposed method for linking exercises to knowledge concepts. In the following, firstly, the Exercises–Concepts dataset of the Data Structure course and the few-shot dataset construction are introduced in detail. Then the compared methods and evaluation metrics of our experiments are shown. Finally, we analyze the experimental results and the influence of the main parameters.

4.1. Datasets

Exercises–Concepts dataset of Data Structure course: To study the problem of linking exercises to knowledge concepts, we construct the Exercises–Concepts dataset of the Data Structure course. Refer to MOOCCube_DS [44] data repository and Several national planning textbooks, we extract 65 classic knowledge concepts. Subsequently, 2027 exercises used in these textbooks are marked with the corresponding knowledge concepts. Details are shown in Table 1.

Few-shot dataset construction: To simulate the few-shot situation, we reconstruct the dataset in to the form of few-shot learning, where each example is the combination of a query instance (e^q, c^q) and the corresponding $K-shot$ support set S. Unlike the single-label classification problem, instances of multi-label classification may be associated with multiple labels. Therefore, there is no guarantee that each label appears exactly K times during sampling. To address the problem, we approximately construct $K-shot$ support set S with the Minimum-including Algorithm [43]. It constructs a support set generally complying with the following two conditions: (1) All labels in the original dataset appear at least K times in support set S. (2) At least one label will appear less than K times in S if any (e^q, c^q) pair is removed from it. For the original dataset, we sampled N_S different support sets. For each support set, we take the remaining data as the query set. Each support-query-set pair constitutes one few-shot episode.

On the test stage, we constructed 10 different few-shot episodes for each selected K-shot. Among them, support set is used to fine tuning model, and query set is used to test the effectiveness of methods.

Table 1. The number of each exercise linking to knowledge concepts. *C* represents the label of the knowledge concept, *N* denotes the number of exercise.

C	*N*	*C*	*N*	*C*	*N*	*C*	*N*
Array	36	Sequential List	46	Bubble Sort	41	Binary Search	48
Logical Structure	48	Linked Storage Structure	48	Time Complexity	91	Generalized table	35
Heapsort	46	Physical Structure	35	Linked List	10	Matrix	35
Adjacency Matrix	35	Linear List	48	BT-Preorder Traversal	37	Tree-Degree	40
Algorithm	56	String	35	BT-Postorder Traversal	35	Tree-Depth	45
Queue	35	Tree	24	Minimum Spanning Tree	53	Graph	18
Recursion	39	Binary Tree (BT)	23	Topological Sort	45	Circular Queue	35
Complete Binary Tree	42	Binary Sort Tree	35	Depth First Search	5	Binary Tree-Threaded BinaryTree	35
Balanced BinaryTree	50	Huffman Tree	35	Breadth First Search	48	Shell's Sort	60
Search	136	Data Structure	35	Connected Graph	47	Binary Tree-Inorder Traversal	13
Sequential Search	53	Sequential Storage Structure	35	Quick Sort	68	Merge Sort	35
Critical Path	60	Stack	35	Full Binary Tree	48	Space Complexity	35
Selection Sort	35	Strongly Connected Graph	57	Graph-Degree	35	Selection Sort	35
HashSearch	35	Muitl-way Search Tree	35	Adjacency List	37	Sort	28
Shortest Path	35	Binary Tree-Order Traversal	56	Doubly Linked List	35	Straight Insertion Sort	44
Cycle Chain	14	Undirected Graph	27	Oriented graph	36	Data	12
Double Circle List	8						

4.2. Baselines and Evaluation

4.2.1. Baselines

Traditional deep-learning-based multi-label text classification methods, such as XML-CNN [12], MAGNET [13], require massive amounts of training data for model optimization, which inevitably leads to performance degradation in the few-shot scenario. However, the PLMs tuning multi-label text classification methods can provide a certain advantage in the few-shot problem. Therefore, three PLMs tuning methods are conducted as compared methods, the details are described as follows:

TextCNN [45]: The method uses a simple CNN with one layer of convolution on top of word vectors for Sentence Classification. In our experiments, PLMs are used to learn the representation of words, in addition, a multi-label classification layer is added to predict labels. Notably, the method is fine-tuned on the support set to select the optimal model and validated on the query set.

TagBert [46]: This is a model based on a large pre-trained model and a multi-label classification layer. Following the parameter setting of a threshold-based multi-label method, a fixed threshold tuned on the support set is used in the experiments.

BertFGM (https://github.com/percent4/keras_bert_multi_label_cls (accessed on 2 April 2021)). Based on the TagBert method, adversarial training [47] is introduced to increase the robustness and generalization of the model.

The experimental setup of all the above methods is the same as that in TextCNN.

4.2.2. Evaluation

In our paper, the *MacroF1* and *MicroF1* are introduced to evaluate the effectiveness of our proposed method. *MacroF1* calculates the average of the F1 scores obtained for each category, which can be formulated as (5):

$$\begin{aligned} P_t &= \frac{TP_t}{TP_t + FP_t} \\ R_t &= \frac{TP_t}{TP_t + FN_t} \\ \text{Macro } F1 &= \frac{1}{|C|} \sum_{t \in C} \frac{2 P_t R_t}{P_t + R_t} \end{aligned} \quad (5)$$

where P_t represents the precision of each category, R_t represents the recall of each category. TP_t, FP_t and FN_t are the true-positive, false-positive and false-negative example of the t-th label in the label set C, respectively. *MicroF1* calculates the overall of the F1 scores, which can be formulated as (6):

$$\begin{aligned} P &= \frac{\sum_{t \in C} TP_t}{\sum_{t \in Y} TP_t + FP_t} \\ R &= \frac{\sum_{t \in C} TP_t}{\sum_{t \in C} TP_t + FN_t} \\ \text{Micro } F_1 &= \frac{2PR}{P+R} \end{aligned} \quad (6)$$

where P represents the overall precision, R represents the overall recall.

4.3. Experimental Results

4.3.1. Experiment Settings

We evaluate the performance of our proposed method on the few-shot Exercises–Concepts dataset. Because some concepts in the dataset have only 5 exercises, we select the value K in K-shot as 1 and 5, respectively. There are some hyper-parameters that need to be initialized in the above methods. Firstly, we introduce uniform settings in all methods. The maximum length sequence is set as 512. These models are optimized by Adam with batch size 4 and learning rate 1×10^{-5}. Then, the size of thresholds has an impact on final performance. The thresholds are set as 0.10, 0.65, 0.82, 0.24 on 1-shot setting in TextCNN,

TagBert, BertFGM and PTMLTC, respectively. On 5-shot setting, the thresholds are 0.08, 0.70, 0.85 and 0.20. The reported results are the mean and variance of the experimental results on 10 randomly generated few-shot datasets.

4.3.2. Performance Comparison

Results of 1-shot setting: The results of the 1-shot exercise linking to knowledge concepts are shown in Table 2. From the experimental results, we can have the following observations. Firstly, we can observe that the results of $MicroF1$ and $MacroF1$ in the PTMLTC method are 54.74% and 46.11%, respectively, which are far better than the other three baselines. In the case of much training data, the performance of BertFGM is better than the TagBert. However, added adversarial training in the few-shot problem obtains interference information, which makes the classifier more indistinguishable. BertFGM achieves worse results than the TagBert. Results of 5-shot setting: The results of the 5-shot exercise linking to knowledge concepts are shown in Table 3. The results are basically consistent with the trend of the 1-shot setting. Compared with the 1-shot setting, the results of all methods have been improved in the 5-shot setting. These results demonstrated that the increasing of training data improves classification performance. In addition, PTMLTC has a smaller margin of advantage in 5-shot setting compared with 1-shot setting. It is proved that the fewer the data, the more obvious the advantages of PTMLTC.

Table 2. Results of 1-shot on our dataset. Metrics marked in bold contain the highest metrics for the dataset.

Method	1-Shot	
	Micro F1	Macro F1
TextCNN	6.60 ± 1.23	5.70 ± 0.89
TagBert	9.83 ± 0.77	6.05 ± 2.16
BertFGM	6.65 ± 2.47	2.11 ± 2.13
PTMLTC	53.86 ± 3.16	**49.04 ± 3.42**

Table 3. Results of 5-shot on our dataset. Metrics marked in bold contain the highest metrics for the dataset.

Method	5-Shot	
	Micro_F1	Macro_F1
TextCNN	29.49 ± 0.62	29.84 ± 2.67
TagBert	47.06 ± 0.18	41.50 ± 6.90
BertFGM	34.72 ± 0.99	26.66 ± 3.12
PTMLTC	**62.37 ± 0.43**	**58.84 ± 0.84**

4.3.3. Ablation Study

We compare the effects with different PLMs. In our proposed methods, Bert [15] and Roberta [48] models are adopted with bert-base-chinese (https://huggingface.co/bert-base-chinese (accessed on 5 February 2022)) and chinese-roberta-wwm-ext (https://huggingface.co/hfl/chinese-roberta-wwm-ext (accessed on 6 February 2022)). Table 4 summarizes The results are summarized in Table 4, which shows the Roberta-based pre-training model achieves better results than Bert.

The success of prompt tuning mainly owes to the template design and label words. Different templates are designed in our method to discuss their effect. The details are shown Table 5. The template was selected as "It belongs to [MASK]", which obtains the better result.

Table 4. Results of different PLMs on our dataset. Metrics marked in bold contain the highest metrics for the dataset.

Method	Micro F1		Macro F1	
	1-Shot	5-Shot	1-Shot	5-Shot
PTMLTC_Bert	50.74 ± 1.53	58.56 ± 1.50	46.11 ± 2.68	54.28 ± 1.47
PTMLTC_Roberta	**53.86 ± 3.16**	**62.37 ± 0.43**	**49.04 ± 3.42**	**58.84 ± 0.84**

Table 5. Results of the different design of the templates. Metrics marked in bold contain the highest metrics for the dataset.

Templates	1-Shot		5-Shot	
	Micro F1	Micro F1	Micro F1	Micro F1
It belongs to [MASK].	**53.86 ± 2.74**	49.04 ± 3.12	**62.37 ± 1.05**	**58.84 ± 0.89**
The concept is [MASK].	50.98 ± 2.92	**51.35 ± 2.15**	58.44 ± 0.77	54.28 ± 1.15
The concept belongs to [MASK].	52.76 ± 3.13	46.83 ± 2.47	60.99 ± 0.37	53.85 ± 0.62

4.3.4. Parameter Sensitivity

Regarding our proposed method, in this section we have studied the influence of the parameter, which is the threshold t in Equation (3). The experimental mode of control variables is adopted, when one variable is changed, the other variables remain unchanged. We randomly selected a dataset from the 1-shot and 5-shot few-shot datasets for verification. After some preliminary tests, we found that the value of t will have a relatively large impact on the effect, it can be ensured that the effect will not excessively fluctuate within a certain range. The value set of t is [0.14, 0.16, 0.18, 0.22, 0.24, 0.26]. It can be observed from Figure 4 that $t = 0.24$ on the 1-shot setting and $t = 0.2$ on the 5-shot setting lead to the best results.

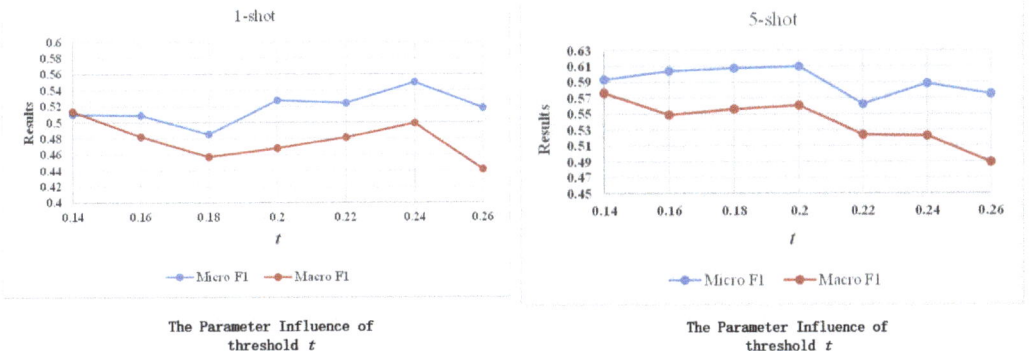

Figure 4. Effects of threshold t on two datasets.

5. Conclusions and Future Work

In this paper, a prompt tuning multi-label text classification method is proposed to realize the link between exercises and knowledge concepts. The main idea is that the relevance scores of exercise content and knowledge concepts are learned by a prompt tuning model with a unified template, and then the multiple associated knowledge concepts are selected with a threshold. On the constructed dataset, we compare the proposed method with other baseline methods. The results show that PTMLTC achieves better performance than other state-of-the-art methods in the evaluation metrics, and with fewer training data, the advantage is more conspicuous. The knowledge concepts in the course bear a natural graph relationship, and our work ignores the relationship between them. Future work will try to introduce the structural relationship between knowledge concepts into the model for achieving better results.

Author Contributions: Methodology, Y.L.; Resources, B.L.; Validation, L.Z.; Writing—original draft L.W.; Writing—review & editing, Y.Z. All authors have read and agreed to the published version of the manuscript.

Funding: This research received no external funding.

Institutional Review Board Statement: Not applicable.

Informed Consent Statement: Not applicable.

Data Availability Statement: Not applicable.

Conflicts of Interest: The authors declare no conflict of interest. The funders had no role in the design of the study; in the collection, analyses, or interpretation of data; in the writing of the manuscript, or in the decision to publish the results.

References

1. Gong, J.; Wang, S.; Wang, J.; Feng, W.; Peng, H.; Tang, J.; Yu, P.S. Attentional graph convolutional networks for knowledge concept recommendation in moocs in a heterogeneous view. In Proceedings of the 43rd International ACM SIGIR Conference on Research and Development in Information Retrieval, Virtual Event, 25–30 July 2020; pp. 79–88.
2. Chen, S.Y.; Wang, J.H. Individual differences and personalized learning: A review and appraisal. *Univers. Access Inf. Soc.* **2021** 20, 833–849. [CrossRef]
3. Khalid, A.; Lundqvist, K.; Yates, A. Recommender systems for moocs: A systematic literature survey (January 1, 2012–July 12 2019). *Int. Rev. Res. Open Distrib. Learn.* **2020**, 21, 255–291.
4. Corbett, A.T.; Anderson, J.R. Knowledge tracing: Modeling the acquisition of procedural knowledge. *User Model. User-Adapt Interact.* **1994**, 4, 253–278. [CrossRef]
5. He, Z.; Li, W.; Yan, Y. Modeling knowledge proficiency using multi-hierarchical capsule graph neural network. *Appl. Intell.* **2021** 52, 7230–7247. [CrossRef]
6. Okpo, J.; Masthoff, J.; Dennis, M.; Beacham, N. Conceptualizing a framework for adaptive exercise selection with personality as a major learner characteristic. In Proceedings of the Adjunct Publication of the 25th Conference on User Modeling, Adaptation and Personalization, Bratislava, Slovakia, 9–12 July 2017; pp. 293–298.
7. Okpo, J.A.; Masthoff, J.; Dennis, M. Qualitative Evaluation of an Adaptive Exercise Selection Algorithm. In Proceedings of the 29th ACM Conference on User Modeling, Adaptation and Personalization, Utrecht, The Netherlands, 21–25 June 2021; pp. 167–174.
8. Gao, W.; Liu, Q.; Huang, Z.; Yin, Y.; Bi, H.; Wang, M.C.; Ma, J.; Wang, S.; Su, Y. Rcd: Relation map driven cognitive diagnosis for intelligent education systems. In Proceedings of the 44th International ACM SIGIR Conference on Research and Development in Information Retrieval, Virtual Event, 11–15 July 2021; pp. 501–510.
9. Piech, C.; Bassen, J.; Huang, J.; Ganguli, S.; Sahami, M.; Guibas, L.J.; Sohl-Dickstein, J. Deep knowledge tracing. In Proceedings of the Advances in Neural Information Processing Systems 28 (NIPS 2015), Montreal, QC, USA, 7–12 December 2015; Volume 28.
10. Zhang, J.; Shi, X.; King, I.; Yeung, D.Y. Dynamic key-value memory networks for knowledge tracing. In Proceedings of the 26th International Conference on World Wide Web, Perth, Australia, 3–7 April 2017; pp. 765–774.
11. Ghosh, A.; Heffernan, N.; Lan, A.S. Context-aware attentive knowledge tracing. In Proceedings of the 26th ACM SIGKDD International Conference on Knowledge Discovery & Data Mining, Virtual Event, 6–10 July 2020; pp. 2330–2339.
12. Liu, J.; Chang, W.C.; Wu, Y.; Yang, Y. Deep learning for extreme multi-label text classification. In Proceedings of the 40th International ACM SIGIR Conference on Research and Development in Information Retrieval, Tokyo, Japan, 7–11 August 2017; pp. 115–124.
13. Pal, A.; Selvakumar, M.; Sankarasubbu, M. Multi-label text classification using attention-based graph neural network. *arXiv* **2020**, arXiv:2003.11644.
14. Chang, W.C.; Yu, H.F.; Zhong, K.; Yang, Y.; Dhillon, I. X-bert: Extreme multi-label text classification with bert. *arXiv* **2019**, arXiv:1905.02331.
15. Devlin, J.; Chang, M.W.; Lee, K.; Toutanova, K. Bert: Pre-training of deep bidirectional transformers for language understanding. *arXiv* **2018**, arXiv:1810.04805.
16. Babbar, R.; Schölkopf, B. Dismec: Distributed sparse machines for extreme multi-label classification. In Proceedings of the Tenth ACM International Conference on Web Search and Data Mining, Cambridge, UK, 6–10 February 2017; pp. 721–729.
17. Yen, I.E.; Huang, X.; Dai, W.; Ravikumar, P.; Dhillon, I.; Xing, E. Ppdsparse: A parallel primal-dual sparse method for extreme classification. In Proceedings of the 23rd ACM SIGKDD International Conference on Knowledge Discovery and Data Mining, Halifax, NS, Canada, 13–17 August 2017; pp. 545–553.

8. Prabhu, Y.; Kag, A.; Harsola, S.; Agrawal, R.; Varma, M. Parabel: Partitioned label trees for extreme classification with application to dynamic search advertising. In Proceedings of the 2018 World Wide Web Conference, Lyon, France, 23–27 April 2018; pp. 993–1002.
9. Jain, H.; Prabhu, Y.; Varma, M. Extreme multi-label loss functions for recommendation, tagging, ranking & other missing label applications. In Proceedings of the 22nd ACM SIGKDD International Conference on Knowledge Discovery and Data Mining, San Francisco, CA, USA, 13–17 August 2016; pp. 935–944.
10. Akbarnejad, A.H.; Baghshah, M.S. An efficient semi-supervised multi-label classifier capable of handling missing labels. *IEEE Trans. Knowl. Data Eng.* **2018**, *31*, 229–242. [CrossRef]
11. Tagami, Y. Annexml: Approximate nearest neighbor search for extreme multi-label classification. In Proceedings of the 23rd ACM SIGKDD International Conference on Knowledge Discovery and Data Mining, Halifax, NS, Canada, 13–17 August 2017; pp. 455–464.
12. Prabhu, Y.; Varma, M. Fastxml: A fast, accurate and stable tree-classifier for extreme multi-label learning. In Proceedings of the 20th ACM SIGKDD International Conference on Knowledge Discovery and Data Mining, New York, NY, USA, 24–27 August 2014; pp. 263–272.
13. Qiang, J.; Chen, P.; Ding, W.; Wang, T.; Xie, F.; Wu, X. Heterogeneous-length text topic modeling for reader-aware multi-document summarization. *ACM Trans. Knowl. Discov. Data (TKDD)* **2019**, *13*, 1–21. [CrossRef]
14. Qiang, J.; Wu, X. Unsupervised statistical text simplification. *IEEE Trans. Knowl. Data Eng.* **2021**, *33*, 1802–1806. [CrossRef]
15. Xiao, Y.; Li, Y.; Yuan, J.; Guo, S.; Xiao, Y.; Li, Z. History-based attention in Seq2Seq model for multi-label text classification. *Knowl.-Based Syst.* **2021**, *224*, 107094. [CrossRef]
16. Ma, Y.; Liu, X.; Zhao, L.; Liang, Y.; Zhang, P.; Jin, B. Hybrid embedding-based text representation for hierarchical multi-label text classification. *Expert Syst. Appl.* **2022**, *187*, 115905. [CrossRef]
17. Chen, G.; Ye, D.; Xing, Z.; Chen, J.; Cambria, E. Ensemble application of convolutional and recurrent neural networks for multi-label text categorization. In Proceedings of the 2017 IEEE International Joint Conference on Neural Networks (IJCNN), Anchorage, AK, USA, 14–19 May 2017; pp. 2377–2383.
18. Yang, P.; Sun, X.; Li, W.; Ma, S.; Wu, W.; Wang, H. SGM: Sequence generation model for multi-label classification. *arXiv* **2018**, arXiv:1806.04822.
19. Xun, G.; Jha, K.; Sun, J.; Zhang, A. Correlation networks for extreme multi-label text classification. In Proceedings of the 26th ACM SIGKDD International Conference on Knowledge Discovery & Data Mining, Virtual Event, 6–10 July 2020; pp. 1074–1082.
20. Ding, N.; Hu, S.; Zhao, W.; Chen, Y.; Liu, Z.; Zheng, H.T.; Sun, M. Openprompt: An open-source framework for prompt-learning. *arXiv* **2021**, arXiv:2111.01998.
21. Schick, T.; Schütze, H. Exploiting cloze questions for few shot text classification and natural language inference. *arXiv* **2020**, arXiv:2001.07676.
22. Zhang, N.; Li, L.; Chen, X.; Deng, S.; Bi, Z.; Tan, C.; Huang, F.; Chen, H. Differentiable prompt makes pre-trained language models better few-shot learners. *arXiv* **2021**, arXiv:2108.13161.
23. Floridi, L.; Chiriatti, M. GPT-3: Its nature, scope, limits, and consequences. *Minds Mach.* **2020**, *30*, 681–694. [CrossRef]
24. Hu, S.; Ding, N.; Wang, H.; Liu, Z.; Li, J.; Sun, M. Knowledgeable prompt-tuning: Incorporating knowledge into prompt verbalizer for text classification. *arXiv* **2021**, arXiv:2108.02035.
25. Chen, X.; Zhang, N.; Xie, X.; Deng, S.; Yao, Y.; Tan, C.; Huang, F.; Si, L.; Chen, H. Knowprompt: Knowledge-aware prompt-tuning with synergistic optimization for relation extraction. *arXiv* **2021**, arXiv:2104.07650.
26. Ma, Y.; Wang, Z.; Cao, Y.; Li, M.; Chen, M.; Wang, K.; Shao, J. Prompt for Extraction? PAIE: Prompting Argument Interaction for Event Argument Extraction. *arXiv* **2022**, arXiv:2202.12109.
27. Cui, L.; Wu, Y.; Liu, J.; Yang, S.; Zhang, Y. Template-based named entity recognition using BART. *arXiv* **2021**, arXiv:2106.01760.
28. Li, X.L.; Liang, P. Prefix-tuning: Optimizing continuous prompts for generation. *arXiv* **2021**, arXiv:2101.00190.
29. Scao, T.L.; Rush, A.M. How many data points is a prompt worth? *arXiv* **2021**, arXiv:2103.08493.
30. Hambardzumyan, K.; Khachatrian, H.; May, J. Warp: Word-level adversarial reprogramming. *arXiv* **2021**, arXiv:2101.00121.
31. Reynolds, L.; McDonell, K. Prompt programming for large language models: Beyond the few-shot paradigm. In Proceedings of the Extended Abstracts of the 2021 CHI Conference on Human Factors in Computing Systems, Yokohama, Japan, 8–13 May 2021; pp. 1–7.
32. Xu, G.; Lee, H.; Koo, M.W.; Seo, J. Convolutional neural network using a threshold predictor for multi-label speech act classification. In Proceedings of the 2017 IEEE International Conference on Big Data and Smart Computing (BigComp), Jeju, Korea, 13–16 February 2017; pp. 126–130.
33. Hou, Y.; Lai, Y.; Wu, Y.; Che, W.; Liu, T. Few-shot learning for multi-label intent detection. *arXiv* **2020**, arXiv:2010.05256.
34. Yu, J.; Luo, G.; Xiao, T.; Zhong, Q.; Wang, Y.; Feng, W.; Luo, J.; Wang, C.; Hou, L.; Li, J.; et al. MOOCCube: A large-scale data repository for NLP applications in MOOCs. In Proceedings of the 58th Annual Meeting of the Association for Computational Linguistics, Online, 5 July 2020; pp. 3135–3142.
35. Chen, Y. Convolutional Neural Network for Sentence Classification. Master's Thesis, University of Waterloo, Waterloo, ON, Canada, 2015.
36. Khezrian, N.; Habibi, J.; Annamoradnejad, I. Tag recommendation for online Q&A communities based on BERT pre-training technique. *arXiv* **2020**, arXiv:2010.04971.

47. Szegedy, C.; Zaremba, W.; Sutskever, I.; Bruna, J.; Erhan, D.; Goodfellow, I.; Fergus, R. Intriguing properties of neural networks. *arXiv* **2013**, arXiv:1312.6199.
48. Liu, Y.; Ott, M.; Goyal, N.; Du, J.; Joshi, M.; Chen, D.; Levy, O.; Lewis, M.; Zettlemoyer, L.; Stoyanov, V. Roberta: A robustly optimized bert pretraining approach. *arXiv* **2019**, arXiv:1907.11692.

Article

Unsupervised Domain Adaptation via Stacked Convolutional Autoencoder [†]

Yi Zhu [1], Xinke Zhou [1] and Xindong Wu [2],*

1 Yangzhou University, Yangzhou 225012, China
2 Key Laboratory of Knowledge Engineering with Big Data (The Ministry of Education of China), Hefei University of Technology, Hefei 230009, China
* Correspondence: xwu@hfut.edu.cn; Tel.: +86-152-2150-7475
† This paper is an extended version of the paper "Domain Adaptation with Stacked Convolutional Sparse Autoencoder" published in 2021 28th International Conference on Neural Information Processing (ICONIP), Bali, Indonesia, 8–12 December 2021.

Abstract: Unsupervised domain adaptation involves knowledge transfer from a labeled source to unlabeled target domains to assist target learning tasks. A critical aspect of unsupervised domain adaptation is the learning of more transferable and distinct feature representations from different domains. Although previous investigations, using, for example, CNN-based and auto-encoder-based methods, have produced remarkable results in domain adaptation, there are still two main problems that occur with these methods. The first is a training problem for deep neural networks; some optimization methods are ineffective when applied to unsupervised deep networks for domain adaptation tasks. The second problem that arises is that redundancy of image data results in performance degradation in feature learning for domain adaptation. To address these problems, in this paper, we propose an unsupervised domain adaptation method with a stacked convolutional sparse autoencoder, which is based on performing layer projection from the original data to obtain higher-level representations for unsupervised domain adaptation. More specifically, in a convolutional neural network, lower layers generate more discriminative features whose kernels are learned via a sparse autoencoder. A reconstruction independent component analysis optimization algorithm was introduced to perform individual component analysis on the input data. Experiments undertaken demonstrated superior classification performance of up to 89.3% in terms of accuracy compared to several state-of-the-art domain adaptation methods, such as SSRLDA and TLMRA.

Keywords: domain adaptation; convolutional autoencoder; sparse autoencoder

1. Introduction

An assumption of traditional machine learning classification methods is that training and test data have independent and identical distributions [1]. Because different domains are usually different but related in real-world scenarios, most existing traditional machine learning methods are not guaranteed to be effective due to the ubiquitous large discrepancy between different domains [2,3]. To address this problem, in recent decades, domain adaptation methods have attracted a great deal of attention and stimulated research studies [4–7], which have primarily focused on the transfer of knowledge between different domains. Because the target domain is usually unknown, unsupervised domain adaptation aims to promote learning tasks in target domains based on knowledge in source domains, which has far-ranging consequences for practical applications, such as speech emotion recognition [8], medical image classification [9], and semantic image segmentation [9].

Among domain adaptation methods, including instance-transfer, parameter-transfer, feature-representation-transfer and relational-knowledge-transfer methods [10], methods based on feature representation learning can be applied to a broader set of scenarios due to loose restrictions on source data [11]. The key issue for feature-representation-transfer methods is how to learn more discriminative and transferable feature representations to minimize deviations between different domains [12].

In recent decades, remarkable progress has been made in the use of feature learning methods based on shallow structure and deep neural networks which have learned how to transfer representations across domains and have performed well in unsupervised domain adaptation. Typical shallow learning methods, such as transfer component analysis [13] aim to reduce domain divergence in new feature space using a kernel function. In comparison to shallow structure methods, deep neural networks have been shown to be more effective by separating the explanatory factors behind different domains [14,15]. Recently mainstream deep neural networks, such as the convolutional neural network (CNN) [16] the recurrent neural network (RNN) [17], the generative adversarial network (GAN) [18] and Autoencoder [19], have been used to learn more discriminative representations for unsupervised domain adaptation and have performed well in reducing domain divergence

Among unsupervised domain adaptation methods that are based on deep neural networks, the autoencoder-based method has achieved superior performance with respect to the no label requirement and fast convergence speed. For example, the stacked denoising autoencoder (SDA) method [20] aims to learn higher-level representations from all available domains to train a classifier that performs classification on new-featured spaces. Similarly to address the issue of high computational cost in SDA, a marginalized stacked denoising autoencoder method [19] has been proposed based on matrix computation, which is as effective as SDA in representation learning for domain adaptation and has been shown to be more efficient. In light of the development of these methods, Wei et al. proposed an unsupervised domain adaptation method based on non-linear representation learning [21] which introduced non-linear coding by kernelization into SDA to enable the extraction of deep features.

While it is possible to explore different domains and learn transferable and discriminative representations using unsupervised domain adaptation methods based on autoencoders, most current approaches depend on use of the classical structure of autoencoders or integration of regularization terms into the objective function [22–24]. For improved understanding of feature representation learning, here, a method is proposed to achieve representation learning based on a stacked convolutional sparse autoencoder for unsupervised domain adaptation which can capture more transferable and distinguishable features by layer mapping of the raw data and unsupervised domain adaptation. Firstly, we utilize the reconstruction independent component analysis (RICA) algorithm [4] with whitening to pre-process the original data in both source and target domains, where "whitening" refers to a transformation of the original data x to $x_{whitened}$, and the covariance matrix of $x_{whitened}$ is the identity matrix. A stacked sparse autoencoder is then introduced to extract features to alleviate domain discrepancy Secondly, based on the new feature space learned by the first component, convolution and pooling are applied to maintain local relevance. Finally, we stack two convolutional sparse autoencoders to achieve more abstract and transferable representation learning. Compared to other state-of-the-art methods, experimental results obtained confirm the effectiveness of our proposed framework for unsupervised domain adaptation.

In summary, this paper makes the following main contributions:

- We explicitly propose a new framework of unsupervised domain adaptation based on a stacked convolutional sparse autoencoder (short for SCSA). There is an obvious distinction between this method and the original method [2,14], which relies on applying the classical structure of the autoencoder to learn representations or integratation of the regularization term into the objective function.
- Our proposed SCSA has two main components in each layer. In the first component, a stacked sparse autoencoder with RICA is introduced for recognition feature learning to reduce the divergence between the source and target domains. In the second component, the convolution and pool layer is utilized to preserve the local relevance of features to achieve enhanced performance.

The remainder of the paper is organized as follows: In Section 2, related work is described. In Section 3, the SCSA proposal is described in detail. Several real-world datasets are presented and the experimental results are analyzed in Section 4. The conclusions are presented in Section 5.

It is worth explaining that we first introduced the unsupervised domain adaptation method in our conference paper [25], titled "Domain Adaptation with Stacked Convolutional Sparse Autoencoder", published in the proceedings of the Twenty-Eighth International Conference on Neural Information Processing (ICONIP), Indonesia, 8–12 December 2021. In our conference paper, we focus on a domain adaptation method with an autoencoder (SCSA). Here, we propose an unsupervised domain adaptation framework. Compared with our previous version, we add the following: (1) further discussion and analysis regarding validation of the proposed method; (2) more detailed description of the proposed method; (3) a more comprehensive survey of related studies; and (4) further experimental analysis of the SCSA and the baselines.

2. Background Studies

Due to strong feature representation learning ability, deep neural networks have attracted considerable attention regarding domain adaptation. For example, Ganin et al. proposed an unsupervised domain adaptation method with deep architectures [26], which trained a model with standard back-propagation on large-scale labeled source data and unlabeled target data. Similarly, Sener et al. proposed a fine-tuned deep neural network to minimize the discrepancy between different domains [27]. An end-to-end model was designed to jointly optimize learned features, to cross-domain transform, and target label prediction. Existing deep domain adaptation methods can be broadly categorized into three classes: discrepancy-based, adversarial-based and PLM-based methods [28].

Discrepancy-based methods aim to embed data from source and target domains into a kernel space to alleviate domain discrepancy. For example, Zhang et al. proposed a deep neural network based on the maximum mean discrepancy (MMD) [29], which was able to learn a common subspace to simultaneously align both marginal and conditional distributions. Long et al. proposed a residual transfer network [30], which not only aligned the feature distributions between different domains, but also transferred the classifier with a residual function. As well as these deep methods, which mainly focus on cross-feature learning, many methods have been proposed to transfer the classifier across different domains. For example, Pinheiro proposed training the classifier with similarity learning [31]; application of this method demonstrated that feature representation learning together with similarity learning can improve domain adaptation.

Inspired by the generative adversarial net (GAN) approach, adversarial-based domain adaptation methods aim to minimize deviations across domains using an adversarial objective. For example, Long et al. designed a conditional domain adversarial network [32], which conditions adversarial adaptation models based on the discriminative information conveyed in the classifier predictions. Kang et al. proposed a contrastive adaptation network for minimizing intra- and inter-class deviations [7], which included an end-to-end update strategy for model optimization. Pei et al. proposed a multi-adversarial domain adaptation method [33]. In this method, multiple class-wise domain discriminators are constructed to reduce the shift of joint distributions between different domains and to achieve fine-grained alignment of different class distributions. In this way, each discriminator only matches samples of source and target data belonging to the same class.

Recently, pre-trained language models (PLMs) have received much attention and achieved remarkable improvements in a series of tasks. As PLMs can learn syntactic, semantic and structural information, there has been some effort to apply PLMs to domain adaptation. For example, Zhang et al. proposed a domain adaptation neural network based on BERT for multi-modal fake-news detection [34]. The pre-trained BERT and VGG-19 model were first introduced to learn text and image features, respectively. Then the multi-modal features were mapped onto the same space by domain adaptation. Finally, a detector was used to distinguish fake news. Guo et al. proposed the creation of input disturbance vectors using soft prompt tuning to optimize domain similarity [35], introducing targeted regularization to minimize domain discrepancy.

Although the deep learning methods described have achieved fairly good results in domain adaptation, the deep neural network training problem remains. Some efficient models, such as graph regularization and sparse constraint, cannot be applied directly in supervised convolutional networks. Moreover, although some optimization methods have been proposed, they have not been shown to be effective in unsupervised deep networks for domain adaptation tasks.

3. Related Work

The goal of domain adaptation is to reduce the discrepancy between different domains and to bridge the chasm among them. Amongst unsupervised domain adaptation methods, methods based on feature learning have been widely applied in multiple disciplines a a result of looser limitations on the data in the source domain. According to the technology used, existing feature-learning-based methods for domain adaptation can be broadly divided into two categories: shallow-learning and deep-learning methods.

3.1. Shallow Learning Methods

Among unsupervised domain adaptation methods based on shallow structure, the transfer component analysis (TCA) model [13] is a typical model that attempts to minimize the distance between source and target domains in a new feature space using the maximum mean discrepancy (MMD). Chen et al. proposed an unsupervised domain adaptation method based on an extreme learning machine network to retain the space information of the target domain [36], which seeks to transfer the source domain for better matching of the data distribution in the target domain by reducing the MMD distance. He et al proposed an unsupervised domain adaptation model for multi-view data [37]; the features extracted from one view of the data are considered privileged information from another view. Chen et al. proposed combination of domain-adversarial learning and self-training with the intention of combining the strengths of both methods [38]. The pseudo-label prediction and the confusion matrix were learned using self-training and using an adversarial approach, respectively. Wang et al. proposed a symmetric and positive-definite matrix network for domain adaptation (daSPDnet) [39]. Inspired by Riemannian manifold methods, daSPDnet aims to enable EEG emotion recognition by overcoming the variability in the physiological responses of subjects.

Some effort has already been invested in applying unsupervised transfer methods to heterogeneous domains. For example, Liu et al. proposed a heterogeneous unsupervised domain adaptation model [40], which introduced an n-dimensional metric of fuzzy geometry to compute the similarity between different vectors. Based on the results, the fuzzy equivalence relations were explored and the cross-domain clustering categories were captured. Yan et al. proposed an optimal matrix transport method for heterogeneous domain adaptation [41], which introduced the entropic Gromov–Wasserstein discrepancy for learning an optimal transport matrix. Luo et al. proposed a distance metric learning method for heterogeneous domain adaptation [42]. This method used existing models to learn the knowledge fragments in the source domain, which can reduce domain divergence.

However, unsupervised domain adaptation methods based on shallow structure have two main drawbacks. The first is utilization of labeled data information, since a small amount of labeled data can significantly improve domain adaptation performance. The second drawback is the capacity for feature learning. How to learn more transferable representations to alleviate domain discrepancy represents a major challenge.

3.2. Autoencoder-Based Methods

Among deep neural networks, autoencoder-based unsupervised domain adaptation methods have performed well with respect to the no label requirement and fast convergence speed. For example, Glorot et al. proposed a stacked denoising autoencoder (SDA) for domain adaptation [43]. A marginalized denoising autoencoder (mSDA) method was proposed for speeding up SDA by two orders of magnitude [19]. Wei et al. introduced non-linear coding by kernelization into the mSDA for domain adaptation [21]. Zhuang et al. proposed an unsupervised domain adaptation framework with deep autoencoders [22]. In this method, the mSDA is utilized to pre-train the whole framework and two encoding and decoding layers are incorporated to learn more transferable representations between the source and target domains. Zhu et al. proposed integration of the manifold regularization term in the objective function [2], involving stacking of two layers of autoencoders to learn more abstract representations for unsupervised domain adaptation. Yang et al. proposed a semi-supervised method using dual autoencoders [1], which extracted more powerful features using two different autoencoders based on mSDA for unsupervised domain adaptation. Nikisins et al. proposed a face presentation attack detection model using an autoencoder and a multi-layer perceptron [44], which transferred the knowledge of facial appearance between different domains. This domain adaptation method reduced the requirements for large-scale labeled data, which avoided labor-intensive work and reduced costs when training face recognition systems. Zhu et al. proposed a deep sparse autoencoder for an imbalanced domain adaptation problem [45], which could adjust the model automatically according to the degree of imbalance to bridge the gap between domains. In this method, a self-adaptive imbalanced cross-entropy loss function is used to highlight minority categories and automatically compensate for training loss bias. In contrast to autoencoder-based methods that rely on application of the classical structure of an autoencoder to learn representations or integrate the regularization term into the objective function, our method introduces convolution and pooling kernels to use local relevance to learn abstract representations for domain adaptation.

4. Our Proposed Method

4.1. Motivation

For domain adaptation, methods based on feature representation learning can be applied to a broader set of scenarios because of the loose restrictions on the source data. Furthermore, among representation-learning-based domain adaptation methods, some typical supervised and unsupervised deep learning models, such as convolutional neural networks and the autoencoder, have achieved fairly good performance. However, there are two main problems that have prevented the further development of these methods. The first is the training problem associated with deep neural networks. Some efficient models, such as graph regularization and sparse constraint, cannot be applied directly in supervised convolutional networks. In addition, although some optimization methods have been proposed [46–48], they have not been demonstrated to be effective in unsupervised deep networks for domain adaptation tasks. The second problem is data redundancy of image data. As the adjacent pixels of an image inside a local area are highly correlated, high-dimensional features of image data are inevitably affected by performance degradation in representation learning. For example, in a local receptive field neural network, the local relationship of replication features leads to a non-uniform distribution of edge detectors. To address these two problems, we propose a stacked convolutional sparse autoencoder method for unsupervised domain adaptation. In contrast to previous autoencoder-based methods that rely on the classical structure or the integration of regularization terms into the objective function, path-wise training is used to optimize the model of the sparse autoencoder and then the convolutional kernels are used to reserve the local relevance for learning abstract representations. Furthermore, the reconstruction independent component analysis (RICA) algorithm with whitening is introduced to pre-process the original data in both the source and target domains to remove correlations inside the local area for representation learning.

In Figure 1, a stacked convolutional sparse autoencoder is illustrated as the proposed unsupervised domain adaptation method. The SCSA consists of several levels: for example, there are two layers in Figure 1; layer 2 is a repeat of layer 1 for more abstract feature learning; each layer is composed of two components. Firstly, the input data information is sphered according to the RICA with whitening. The overall goal of this part is to perform a separate part analysis of the imported data. Then, the transferable features are learned by training on patches with a sparse autoencoder. Secondly, the CNN feature maps are generated with the help of practical convolution operations and pooling in different domains. According to the projection layer, a classifier is built from the final features by transforming and reshaping them in the overall target domain.

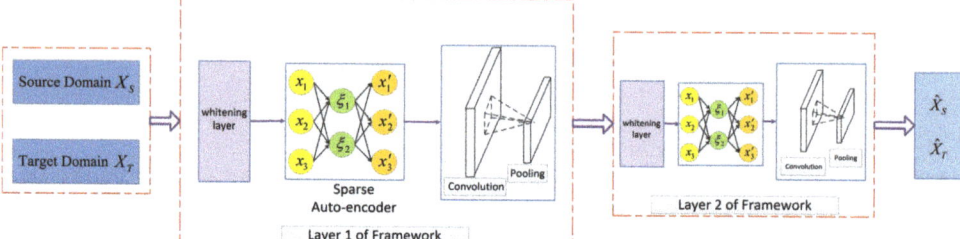

Figure 1. Illustration of our proposed SCSA. Each layer is composed of two main components: a stacked sparse autoencoder and the convolution and pooling kernels. The whitening layer is first introduced for recognition feature learning.

4.2. Stacked Sparse Autoencoder

The first component is composed of a sparse autoencoder with a whitening layer that learns the latent feature representations from the data in the source domain. As the target domain is unlabeled in unsupervised domain adaptation, the source domain D_s with labeled data and target domain D_t with unlabeled data is $D_s = \{x_i^{(s)}, y_i^{(s)}\}|_{i=1}^{n_s}$ with $x_i^{(s)} \in R^{m \times 1}$ and $D_t = \{x_i^{(t)}\}|_{i=1}^{n_t}$, where $x_i^{(s)} \in R^{m \times 1}$ and $x_i^{(t)} \in R^{m \times 1}$ denote the instances in the source and target domain and n_s and n_t denote the number of instances in the source and target domain, respectively; $y_i^{(s)} \in \{1, 2, \ldots, c\}$ denotes the label information in the source domain, m denotes the feature dimension of the input data and c denotes the number of labels. In a sparse autoencoder, at the encoder stage, the data from both the source and the overall target domains are projected onto vectors in the hidden layer, respectively, expressed as $\xi^{(s)}$ and $\xi^{(t)}$. Then, in the decoder stage, the $\xi^{(s)}$ and $\xi^{(t)}$ are mapped to the output layer as $\hat{x}_i^{(s)}$ and $\hat{x}_i^{(t)}$. To obtain more powerful feature representations for knowledge transfer, we introduce a softmax encoder weight regularization to apply the labeled information in the source domain to train the whole model.

First, we introduce the RICA algorithm to perform the independent component analysis from the original data in both source and target domains. We utilize the whitening layer before the RICA to make the input less redundant. The objective function can be shown as (1):

$$J_{\text{RICA}}(W_R) = \lambda \|W_R X\|_1 + \frac{1}{m} \left\| W_R^T W_R X - X \right\|_2^2 \tag{1}$$

X denotes the original data in both source and target domains, W_R denotes the weight matrix, and λ are the tuning parameters. To scale the reconstruction item, i.e., the second item in (1), the L1 regularization expressed as $f(x) = \sqrt{(WX)^2 + \varepsilon}$ is introduced to (1). In our method, we select $\varepsilon = 0.1$ as a small constant to prevent the L1 regularization item from being numerically close to zero. Thus, (1) can be expressed as (2):

$$J_{\text{RICA}}(W_R) = \lambda \sum (\sqrt{(W_R x_i)^2 + \varepsilon}) + \frac{1}{2n} \sum_{i=1}^{n} \left(\frac{1}{m} \left\| W_R^T W_R x_i - x_i \right\|_2^2 \right) \tag{2}$$

The partial derivatives of $J_{\text{RICA}}(W_R)$ can be formalized as (3):

$$\nabla_{W_R} J_{\text{RICA}}(W_R) = \frac{2}{m}(W_R(W_R^T W_R X - X)X^T \\ + (W_R X)(W_R^T W_R X - X)^T) \\ + \lambda((W_R X)^2 + \varepsilon)^{-1/2}(W_R X)X^T \qquad (3)$$

According to the partial derivatives of (3), the output $W_R^T W_R X$ of the RICA is fed into the next autoencoder as the input.

After the RICA, we introduce the stacked sparse autoencoder with softmax weight regression to learn more abstract features across the source and target domains. In the stacked sparse autoencoder, the desired partial derivatives regrading W and b can be shown as (4) and (5):

$$\nabla_{W^{(l)}} J(W, b) = \delta^{(l+1)}(\xi^{(l)})^T \qquad (4)$$

$$\nabla_{b^{(l)}} J(W, b) = \delta^{(l+1)} \qquad (5)$$

$W^{(l)}$, $b^{(l)}$ and $\xi^{(l)}$ are the weight matrix, bias vector and output of the lth hidden level in the autoencoder, respectively. Taking the added sparsity penalty term in the sparse autoencoder into consideration, δ^l can be calculated in (6).

$$\delta^l = \left(\left(\sum_{r=1}^{s} W_{ri}^l \delta^{(l+1)}\right) + \beta\left(-\frac{p}{\hat{p}_i} + \frac{1-p}{1-\hat{p}_i}\right)\right) f'(z_i^l) \qquad (6)$$

where $f'(z_i^l) = W^l x_i + b^l$. The output of the sparse autoencoder is represented as $W_2(W_1 x_i + b_1) + b_2$. Due to space limitation, more details for (4)–(6) are provided in Appendix A.

To utilize the labeled information in the source domain to alleviate domain discrepancy, we follow the approach used in [2]; the softmax encoder weight regularization is introduced into the stacked sparse autoencoder. The objective function is described in (7):

$$J = J_1(x, \hat{x}) + \alpha J_2(\xi, \theta) + \beta J_3(W_1, W_2, b_1, b_2) \qquad (7)$$

where α and β are the trade-off parameters, which aim to balance the effectiveness of each item in (7).

The first term $J_1(x, \hat{x})$ in (7) is the reconstruction error, which can be defined as (8):

$$J_1(x, \hat{x}) = \sum_{i=1}^{n} \left\| x^{(i)} - \hat{x}^{(i)} \right\|^2 \qquad (8)$$

The second term $J_2(\xi, \theta)$ in (7) is the cost function of the softmax encoder weight regularization, which can be formalized as (9):

$$J_2(\xi, \theta) = -\frac{1}{n} \sum_{i=1}^{n} \sum_{j=1}^{c} 1\{y_i^{(s)} = j\} \log \frac{e^{\theta_j^T \xi_i^{(s)}}}{\sum_{l=1}^{c} e^{\theta_l^T \xi_i^{(s)}}} \qquad (9)$$

where θ_j^T denotes the j-th row of W_2, and $y_i^{(s)}$ denotes the label x_i in the source domain.

The last term $J_3(W_1, W_2)$ in (7) is the total weight regularization, which can be written as (10):

$$J_3(W_1, W_2) = \|W_1\|^2 + \|W_2\|^2 + \|b_1\|^2 + \|b_2\|^2 \qquad (10)$$

As the objective function is an unconstrained optimization problem, the minimization of J with respect to W_1, W_2, b_1, b_2 and θ_j is adopted using the l-bfgs method, which has been demonstrated to be a more efficient backtracking method [22]. The partial derivatives of θ_j can be formalized as (11):

$$\frac{\partial J}{\partial \theta_j} = \alpha(-\frac{1}{n}\sum_{i=1}^{n}\sum_{j=1}^{c}1\{y_i = j\}(1-\frac{e^{\theta_j^T \xi_i}}{\sum_{l=1}^{c}e^{\theta_l^T \xi_i}})\xi_i) \quad (11)$$

The alternate optimization method is adopted to derive the solutions as follows: $W_j \leftarrow W_j - \eta \frac{\partial J}{\partial W_j}$, $b_j \leftarrow b_j - \eta \frac{\partial J}{\partial b_j}$, $\theta_j \leftarrow \theta_j - \eta \frac{\partial J}{\partial \theta_j}$ where η is the step length, which determines the speed of convergence.

4.3. Convolution and Pool Layer

After feature learning via the stacked sparse autoencoder, the convolution and pool kernel is utilized to preserve the local relevance of features. Given $x^{(l)} \in R^{m_1 \times m_2 \times d}$ are the whole sample representation of both source and target domain maps of layer l, where m_1 and m_2 represent the height and width of each input map, respectively, and d represents the number of channels. The patches $P \in R^{(n_1 \times n_2 \times d) \times K}$ are extracted from $x^{(l)}$ to compose the training set for learning latent features, where K denotes the number of patches, n_1 and n_2 are the size of patches, respectively, and $n_1 \times n_2 \times d$ denotes the convolution kernel size Each input is reshaped to the vector of $(n_1 \times n_2 \times d) \times 1$ for the convenience of training the autoencoder. The number of neurons in hidden layer l can be manually designed.

After the convolved features are extracted, we divide the input features into disjoint $n_1 \times n_2$ regions, and the mean (or maximum) activation function is utilized to obtain the pooled convolution feature representations, where n_1 and n_2 denote the size of patches Different pooling methods are selected for different distributed datasets. For example, the mean pool objective function is (12):

$$P = \frac{P - mean(P)}{std(P)} \quad (12)$$

In the experiments performed, the parameter ϑ in the objective function $J(\vartheta)$ is updated as (13):

$$\vartheta = \vartheta - \gamma \nabla_\vartheta J\left(\vartheta; x^{(i)}\right) \quad (13)$$

where x_i is derived from the projection and γ is the learning rate, which is usually much lower than the corresponding learning rate in batch gradient descent due to larger variance in the update. In the experiments undertaken, the momentum method is introduced to rapidly facilitate the objective along the shallow ravine.

$$v = \phi v + \gamma \nabla_\vartheta J\left(\vartheta; x^{(i)}\right)$$
$$\vartheta = \vartheta - v \quad (14)$$

where v is the current velocity vector with the same dimension as the parameter vector ϑ. $\phi \in (0, 1]$ determines how many iterations from the previous gradients are incorporated into the current update.

It is of note that the pooling operation can both reduce the representation dimensions and select more significant features. For example, the pervasive pooling tools, such as max-pooling [49], mean-pooling [50] and stochastic pooling [51] have achieved promising performance in feature representation learning. Therefore, in the experiments, two different pooling tools, max and mean pooling, were used according to the distribution of the datasets.

5. Experiments

5.1. Datasets

Corel Data Set http://archive.ics.uci.edu/ml/datasets/Corel+Image+Features, accessed on 1 June 2022. In the experiments, two different top categories in the dataset, such as flower and traffic, were selected as positive and negative [4]. The source domain was built by randomly choosing a subcategory from flower and traffic and the target domain was built by choosing another subcategory from flower and traffic. In this way, 144 domain adaptation classification tasks were constructed.

ImageNet Data Set http://www.image-net.org/, accessed on 1 February 2021. In the experiments, five domains where the ImageNet data information was centralized were selected [52], including ambulance, taxi, jeep, minivan and scooter. The scooter is considered as a set of negative cases, randomly divided into four other datasets. To better build the classification, we randomly selected two domains from the four domains as the source domain and target domain, respectively. Therefore, 12 domain adaptation classification tasks were constructed in this way. The number of positive and negative instances in four domains was 1000, and the number of features was 900. Details of the ImageNet datasets used in the experiments are listed in Table 1.

Table 1. Details of the ImageNet dataset used in our experiment.

	Domain1	Domain2	Domain3	Domain4
Number of Positive Instances	1000	1000	1000	1000
Number of Negative Instances	1000	1000	1000	1000
Feature	900	900	900	900

Leaves Data Set http://www.cse.wustl.edu/mchen/, accessed on 1 January 2021. In this dataset, there are 100 plant species in total, divided into 32 genera, with 16 species for each genus [53]. In the experiments, we selected four different genera from this dataset and four class classification problems were constructed with 64-margin descriptors. Therefore, 12 domain adaptation classification tasks were constructed.

5.2. Compared Methods

The following baseline methods were compared with our proposed SCSA:

- The standard classifier without unsupervised domain adaptation technique; we introduced support vector machine (SVM) in the experiments.
- Transfer component analysis (TCA) [13], which aims to project the original data into the common latent feature space via dimension reduction for unsupervised domain adaptation.
- Marginalized stacked denoising autoencoders (mSDA) [19], which are elaborated to learn more abstract and invasive feature representations so that domain integration can be carried out.
- Transfer learning with deep autoencoders (TLDA) [14]. The dual-level autoencoder is designed to learn more transferable features for domain adaptation.
- Transfer learning with manifold regularized autoencoders (TLMRA) [2]. To obtain more abstract representations, the method combines manifold regularization and softmax weight regression.
- Semi-supervised representation learning framework via dual autoencoders (SSRLDA) [1]. The mSDA with adaptation distributions and multi-class marginalized denoising autoencoder are applied to obtain global and local features for unsupervised domain adaptation.

5.3. Experiment Settings

For the trade-off parameters, $\alpha = 0.01$, $\beta = 0.005$ and $\lambda = 0.01$ were set for the Corel and ImageNet datasets, while $\alpha = 0.05$, $\beta = 0.001$ and $\lambda = 0.001$ were set for the Leaves dataset in our experiments. The hyper-parameters in the convolutional layers, such as the total number of maps, the kernel size, and the pooling type and size, are shown in Table 2. Among the methods compared, the best parameters were measured in the experiments using the mSDA method http://multitask.cs.berkeley.edu, accessed on 1 February 2021.

For TCA, the total number of latent subspace dimensions was intentionally fixed and the best results were reported. For TLDA, the main parameters of the default settings were reported in [14]. We implemented the source code of TLMRA and SSRLDA under optimal parameter settings.

Table 2. Main configurations of SCSA on Datasets.

Data Sets	Configurations	
Corel Data Set	Kernel Size	$11 \times 11 \times 3$
	Maps Number	1000
	Pool Type	max
	Pool Size	12×12
ImageNet Dataset	Kernel Size	$10 \times 10 \times 3$
	Maps Number	500
	Pool Type	max
	Pool Size	24×24
Leaves Dataset	Kernel Size	$6 \times 6 \times 3$
	Maps Number	800
	Pool Type	mean
	Pool Size	3×3

5.4. Experimental Results

All the experimental results for the three datasets are listed in Table 3. Our experiments were conducted five times and the results presented are the average performances of all domain adaptation tasks. Figures 2 and 3 show the results for the ImageNet and Leaves datasets, respectively. The following conclusions are drawn from the experimental results

- All the domain adaptation methods significantly and consistently outperformed the standard SVM classifier, demonstrating the advantages of the feature-representation method in a broader set of scenarios.
- Compared to shallow learning methods, such as TCA, autoencoder-based methods, such as TLDA, TLMRA, and SSRLDA, all achieved superior results in unsupervised domain adaptation, indicating the superiority of deep-learning-based methods in learning transferable and discriminative features across domains. Notably, mSDA achieved comparable performance to TCA, demonstrating that the traditional structure of the autoencoder cannot learn sufficient features. This is why other autoencoder-based methods require improvements in architecture.
- In comparison with mSDA, our SCSA achieved better performance in all tasks for three different datasets, demonstrating the superiority of our framework for exploring different domains compared to autoencoder-based domain adaptation methods.
- By comparison to other autoencoder-based deep methods, such as TLDA and TLMRA, our proposed SCSA achieved better performance for overall tasks in the same target domains and for the same problems. These methods rely on the classical structure of autoencoders (i.e., TLMRA) or the integration of regularization terms into the objective function (i.e., TLDA). The results confirm that our SCSA can explore abstract and distinctive features for domain adaptation.
- For all three experimental datasets, our method was better than SSRLDA. From Figures 2 and 3, it can be seen that our method achieved better results for most tasks in the same target domains and for the same problems. Our SCSA also achieved comparable performance to SSRLDA in other tasks. As a semi-supervised method, our method achieved superior performance for all three image datasets, indicating

that the convolution and pooling layer can maintain the local relevance and learn features better for domain adaptation in image datasets.
- Generally, compared with alternative methods, our SCSA achieved the best results in all groups for three different datasets, confirming the effectiveness of our proposed method.

Table 3. Average accuracy on all three datasets (%).

SVM	TCA	mSDA	TLDA	TLMRA	SSRLDA	SCSA
			ImageNet Data Set			
62.6 ± 0.9	75.6 ± 1.1	77.6 ± 1.2	83.6 ± 1.1	88.9 ± 1.1	89.1 ± 0.7	**89.3 ± 0.9**
			Corel Data Set			
52.9 ± 0.8	76.5 ± 0.7	73.4 ± 0.6	80.2 ± 0.6	84.5 ± 0.5	84.9 ± 0.6	**85.1 ± 0.4**
			Leaves Data Set			
60.0 ± 0.4	72.0 ± 0.5	70.1 ± 0.4	67.5 ± 0.4	73.6 ± 0.7	75.0 ± 0.5	**76.2 ± 0.6**

Tip: The bolder ones mean better.

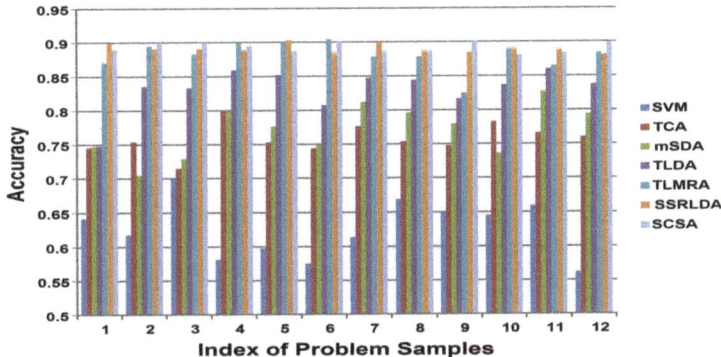

Figure 2. Performances on ImageNet dataset. The y-axis represents the classification accuracy of the target domain; the x-axis represents the index of the problem sample.

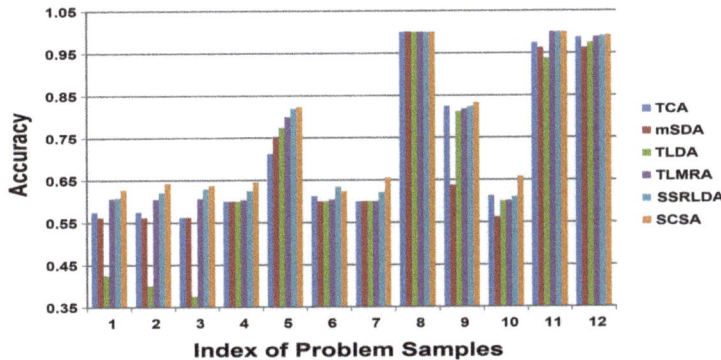

Figure 3. Performances on Leaves dataset. The y-axis represents the classification accuracy of target domain; the x-axis represents the index of the problem sample.

5.5. Analysis of Properties in SCSA

SCSA with and without RICA: In our SCSA, the RICA with whitening played a foundation and optimization role in the experiments. Therefore, we conducted additional experiments to evaluate its optimizing ability. Table 4 shows the results for the SCSA with and without RICA for all three datasets. From the results, it can be observed that the proposed SCSA with RICA outperformed SCSA without RICA for all three datasets, indicating that the RICA can pre-process all the image datasets and make the input less redundant, which is obviously helpful for more transferable and discriminative feature learning. With less redundant input data, the cross-domain and invariant feature representations can improve performance in domain adaptation.

Table 4. Average accuracy of SCSA without or with RICA for three datasets (%).

Without RICA	With RICA
ImageNet Data Set	
89.0 ± 0.7	89.3 ± 0.9
Corel Data Set	
84.8 ± 0.5	85.1 ± 0.4
Leaves Data Set	
74.1 ± 0.5	76.2 ± 0.6

Computational Cost: The time complexity of a stacked sparse auto-encoder is $O(h_1 + h_2)$, where h_1 and h_2 are the hidden unit numbers of two layers, respectively. For our method, we took the labeled information into consideration, given c as the number of classes; the time complexity is $O(h_1 + h_2 + h_2 \bullet c) = O(h_1 + h_2 \bullet (1 + c)) = O(h_1 + h_2)$. For the convolution and pooling kernels, the time complexity is $O(m \times m \times p \times p \times d) = O(m^2 \times p^2 \times d)$, where $m \times m$ and $p \times p \times d$ represent the size of the input and the patches, respectively. The time complexity of our SCSA is $O(m^2 \times p^2 \times d + h_1 + h_2)$.

5.6. Transfer Distance

The transfer distance that can be defined as the $\mathcal{A}$-distance is widely used as a similarity measure between the source and target domains [2,15,54]. The $\mathcal{A}$-distance can be defined as $\mathcal{A}-\text{distance} = 2(1 - 2error)$, where $error$ is the generalization error of classifiers, such as the linear SVM trained on the binary classification problem, which is used to distinguish the source domain from the target domain. If the new features are more suitable for domain adaptation tasks, the $\mathcal{A}$-distance increases in the new representation space. The results on the Corel and ImageNet datasets with and without our proposed SCSA are shown in Figure 4. It can be observed that the distance increases with the new features after the proposed method is applied. It appears that the representations obtained by SCSA are more appropriate for transfer learning applications.

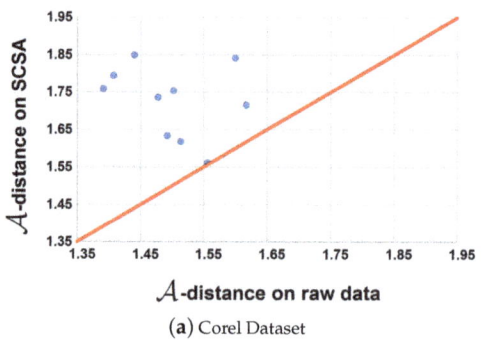

(**a**) Corel Dataset

Figure 4. *Cont.*

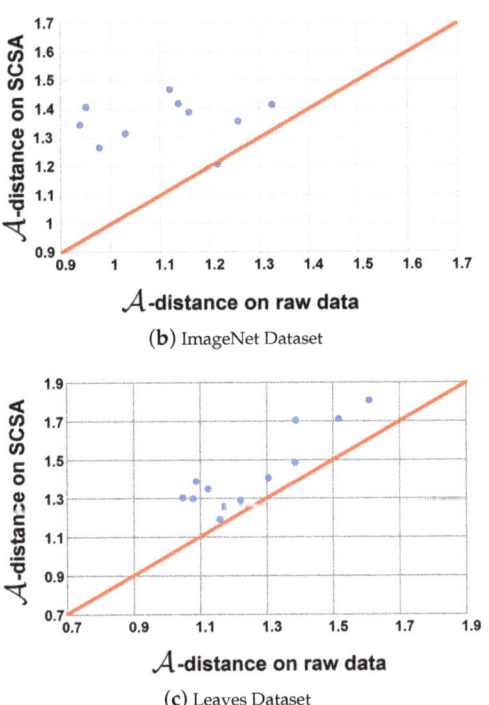

(b) ImageNet Dataset

(c) Leaves Dataset

Figure 4. $\mathcal{A}$-distance on Corel, ImageNet and Corel datasets. The x-axis and y-axis represent the $\mathcal{A}$-distance on the raw data and learned features space.

5.7. Parameter Sensitivity

The influence of hyper-parameters is investigated in this section, which includes λ, α and β in (3) and (7), respectively. In the experiments, when one parameter is changed, the values of the other parameters are fixed. α is sampled from $\{10^{-4}, 5 \times 10^{-4}, 0.01, 0.05, 0.1, 0.5, 1\}$, β is sampled from $\{10^{-4}, 5 \times 10^{-4}, 10^{-3}, 5 \times 10^{-3}, 0.01, 0.05, 0.1, 0.5, 1\}$, and λ is sampled from $\{10^{-4}, 10^{-3}, 0.01, 0.1, 1, 10\}$, respectively. All the results for the ImageNet datasets are reported in Figures 5–7. According to the observations, we set $\alpha = 0.01$, $\beta = 0.005$ and $\lambda = 0.01$ to obtain the best and most stable results.

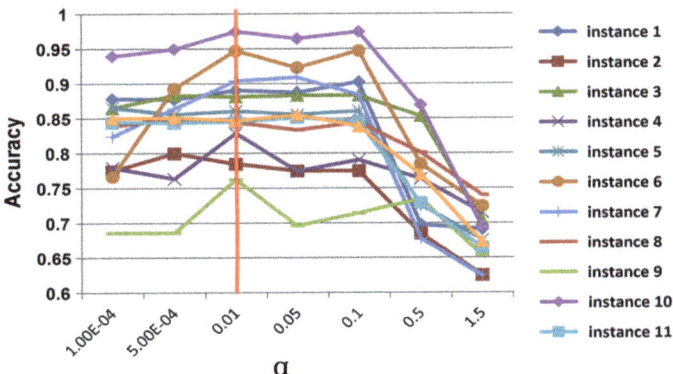

Figure 5. Parameter Influence on α of SCSA on ImageNet dataset. The y-axis represents the classification accuracy of the target domain; the x-axis represents the value range of α.

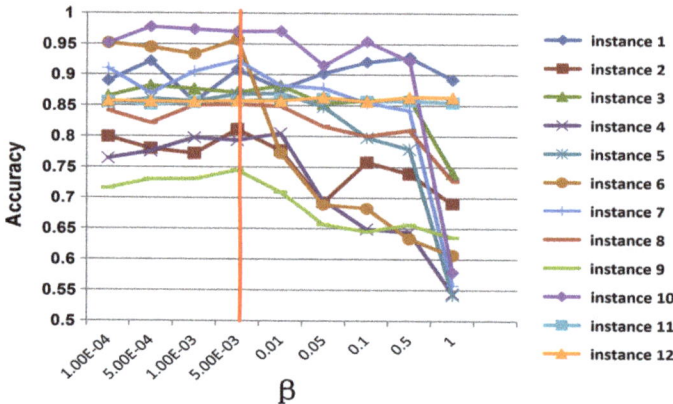

Figure 6. Parameter influence on β of SCSA on ImageNet dataset. The y-axis represents the classification accuracy of the target domain; the x-axis represents the value range of β.

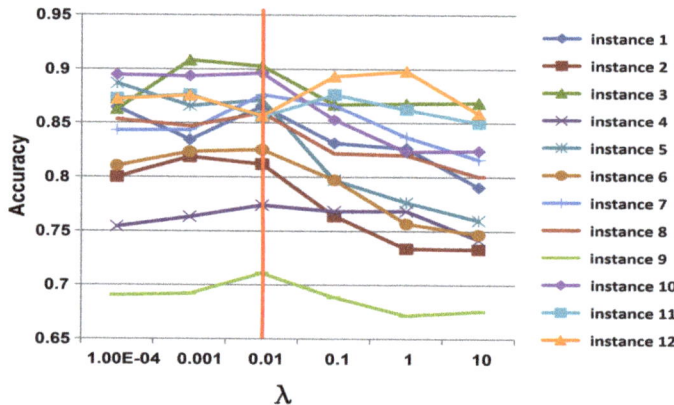

Figure 7. Parameter influence on λ of SCSA on ImageNet dataset. The y-axis represents the classification accuracy of the target domain; the x-axis represents the value range of λ.

6. Conclusions

In this paper, we proposed an unsupervised domain adaptation framework based on a stacked convolution sparse autoencoder, called SCSA. Our method can learn more transferable and discriminative representations across domains. Firstly, the original data is pre-processed by the layer-wise RICA with whitening. Then, the labeled data information in the source domain is encoded via softmax encoder weight regularization in a sparse autoencoder model. Finally, the convolutional kernels are used to reserve the local relevance for learning abstract representations. The proposed method was extensively tested on several datasets and was found to be more effective than state-of-the-art domain adaptation methods. The proposed method was extensively tested on several datasets and an accuracy of up to 89.3% was obtained, outperforming other state-of-the-art autoencoder-based domain adaptation methods, such as SSRLDA.

The designed SCSA is only concerned with the unsupervised domain adaptation of image data and is not concerned with other types of data, such as text data. In the future, we intend to focus on learning better feature representations in text data for unsupervised domain adaptation.

Author Contributions: Conceptualization, Y.Z. and X.W.; methodology, Y.Z. and X.W.; software, Y.Z. and X.Z.; validation, X.Z.; formal analysis,Y.Z.; investigation, X.W.; resources, X.Z.; data curation, X.Z.; writing—original draft preparation, Y.Z. and X.Z.; writing—review and editing, X.W.; visualization, X.W.; supervision, X.W.; project administration,Y.Z. and X.W. All authors have read and agreed to the published version of the manuscript.

Funding: This research is partially supported by the National Natural Science Foundation of China under grants (61906060,62120106008), Yangzhou University Interdisciplinary Research Foundation for Animal Husbandry Discipline of Targeted Support (yzuxk202015,yzuxk202008), the Opening Foundation of Key Laboratory of Huizhou Architecture in Anhui Province under grant HPJZ-2020-02.

Informed Consent Statement: Not applicable.

Conflicts of Interest: The authors declare no conflict of interest. The funders had no role in the design of the study; in the collection, analyses, or interpretation of data.

Appendix A

The aim of the sparse autoencoder is to constrain the neurons in the hidden layers to be inactive most of the time. Given an input set $\{x_1, \ldots, x_i, \ldots, x_n\}$, $x_i \in R^{m \times 1}$, and the hidden unit set $\{\xi_1, \ldots, \xi_r, \ldots, \xi_s\}$, $\xi_i \in R^{k \times 1}$, the average activation of the hidden unit can be calculated as (A1).

$$\hat{p}_r = \frac{1}{n} \sum_{i=1}^{n} [\xi_r(x_i)] \tag{A1}$$

To ensure that the hidden unit's activation status is inactive, the constraint $\hat{p}_r = p$ is enforced, where p is the sparsity parameter, which is close to zero. The KL divergence method can be used to penalize $\hat{p}_r$ if it deviates significantly from p, as shown in (A2):

$$\sum_{r=1}^{s} \mathrm{KL}(p||\hat{p}_r) = \sum_{r=1}^{s} p \log \frac{p}{\hat{p}_r} + (1-p) \log \frac{1-p}{1-\hat{p}_r} \tag{A2}$$

The overall cost function of the sparse auto-encoder can be shown as (A3):

$$J_{\mathrm{sparse}}(W, b) = J_r(W, b) + \beta \sum_{r=1}^{s} \mathrm{KL}(p||\hat{p}_r) \tag{A3}$$

where $J_r(W, b)$ is defined as (6) and β is the hyper-parameter which controls the weight of the sparsity penalty term. Since the term $\hat{p}_r$ is the average activation of the hidden unit, it also depends on W and b.

References

1. Yang, S.; Wang, H.; Zhang, Y.; Li, P.; Zhu, Y.; Hu, X. Semi-supervised representation learning via dual autoencoders for domain adaptation. *Knowl.-Based Syst.* **2020**, *190*, 105161. [CrossRef]
2. Zhu, Y.; Xindong, W.; Li, P.; Zhang, Y.; Hu, X. Transfer learning with deep manifold regularized auto-encoders. *Neurocomputing* **2019**, *369*, 145–154. [CrossRef]
3. Wilson, G.; Cook, D.J. A survey of unsupervised deep domain adaptation. *ACM Trans. Intell. Syst. Technol. (TIST)* **2020**, *11*, 1–46. [CrossRef] [PubMed]
4. Yi, Z.; Hu, X.; Zhang, Y.; Li, P. Transfer Learning with Stacked Reconstruction Independent Component Analysis. *Knowl.-Based Syst.* **2018**, *152*, 100–106.
5. Wang, M.; Deng, W. Deep visual domain adaptation: A survey. *Neurocomputing* **2018**, *312*, 135–153. [CrossRef]
6. You, K.; Long, M.; Cao, Z.; Wang, J.; Jordan, M.I. Universal domain adaptation. In Proceedings of the IEEE/CVF Conference on Computer Vision and Pattern Recognition, Long Beach, CA, USA, 15–20 June 2019; pp. 2720–2729.
7. Kang, G.; Jiang, L.; Yang, Y.; Hauptmann, A.G. *Contrastive Adaptation Network for Unsupervised Domain Adaptation*; IEEE: Piscataway, NJ, USA, 2019; pp. 4893–4902.
8. Deng, J.; Zhang, Z.; Eyben, F.; Schuller, B. Autoencoder-based Unsupervised Domain Adaptation for Speech Emotion Recognition. *IEEE Signal Process. Lett.* **2014**, *21*, 1068–1072. [CrossRef]

9. Ahn, E.; Kumar, A.; Fulham, M.; Feng, D.; Kim, J. Unsupervised Domain Adaptation to Classify Medical Images Using Zero Bias Convolutional Auto-Encoders and Context-Based Feature Augmentation. *IEEE Trans. Med. Imaging* **2020**, *39*, 2385–2394. [CrossRef]
10. Pan, S.J.; Yang, Q. A survey on transfer learning. *IEEE Trans. Knowl. Data Eng.* **2009**, *22*, 1345–1359. [CrossRef]
11. Feng, S.; Yu, H.; Duarte, M.F. Autoencoder based sample selection for self-taught learning. *Knowl.-Based Syst.* **2020**, *192*, 105343. [CrossRef]
12. Tzeng, E.; Hoffman, J.; Saenko, K.; Darrell, T. Adversarial discriminative domain adaptation. In Proceedings of the IEEE Conference on Computer Vision and Pattern Recognition, Honolulu, HI, USA, 21–26 July 2017; pp. 7167–7176.
13. Pan, S.J.; Tsang, I.W.; Kwok, J.T.; Yang, Q. Domain adaptation via transfer component analysis. *IEEE Trans. Neural Netw.* **2011**, *22*, 199–210. [CrossRef]
14. Zhuang, F.; Cheng, X.; Luo, P.; Pan, S.J.; He, Q. Supervised representation learning: Transfer learning with deep autoencoders. In Proceedings of the International Joint Conference on Artificial Intelligence, IJCAI, Buenos Aires, Argentina, 25–31 July 2015; pp. 4119–4125.
15. Yang, S.; Zhang, Y.; Wang, H.; Li, P.; Hu, X. Representation learning via serial robust autoencoder for domain adaptation. *Expert Syst. Appl.* **2020**, *160*, 113635. [CrossRef]
16. Xie, G.S.; Zhang, X.Y.; Yan, S.; Liu, C.L. Hybrid CNN and dictionary-based models for scene recognition and domain adaptation. *IEEE Trans. Circuits Syst. Video Technol.* **2015**, *27*, 1263–1274. [CrossRef]
17. Jaech, A.; Heck, L.; Ostendorf, M. Domain adaptation of recurrent neural networks for natural language understanding. *arXiv* **2016**, arXiv:1604.00117.
18. Choi, J.; Kim, T.; Kim, C. Self-ensembling with gan-based data augmentation for domain adaptation in semantic segmentation. In Proceedings of the IEEE/CVF International Conference on Computer Vision, Seoul, Republic of Korea, 27 October–2 November 2019; pp. 6830–6840.
19. Chen, M.; Xu, Z.; Weinberger, K.; Fei, S. Marginalized Denoising Autoencoders for Domain Adaptation. In Proceedings of the ICML, Edinburgh, UK, 26 June–1 July 2012; pp. 767–774.
20. Vincent, P.; Larochelle, H.; Lajoie, I.; Bengio, Y.; Manzagol, P.A. Stacked Denoising Autoencoders: Learning Useful Representations in a Deep Network with a Local Denoising Criterion. *J. Mach. Learn. Res.* **2010**, *11*, 3371–3408.
21. Wei, P.; Ke, Y.; Goh, C.K. Deep nonlinear feature coding for unsupervised domain adaptation. In Proceedings of the International Joint Conference on Artificial Intelligence, IJCAI, New York, NY, USA, 9–15 July 2016; pp. 2189–2195.
22. Zhuang, F.; Cheng, X.; Luo, P.; Pan, S.J.; He, Q. Supervised representation learning with double encoding-layer autoencoder for transfer learning. *ACM Trans. Intell. Syst. Technol. (TIST)* **2017**, *9*, 1–17. [CrossRef]
23. Clinchant, S.; Csurka, G.; Chidlovskii, B. A Domain Adaptation Regularization for Denoising Autoencoders. In Proceedings of the Annual Meeting of the Association for Computational Linguistics (Volume 2: Short Papers), Berlin, Germany, 7–12 August 2016; pp. 26–31.
24. Yang, S.; Zhang, Y.; Zhu, Y.; Li, P.; Hu, X. Representation learning via serial autoencoders for domain adaptation. *Neurocomputing* **2019**, *351*, 1–9. [CrossRef]
25. Zhu, Y.; Zhou, X.; Li, Y.; Qiang, J.; Yuan, Y. Domain Adaptation with Stacked Convolutional Sparse Autoencoder. In Proceedings of the International Conference on Neural Information Processing, Sanur, Bali, Indonesia, 8–12 December 2021; pp. 685–692.
26. Ganin, Y.; Lempitsky, V. Unsupervised Domain Adaptation by Backpropagation. In Proceedings of the International Conference on Machine Learning, ICML, Lille France, 6–11 July 2015; pp. 1180–1189.
27. Sener, O.; Song, H.O.; Saxena, A.; Savarese, S. Learning transferrable representations for unsupervised domain adaptation. *Adv. Neural Inf. Process. Syst.* **2016**, *29*, 1–9.
28. Farahani, A.; Voghoei, S.; Rasheed, K.; Arabnia, H.R. A brief review of domain adaptation. *Adv. Data Sci. Inf. Eng.* **2021**, 877–894.
29. Zhang, X.; Yu, F.X.; Chang, S.F.; Wang, S. Deep transfer network: Unsupervised domain adaptation. *arXiv* **2015**, arXiv:1503.00591.
30. Mingsheng, L.; Han, Z.; Jianmin, W.; Jordan, M.I. Unsupervised Domain Adaptation with Residual Transfer Networks. In Proceedings of the Advances in Neural Information Processing Systems, Barcelona, Spain, 5–10 December 2016; Volume 29, pp. 1–9.
31. Pinheiro, P.O. Unsupervised Domain Adaptation With Similarity Learning. In Proceedings of the IEEE Conference on Computer Vision and Pattern Recognition (CVPR), Salt Lake City, UT, USA, 18–23 June 2018; pp. 8004–8013.
32. Long, M.; Cao, Z.; Wang, J.; Jordan, M.I. Conditional adversarial domain adaptation. *Adv. Neural Inf. Process. Syst.* **2018**, *31*, 1647–1657.
33. Pei, Z.; Cao, Z.; Long, M.; Wang, J. Multi-adversarial domain adaptation. In Proceedings of the Thirty-Second AAAI Conference on Artificial Intelligence, New Orleans, LA, USA, 2–7 February 2018; pp. 877–894.
34. Zhang, T.; Wang, D.; Chen, H.; Zeng, Z.; Guo, W.; Miao, C.; Cui, L. BDANN: BERT-based domain adaptation neural network for multi-modal fake news detection. In Proceedings of the 2020 international joint conference on neural networks (IJCNN), Glasgow, UK, 19–24 July 2020; pp. 1–8.
35. Guo, X.; Li, B.; Yu, H. Improving the Sample Efficiency of Prompt Tuning with Domain Adaptation. *arXiv* **2022**, arXiv:2210.02952.
36. Chen, Y.; Song, S.; Li, S.; Yang, L.; Wu, C. Domain space transfer extreme learning machine for domain adaptation. *IEEE Trans. Cybern.* **2019**, *49*, 1909–1922. [CrossRef] [PubMed]

7. He, Y.; Tian, Y.; Liu, D. Multi-view transfer learning with privileged learning framework. *Neurocomputing* **2019**, *335*, 131–142. [CrossRef]
8. Chen, M.; Zhao, S.; Liu, H.; Cai, D. Adversarial-Learned Loss for Domain Adaptation. In Proceedings of the AAAI Conference on Artificial Intelligence, New York, NY, USA, 7–12 February 2020; pp. 3521–3528.
9. Wang, Y.; Qiu, S.; Ma, X.; He, H. A prototype-based SPD matrix network for domain adaptation EEG emotion recognition. *Pattern Recognit.* **2021**, *110*, 107626. [CrossRef]
10. Liu, F.; Lu, J.; Zhang, G. Unsupervised heterogeneous domain adaptation via shared fuzzy equivalence relations. *IEEE Trans. Fuzzy Syst.* **2018**, *26*, 3555–3568. [CrossRef]
11. Yan, Y.; Li, W.; Wu, H.; Min, H.; Tan, M.; Wu, Q. Semi-Supervised Optimal Transport for Heterogeneous Domain Adaptation. In Proceedings of the International Joint Conference on Artificial Intelligence, IJCAI, Stockholm, Sweden, 13–19 July 2018; Volume 7, pp. 2969–2975.
12. Luo, Y.; Wen, Y.; Liu, T.; Tao, D. Transferring knowledge fragments for learning distance metric from a heterogeneous domain. *IEEE Trans. Pattern Anal. Mach. Intell.* **2019**, *41*, 1013–1026. [CrossRef]
13. Glorot, X.; Bordes, A.; Bengio, Y. Domain adaptation for large-scale sentiment classification: A deep learning approach. In Proceedings of the International Conference on Machine Learning, Bellevue, WA, USA, 28 June–2 July 2011; pp. 513–520.
14. Nikisins, O.; George, A.; Marcel, S. Domain Adaptation in Multi-Channel Autoencoder based Features for Robust Face Anti-Spoofing. In Proceedings of the 2019 International Conference on Biometrics (ICB), Crete, Greece, 4–7 June 2019; pp. 1–8.
15. Zhu, Y.; Wu, X.; Li, Y.; Qiang, J.; Yuan, Y. Self-Adaptive Imbalanced Domain Adaptation With Deep Sparse Autoencoder. *IEEE Trans. Artif. Intell.* **2022**, 1–12. [CrossRef]
16. Oquab, M.; Bottou, L.; Laptev, I.; Sivic, J. Learning and transferring mid-level image representations using convolutional neural networks. In Proceedings of the IEEE Conference on Computer Vision and Pattern Recognition, Columbus, OH, USA, 23–28 June 2014; pp. 1717–1724.
17. Hoffman, J.; Guadarrama, S.; Tzeng, E.S.; Hu, R.; Donahue, J.; Girshick, R.; Darrell, T.; Saenko, K. LSDA: Large scale detection through adaptation. In Proceedings of the Advances in Neural Information Processing Systems, Montreal, QC, Canada, 8–13 December 2014; pp. 3536–3544.
18. Girshick, R. Fast R-CNN. In Proceedings of the IEEE Conference on Computer Vision and Pattern Recognition, Boston, MA, USA, 7–12 June 2015; pp. 1440–1448.
19. Murray, N.; Perronnin, F. Generalized max pooling. In Proceedings of the IEEE Conference on Computer Vision and Pattern Recognition, Columbus, OH, USA, 23–28 June 2014; pp. 2473–2480.
20. Boureau, Y.L.; Ponce, J.; LeCun, Y. A theoretical analysis of feature pooling in visual recognition. In Proceedings of the ICML, Haifa, Israel, 21–24 June 2010; pp. 111–118.
21. Li, X.; Armagan, E.; Tomasgard, A.; Barton, P. Stochastic pooling problem for natural gas production network design and operation under uncertainty. *AIChE J.* **2011**, *57*, 2120–2135. [CrossRef]
22. Krizhevsky, A.; Sutskever, I.; Hinton, G.E. ImageNet classification with deep convolutional neural networks. In Proceedings of the ICNIPS, Lake Tahoe, NV, USA, 3–6 December 2012; pp. 1097–1105.
23. Jin, X.; Zhuang, F.; Xiong, H.; Du, C.; Luo, P.; He, Q. Multi-task Multi-view Learning for Heterogeneous Tasks. In Proceedings of the ACM International Conference on Conference on Information and Knowledge Management, Shanghai, China, 3–7 November 2014; pp. 441–450.
24. Ben-David, S.; Blitzer, J.; Crammer, K.; Pereira, F.; et al. Analysis of representations for domain adaptation. *Adv. Neural Inf. Process. Syst.* **2007**, *19*, 137–145.

Disclaimer/Publisher's Note: The statements, opinions and data contained in all publications are solely those of the individual author(s) and contributor(s) and not of MDPI and/or the editor(s). MDPI and/or the editor(s) disclaim responsibility for any injury to people or property resulting from any ideas, methods, instructions or products referred to in the content.

Article

Web Page Content Block Identification with Extended Block Properties

Kiril Griazev * and Simona Ramanauskaitė

Department of Information Technologies, Vilnius Gediminas Technical University, Sauletekio al. 11, LT-10223 Vilnius, Lithuania
* Correspondence: kiril.griazev@vilniustech.lt

Abstract: Web page segmentation is one of the most influential factors for the automated integration of web page content with other systems. Existing solutions are focused on segmentation but do not provide a more detailed description of the segment including its range (minimum and maximum HTML code bounds, covering the segment content) and variants (the same segments with different content). Therefore the paper proposes a novel solution designed to find all web page content blocks and detail them for further usage. It applies text similarity and document object model (DOM) tree analysis methods to indicate the maximum and minimum ranges of each identified HTML block. In addition, it indicates its relation to other blocks, including hierarchical as well as sibling blocks. The evaluation of the method reveals its ability to identify more content blocks in comparison to human labeling (in manual labeling only 24% of blocks were labeled). By using the proposed method, manual labeling effort could be reduced by at least 70%. Better performance was observed in comparison to other analyzed web page segmentation methods, and better recall was achieved due to focus on processing every block present on a page, and providing a more detailed web page division into content block data by presenting block boundary range and block variation data.

Keywords: web segmentation; hierarchical segments; web page labeling

Citation: Griazev, K.; Ramanauskaitė, S. Web Page Content Block Identification with Extended Block Properties. *Appl. Sci.* 2023, 13, 5680. https://doi.org/10.3390/app13095680

Academic Editors: Jing Zhang, Jipeng Qiang and Cangqi Zhou

Received: 12 March 2023
Revised: 25 April 2023
Accepted: 28 April 2023
Published: 5 May 2023

Copyright: © 2023 by the authors. Licensee MDPI, Basel, Switzerland. This article is an open access article distributed under the terms and conditions of the Creative Commons Attribution (CC BY) license (https://creativecommons.org/licenses/by/4.0/).

1. Introduction

The vast majority of data are presented in web systems in HTML format. The purpose of designing this technology was to present data to humans. However, current technologies are increasingly interconnected, so the content must be designed for machines to read rather than just humans [1]. Machine-adapted labeling of content on web pages is a base for automated content extraction, data mining, content transformation, and other needs [2]. However, the existing HTML standard is slowly moving away from presentation over data. Content-related semantic tags like header, nav, section, article, figure, etc., are introduced but are mixed with general-purpose tags to build the needed design. Thus, web page content block identification is a relevant task that should be automated rather than performed manually.

For automated data gathering from web pages, after the HTML code is obtained, it should be divided into content blocks and then the type of each block should be defined [3]. The first part is conducted by segmenting the HTML code or dividing it into content blocks. The second part uses intelligent solutions to classify the blocks into predefined types [4]. However, both of these parts currently are facing some challenges, which are related to the hierarchical nature of web page blocks [5]:

- Some content blocks might be divided into smaller internal blocks. For example, menu can have menu items, and article paragraph can have some highlighted words or phrases. In the first case, the division into internal blocks is meaningful, while in the case of text formatting, it mostly will be redundant. Therefore, the level of detailing might cause redundancy of blocks.

- Content block might have HTML code ranges, caused by its presentation structure. If the block content is surrounded by several tags, it can be gathered by using different selectors, and the path to the segment and its content might vary. Therefore, for more accurate block classification, knowledge of the possible ranges would be beneficial.
- Hierarchical and sibling relations between different blocks might positively affect the block classification accuracy. Blocks like navigation menus and lists have a hierarchical structure, therefore keeping the links between the blocks would bring more features for correct block type identification. At the same time, identification of relations between blocks might lead to a reduced size of the dataset without losing any of the data. Only one sibling element could have a label, while the remaining ones could be associated as sibling blocks of the same type.

The mentioned issues in conjunction with other limitations affect the fact there is no solution capable of automatic extraction of unknown structure website data and linking it to the appropriate content type [6]. The existing solutions require a predefined website structure or extraction of specific data, such as listed items, links or other blocks only.

Our goal in this paper is to propose a novel approach to web page block identification, which would provide a bigger variety of content blocks and more detailed information about the content blocks, in comparison to existing web page segmentation solutions. Each identified block should contain a content reflecting certain structural element of the web page (menu, header, title, contacts, paragraph, etc.). The method should identify all content blocks with its internal structure and provide more detailed block data than traditional web page segmentation solutions, such as block's ranges, hierarchical relations, and siblings. Such an extension of content block information would extend the capabilities of the segmentation data application and lead to a better website content block classification.

2. Related Work

Currently, the content block extraction from web pages is mostly conducted by web page segmentation methods [7,8] as the main part of content blocks match the web page segments, while selected segments can be repeatedly analyzed to get internal structure of segments of it. A significant portion of existing solutions for web page segmentation is based on visual page segmentation. M. Cormier et al. [9] and J. Zaleny et al. [10] rely on visual analysis only, eliminating the dependency on web page implementation technologies. However, image segmentation-based solutions usually are more expensive in computational time in comparison to document object model (DOM)-based methods [11]. J. Kiesel et al.'s [12] research indicates that segmenting web pages visually provides high performance. However, in the research, the Vision-based Page Segmentation (VIPS) method, which uses both DOM and visual segmentation solutions, had the highest performance.

By integrating DOM tree analysis, a wide range of metadata can be analyzed. We can, for example, apply text analysis to identify related text on a web page [13], detect malicious websites [14], and segment blocks [15]. In addition to text, it also includes content analysis and text density for web page segmentation [16].

Furthermore, DOM structure and its related features are also relevant for web page segmentation [17,18]. Language-independent solutions for dedicated content extraction are available [19]. Some existing web page segmentation solutions are oriented to specific application areas. For example, A. Sonaja and S. Gancarski [20] proposed a solution to convert HTML code from version 4 to version 5. The project involves web page segmentation and its migration to HTML 5. Image segmentation is used to identify different types of images on a web page [21]. However, the existing solutions do not provide a means of obtaining complete data on the web page block, which would be necessary for extending web mining capabilities [22]. Existing methods do not focus on the range of HTML code corresponding to the same block (additional tags can be used to surround the content and affect the presentation and variety of selectors or paths to extract the content). Block variations (relationships between siblings or hierarchically related blocks) are not linked to obtaining a more interconnected block map as well.

To compare the existing segmentation methods, several datasets are prepared. One of the most used was created in 2014 and presents a list of web pages that were popular at that moment [23]. The labeling of the dataset presents a few main blocks on each web page with no details on composite elements. On average, this dataset has 13 labeled blocks for each web page, while the median is 16 blocks. The summary of accuracy metrics using different segmentation methods is presented in Table 1.

Table 1. Summary of proposed method accuracy metrics and comparison to other methods.

Method	Precision	Recall	Accuracy	F-Score
BoM [16]	31%	26%	26%	28%
VIPS [17]	24%	26%	24%	25%
SegBlock [18]	38%	40%	38%	39%
Semantic-Block [19]	40%	43%	42%	42%
Fusion-Block [20]	45%	54%	48%	49%
Integrated-Block [20]	52%	62%	54%	53%

Results of other methods were gathered from previous research papers [22] and include the following web page segmentation methods:

- BoM [24] combines the structural, visual, and logical features of web pages.
- VIPS [25] is visual analysis of web pages only.
- SegBlock [26] combines the visual appeal, logic, and features of the content on a web page.
- Semantic-Block [27] uses Gestalt laws.
- Fusion-Block [28] is Gestalt law-inspired and subsequential re-segmentation, which uses semantic text similarity.
- Integrated-Block [28] uses DOM structure, is vision-based, and uses text-based similarity metrics analysis based on web page segmentation.

Research works on specifically web page content block identification exist as well [29,30]. Those are able to identify main web page structure blocks with almost perfect accuracy, however, they are oriented on content block identification based on an analysis of multiple web pages in the same website. This approach is not suitable for one page websites or those, who use different design for different sections or even pages. As well the block bounds or block variations are not estimated in those early web page content block identification solutions. Meanwhile the relations of similar DOM elements is an important aspect [31].

Another web page content block identification direction in research papers is search for some specific content block in the web page [32]. In most of the cases it is based on the content block text analysis. However the full potential of the area is limited because of lack of high quality datasets, suitable for machine learning based models.

The existing datasets and methods are mostly oriented on web page segments, which usually identify segments, not content block. One segment can combine multiple content blocks into bigger, visually consistent segment. Despite the fact, the dataset has just segments, main content blocks, and no details of internal blocks, or code ranges of the blocks, the accuracy metrics are far from perfect. This illustrates the area is complex and requires different solutions to fully master the web page content segmentation and division into content blocks.

3. Block Identification Method for Block Range and Variation Estimation

3.1. Definition of Block Range and Variation

HTML code has a hierarchical structure, where one tag contains other tags that define smaller components of the parent tag. An example of a hierarchical relationship can be seen in Figure 1. Menu elements are blocks of information that can be visually identified on the website. They also have smaller components—menu items. Menu items are arranged according to the hierarchy of the menu element. Additionally, those menu items are siblings since they are presented in the same block and have the same structure.

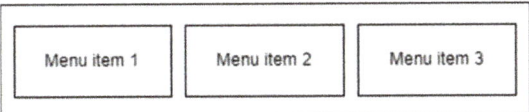

Figure 1. Example of block (menu) with three hierarchically related inner blocks (menu items).

With different tags and their combinations, the example menu case with multiple menu items can be realized. Figure 2 shows one of the examples. It demonstrates how the boundaries of the menu can be indicated by different tags (<header>, <div> or <nav>). All three possible boundaries visually produce the same block. In all cases, the user would treat it as a menu regardless of the possible boundaries of the menu. However, in some cases (machine learning, block structure matching, etc.) the usage of specific or all available tags can affect the desired result. To extend machine-oriented block segmentation properties, we define the range (maximum and minimum boundaries) of HTML blocks.

```
<header><!-- maximum boundary start for block B1 -->
    <div class="container">
        <section><!-- minimum boundary start for block B1 -->
            <div><!-- maximum/minimum boundary start for block B1.1 -->
                <img src="logo.jpg" alt="logo"/>
            </div><!-- maximum/minimum boundary end for block B1.1 -->
            <nav><!-- maximum boundary start for block B1.2 -->
                <ul><!-- minimum boundary start for block B1.2 -->
                    <li><a href="page1.html">Menu item 1</a></li><!-- B1.2.1 -->
                    <li><a href="page2.html">Menu item 2</a></li><!-- B1.2.2 -->
                    <li><a href="page3.html">Menu item 3</a></li><!-- B1.2.3 -->
                </ul><!-- minimum boundary end for block B1.2 -->
            <nav><!-- maximum boundary end for block B1.2 -->
        </section><!-- minimum boundary end for block B1 -->
    </div>
</header><!-- maximum boundary end for block B1 -->
```

Figure 2. HTML code example, illustrating the range between the maximum and minimum boundaries of the blocks.

The maximum boundary is the tag (element in the DOM tree), which defines the widest possible area, covering only the content of the block. In the DOM tree, it would be the highest element, containing only the content of the block and its child blocks, excluding siblings. Meanwhile, the minimum boundary is the tag, which will produce a child block with just partial content of the block, not the full content. If it were in the DOM tree, it would be the last element, before the child elements are visible.

In the example, presented in Figure 2, <section> tag contains both image and the navigation items, therefore it is a minimal bound of block B1. Consequently block B1.1 has matching maximum and minimum boundaries as going deeper than the div would produce the content itself (image) and going wider would include other sibling block content. The area between minimum and maximum boundaries of each block is the part, which has no content in it.

Block variations are defined as similar blocks belonging to the same parent block. In the case of menu items, as shown in Figure 2, the three menu items are variants of each other. Not all child tags are variants of one another (blocks B1.1 and B1.2 are not variants, just siblings as has completely different structure). Whether those siblings are variants or not depends on their structural similarity. The variant blocks must share the same parent block and internal structure, but not the content. In case of Figure 2 example, the path of tags for all B1.2 child elements is the same (<header>,<div>,<section>,<nav>,<ul>,<li>,<a>), while the path between B1.1 and B1.2 is different. The level of similarity can be adjusted based on the web page type or segmentation requirements.

3.2. General Idea of Web Page Division to Content Blocks with Extended Properties

Combining the above two features (block boundaries and variations) we can achieve additional flexibility in the identified content block data in both manual and automated labeling processes. This additional flexibility comes from the fact that by using these features we can reduce the total number of blocks per page by using relationship connections between them. That way when a user is manually marking blocks he or she only needs to label one variant of similar blocks, while the others will be picked up automatically. This would require less work than labeling the whole page.

Figure 3 shows an example of how block relationships make a difference. If we had no block relationships then this code snippet alone would have 8 distinct blocks that would need to be identified to fully process this code snippet (numbered in red circles). To extract only the content-filled blocks, without taking the boundaries into account, we would need to label fewer blocks; four would be sufficient—one for the menu (red dot no. 1) and three for its items (red dot no. 4, 6 and 8). But this can lead to results that are more difficult to verify even if they are correct. The difficulty arises from the fact that during validation only exactly labeled blocks would be deemed correct, so that approach requires a lot of precision. Through the use of block relationships, we can greatly reduce the number of distinct blocks. However, we are also able to maintain information about the complete structure that allows the extraction of all data. With relationships, we would technically have only 2 blocks (marked in blue circles—one for menu and one for menu item) while all other related blocks would be accessible either by hierarchical relation or by structure variations.

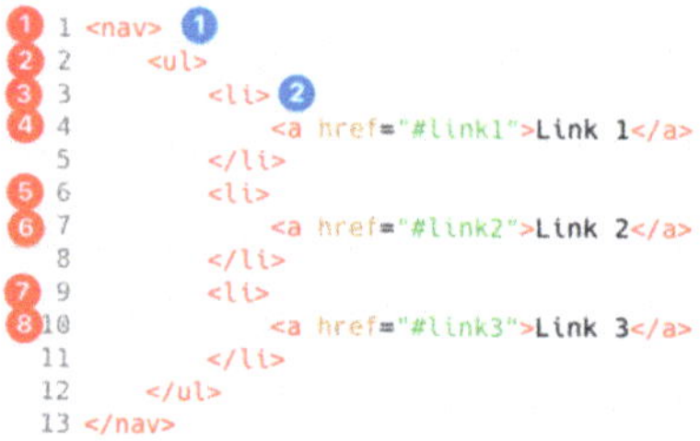

```
 1  <nav>
 2      <ul>
 3          <li>
 4              <a href="#link1">Link 1</a>
 5          </li>
 6          <li>
 7              <a href="#link2">Link 2</a>
 8          </li>
 9          <li>
10              <a href="#link3">Link 3</a>
11          </li>
12      </ul>
13  </nav>
```

Figure 3. HTML code example, illustrating the reduction of labeled blocks when instead of 8 blocks (marked with red dots), a person needs to assign labels to two (marked with blue dots) of them.

To implement web page division into blocks with extended properties, we analyze the DOM tree from top to bottom, starting with the <body> tag (see Algorithm 1). This tag would represent the most general block—web page content. The estimation of block boundaries will provide additional value, as the minimal boundary will define where the actual content and inner blocks start. At the same time, the relationship between child blocks will be able to estimate the repeating structures of variant blocks.

The web page division into blocks solution was implemented to match the dataset data structure provided in our earlier research [22]. It takes an URL address as input and stores all the identified blocks, and the relations between them, in the database. The methods responsible for block maximum and minimum boundary identification and variation estimation are presented in further sections.

Algorithm 1: segmentation

input: DOM tree of the rendered web page HTML code
set analyzed block to <body>
set analyzed parentBlock to <body>
if analyzed block is not empty **then**
    call boundaryEstimation with block and parentBlock **return** minBlock
    call getChildren with minBlock **return** children
    call getVariations with children
    for each children
        call segmentation with children
    end
end

3.3. Method for Block Range Estimation

Due to various design requirements blocks that store the same information, but have different visual representations can often use different HTML structures. Additional HTML elements may be required solely to achieve the required visual representation. As a result, it is crucial to detect the minimum and maximum boundaries of a content block.

As the HTML is analyzed from top to bottom, we can assume the block starts with the maximum block boundary. Deeper elements are analyzed to find the bare minimum. To achieve this we calculate content similarity while traversing the HTML tree. The maximum boundary of Figure 2 starts at line 1 and ends in the last line. The whole code represents the maximum boundary.

The minimum boundary of this block is defined by the <section> element. Comparing the content of these 2 boundaries, we would get the same content that the user sees in both cases. Only the actual data that the user would see, ignoring any other elements, carrying no information, is used for block content similarity estimation.

There are times when small blocks of content can be added to create a visual effect without impacting the content. The symbols can be applied to separate elements (at the beginning or the end of a menu, etc.). A similar problem is addressed by F. Fauzi et al. [33] only meaningful images are extracted, ignoring non-relevant images. We used the Hamming normalized distance [34] to measure the similarity between the content of the blocks to account for noise in the content. The content was extracted by stripping HTML blocks and leaving only clean text for comparison. The threshold value was set at 0.1, by analyzing existing tendencies in web pages. Any comparison of parent and child tags that produces a value below 0.1 means that we still haven't found the minimum boundary. As soon as we get a comparison value of 0.1 or above we know that the minimum boundary was reached during the previous iteration. All blocks between the maximum and minimum boundaries (including the boundary blocks) are saved in the dataset as blocks' length boundaries.

One of the disadvantages of this approach is that it does not cover blocks that have no text content. Such situations can occur when self-closing HTML tags are used. One of the most common self-closing tags is <img> (see Figure 4). Its data are all stored in attributes, thus the content of such a block is empty after HTML tags are removed from the text. Another situation where this issue can arise is when content is added via CSS rules. To represent links to the corresponding website, social media icons (logos of social media networks) are commonly used. In such cases, it is often an icon being applied to an HTML tag via CSS rather than via HTML. This would again result in no content in the HTML tag. But these are edge cases that deal mostly with visual information.

```
1  <section><!-- maximum boundary start -->
2      <div>
3          <div><!-- minimum boundary start -->
4              <div><!-- minimum boundary start if image is ignored -->
5                  <h1>Heading</h1>
6                  <p>Paragraph</p>
7                  <a href="url"><i class="fa fa-play"></i> Link text</a>
8              </div><!-- minimum boundary end if image is ignored -->
9
10             <img src="image" alt="">
11         </div><!-- minimum boundary end -->
12     </div>
13 </section><!-- maximum boundary end -->
```

Figure 4. HTML code example, illustrating the range between maximum and minimum boundaries when empty content elements are included.

To capture such blocks correctly, we added additional checks to the algorithm. First, we check whether the parent block contains any content. If there's no content and the analyzed block is the only child block, then we can safely assume that the child block can be added as the block length boundary.

When analyzing blocks that have content we should still check for images to make sure that the correct block boundaries are determined. To do this we count the occurrences of image tags within parent and child blocks. This is only conducted when the textual content of parent and child blocks is the same and there is more than one child block present. In the simplified HTML code example in Figure 3, we present a case when an incorrect block length variation can be captured. This is because image-like blocks are not accounted for. If the image tag is ignored in this example, then the minimum content block boundary would be incorrectly determined and increased by 1 level, compared to the correct detection.

The schema of HTM block boundary range estimation is presented in Algorithm 2. It takes into account content similarity and the existence of <img> tags. For each candidate to the minimal boundary, the method will be called recursively, and for each child block accordingly, while traversing all DOM trees from top to bottom.

Algorithm 2: boundaryEstimation

    input: block for analysis and its parent block
    set minBoundary to block
    set maxBoundary to block
    set distance to 0
    repeat
      call getChildren with block **return** children
      if parentBlock clean text is empty **then**
        if number of children <= 1 **then**
          set distance to 0
        else
          set distance to 1
        end
      else
        if parentBlock clean text = block clean text and number of children >1 **then**
          call getImageCount with parentBlock **return** parentImages
          call getImageCount with block **return** blockImages
          if parentImages = blockImages **then**
            set distance to 0
          else
            set distance to 1
          end
        else
          call hammingDist with block text and parentBlock text **return** distance
        end
      end
      set block to first children
      set minBoundary to first children
    until distance >= 0.1
    store block data with minBoundaries and maxBoundaries
    store block data with children relations
    retrun minBoundary

3.4. Method for Block Variation Estimation

Block type variation means that we're identifying blocks of the same purpose but with different content. This would allow us to identify clusters of blocks of the same type. Clusters in this case are defined by a common parent block. To achieve this we traverse the HTML tree and look for adjacent HTML blocks that have a similar HTML structure. Structure similarity is evaluated with the help of the HTML path similarity estimation algorithm. When traversing the HTML tree, we are looking for blocks that have multiple child blocks. Blocks with a single child block are ignored. After encountering multiple child blocks we compare them to see whether their structure is similar. At this step we look at the structure, no content is evaluated. Structural similarity is calculated using the Sequence Matcher method [35]. We employed a slightly modified version of the algorithm with the autojunk heuristic disabled since we passed preprocessed HTML structure for analysis.

The basic schema is presented in Algorithm 3. Its principle is to compare each block with its sibling, whether they are similar or not. Experiments with different situations and their similarity estimation were conducted to measure the threshold value for similarity. The situations for experiments were selected independently from the further used web pages. We have found that a sequence matcher similarity of more than 0.92 is enough to determine whether two sibling blocks are variants of each other. Experiments with XML schema similarity [36] indicate the best results can be achieved with weight of 0.8–0.9. HTML tags are more general, therefore we increased the threshold value to 0.92. It allows interconnections and estimation of block clusters. Therefore in transformations, by applying the transformation to one of the blocks, links to other blocks exist and can be used to transform the variations of the block as well.

Algorithm 3: getVariations

    input: blocks for analysis
    for each block in blocks
      call getSiblings with block **return** siblings
      for each sibling in siblings
        call structuralSimilarity with block and sibling **return** similarity
        if similarity > 0.92
          store variation between block and sibling
        end
      end
    end

3.5. Novelty of the Proposed Methods

The main novelty of the paper is expressed in multiple perspectives:

- A more detailed extraction of data from content blocks is the focus of the proposed method. It not only identifies content blocks but also defines variation bounds. Such data can be used for more accurate comparisons between web page blocks.
- Methods are proposed to divide web page into content blocks. Using this approach can simplify the manual work of web page data labeling. Therefore the identified content blocks are additionally grouped to reduce the number of blocks to label. In addition, the proposed architecture allows traceability of all blocks, so labels of one element of the group can be associated with the rest of the group.
- Unique in the sense that it integrates web page block text and structure similarity. Close to Hamming distance for text similarity estimation, both parent and child relations are taken into account to identify group bounds.

In comparison to Andrew Judith et al. solution [37], our method defines as many content blocks as there are on the page, not limiting the number of blocks. In comparison to other segment number not fixed solutions [38], this method is faster, as it does not require two stages (to identify the number of clusters and then to divide the web page into this number of blocks) and extracts all possible content blocks from the web page. The blocks are not limited to text containing structured blocks only [39] and extract all, not only structured blocks [40].

4. Results of Web Page Division to Content Blocks

4.1. Data for Web Page Division to Content Blocks Validation

The validation of the proposed methods is complicated as all existing datasets are dedicated for web page segmentation and do not have extended information about block boundaries and block variations [41]. Furthermore, most of the data sources used in existing research papers are not available for repeating experiments. Nevertheless, the purpose of the methods is different, therefore, an accurate comparison would be difficult to implement. Due to the above, for the purpose of validation of the proposed solutions, a series of experiments were executed to gather the dataset.

For the experimentation, 10 existing web pages were used. Additionally, three web pages (https://1.kiril.dev/, https://5.kiril.dev/, https://6.kiril.dev/, all accessed on 27 April 2023) were prepared to reflect typical one-page websites with different content blocks. The web pages were randomly chosen from one-page website designs and stored in the selected repository to ensure they would not be modified in the future. As they were designed by web designers using the Bootstrap framework, each of them includes both the main structure of the web page and a creative approach. All the web pages were manually revised by labeling as many as possible unique content blocks.

The one-page websites or one web page of the site were chosen to illustrate a wide variety of blocks on one page. A fragment of one of the web pages and its manual block identification example is presented in Figure 5. The red border defines first-level blocks. Its internal blocks are marked in purple, while its inner blocks are presented with green borders. The example lists all content blocks and their hierarchy can be traced, while sibling block estimate (in the case of menu items, contact components or contact form fields) might reduce the need for manual segmentation actions.

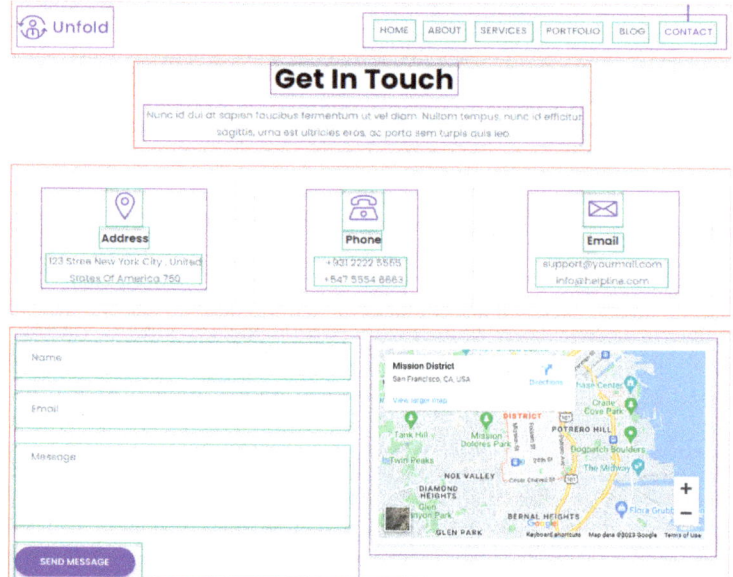

Figure 5. A visual view of a web page fragment with identified blocks and their hierarchy.

To label data more accurately (not only labels, but block coordinates, and block selectors are critical), a web system was created. Web page labeling participants were asked to name all content blocks they saw, including different granularity blocks. However, they were allowed to identify just one block of equivalent blocks with different content (for example, one menu item instead of all menu items one by one within the same menu). All labeled data were stored in the database for further comparison with automatically identified web page content blocks. In this study, the label of the block was not required. However, this information is stored in the same database so that it can be used in future research.

During the manual web page labeling, in total, 40,492 tags existed and 16,453 if YouTube is excluded (WYT) (see Table 2). We will further provide two values for most of the metrics, due to YouTube using a lot of proprietary tags, meaning that in some cases, statistics can be greatly affected. In any case, this amount of labeling data are too big for regular users, while expert labeling for a large number of websites might be too expensive.

Table 2. Summary of manually labeled data.

No.	Web Page	No. of Tags	Labeled Blocks	Percentage of Labeled Tags
1	https://1.kiril.dev/, accessed on 27 April 2023	521	89	17%
2	https://5.kiril.dev/, accessed on 27 April 2023	531	84	16%
3	https://6.kiril.dev/, accessed on 27 April 2023	393	64	16%
4	https://www.youtube.com/, accessed on 27 April 2023	24039	75	0%
5	https://addons.mozilla.org/en-US/firefox/, accessed on 27 April 2023	981	61	6%
6	https://www.apple.com/, accessed on 27 April 2023	1087	69	6%
7	https://www.apple.com/retail/business/, accessed on 27 April 2023	826	74	9%
8	https://www.buzzfeednews.com/, accessed on 27 April 2023	1523	98	6%
9	https://gridbyexample.com/, accessed on 27 April 2023	111	17	15%
10	https://www.nytimes.com/, accessed on 27 April 2023	2474	203	8%
11	https://slack.com/, accessed on 27 April 2023	768	87	11%
12	https://stripe.com/en-gb-lt/connect, accessed on 27 April 2023	4990	144	3%
13	https://www.telegraph.co.uk/news/, accessed on 27 April 2023	2248	114	5%
	In total	40,492	1179	3%
	In total without YouTube (WYT)	16,453	1104	7%

The labeling was conducted by persons with a basic knowledge of HTML and no experience in data labeling. They labeled 1179 (1104 WYT) blocks in total across all websites. This is just 2.9% (6.7% WYT) of the total number of HTML blocks on the surveyed web pages. Labeled data percentages across all web page tags illustrate the ratio between unique labels and tags needed to achieve a one-page website. Meanwhile, if accurate machine learning web page labeling solutions have to be created, these require a detailed dataset which would reflect all tag paths. This is an increase of labeling effort by almost 35 times or almost 15 times if we exclude YouTube data. Therefore, the labels should be duplicated or linked for different tag path variations to obtain a more accurate dataset.

4.2. Results of Web Page Division to Content Blocks Test Cases

The same web pages were divided into content blocks with the proposed methods. The summary of identified web page content blocks is presented in Table 3. It illustrates that the total number of content tags has been reduced by 80% (71% WYT).

Table 3. Summary of data for automated web page division to content blocks.

Web Page No.	No. of Web Page Tags	No. of Potential Content Blocks	Filtered Content Blocks	Reduced Content Blocks	Boundary Range		No. of Blocks with Siblings	Siblings	
					Single Length	Max–Min Range		Main Sibling	Related Sibling
1	521	502	469	238	166	72	114	42	72
2	531	518	494	192	88	104	91	24	67
3	393	379	305	136	87	49	72	23	49
4	24,039	23,983	5743	3458	1772	2816	621	226	395
5	981	899	511	256	136	242	128	48	80
6	1087	919	718	281	216	239	218	59	159
7	826	763	612	285	185	262	148	42	106
8	1523	1433	975	472	264	444	144	32	112
9	111	87	82	45	38	27	21	4	17
10	2474	2410	2174	778	425	797	661	188	473
11	768	702	364	168	116	137	111	29	82
12	4990	4375	2866	1346	888	1091	909	251	658
13	2248	2125	1344	436	184	557	223	55	168
In total	40,492	39,095	16,657	8091	4565	6837	3461	1023	2438
WYT	16,453	15,112	10,914	4633	2793	4021	2840	797	2043

The reduction of content blocks was achieved in several steps. We know that some tags have nothing to do with content (head tag with its contents, scripts, styles, etc.). Some of these tags (<base/>, <link/>, <meta/>, <style>) are easy to exclude, by selecting only the content of the body tag. This way, we reduce the total amount of tags from 40,492 to 39,095 (16,453 to 15,112 WYT). This amounts to a 3.5% (8% WYT) reduction. The body content should also be filtered since it usually contains tags that add value to the content. However, they do not store content themselves. For example, script tags are often included in the body tag. By filtering body content for tags that are not used to display content, we reduce the number of content tags from 39,095 to 16,657 (15,112 to 10,914 WYT). This equates to a 57% (28% WYT) reduction. In total, the reduction amounts to 59% (27% WYT) compared to the starting value of 40,492 (16,453 WYT) tags.

A more advanced reduction cannot be conducted without those simple tag reductions. Detecting content block boundaries rather than all instances of possible content tags allows us to further reduce content blocks to the mentioned 80% (71% WYT) reduction. From the filtered 16,657 (10,914 WYT) blocks, only 8091 (4633 WYT) were left by applying the proposed web page division to content blocks method. The reduction was achieved by identifying variants of different block boundaries and by leaving just one of the multiple identified sibling segments.

By grouping content block boundaries and identifying sibling variants of the block, filtered content blocks were reduced. The analysis of these two methods shows that about 51% (58% WYT) of the tags can be classified into boundary ranges. The boundary block typically groups 5 (3 WYT) tags into one block with min–max boundaries for the block.

Another form of content block reduction is the identification of relevant blocks and counting the path of one content block rather than all of them. In the analyzed web pages 3461 (2840 WYT) blocks had a sibling block. In the reduced set of content blocks, 1023 (797 WYT) were selected to represent sibling blocks, while 2438 (2043 WYT) were linked to them but eliminated. According to this, sibling blocks have, on average, three instances, but only one-third of them can be stored to represent the block pattern.

4.3. Results of Web Page Division to Content Blocks Comparison to Manual Labeling

The web page division to content blocks for manual and automated labeling were stored identically (except the label was not set in automated segmentation) in the same database structure but in different instances of it. Due to the database structure matching, a comparison of manual and automated division is possible. On the other hand, it is not a straightforward process, as in manual labeling, the user could identify some tags and content blocks but not others. The grouping of tags into maximum and minimum boundary blocks was not requested either. Therefore, additional methods were prepared to match a manually labeled tag to an automated division to content block with an estimation of whether the manually labeled tag fits within the content block boundaries (minimum bounds <= labeled tag <= maximum bounds). By using this method, we can estimate the match between labels, even in cases where the boundaries are labeled similarly but not identically. Another method estimates whether a labeled tag corresponds to another content block based on its structure. The feature gathers data about sibling blocks, which were ignored for simplicity, however, correspond to some of the already identified blocks but with different content.

This matching between automated web page division to content blocks and manual labeling enabled us to estimate whether our solution was able to identify all content blocks labeled by humans. In total, 1179 content blocks were labeled by human experts (1104 WYT). The dependency of a number of tags in the web page and our method of identified blocks are presented in Figure 6 which indicates the linear dependency.

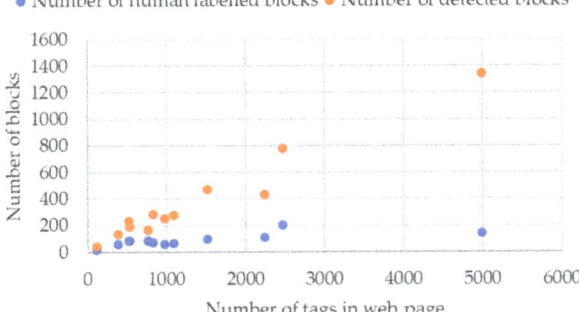

Figure 6. Dependency between human-labeled number of blocks and tags in the appropriate web page.

The labeled blocks were mapped to the identified by using our proposed content block identification method. For further performance analysis, the standard classification metrics were used. The true positive (TP) was assumed for the number of blocks, indicated by our method and matching the dataset-defined segments or user-labeled blocks. False positive (FP) were the other blocks our method detected, but which were not labeled in the dataset. False negative (FN) was for a number of blocks which were labeled in the dataset but were missing in our output, while the true negative (TN) was calculated by subtracting TP, FP, and FN from the total number of tags in the web page. The summary of the metrics is presented in Table 4.

Table 4. Summary of proposed method accuracy metrics comparing reduced content blocks.

Web Page No.	Number of Blocks	Number of True Positive	True Negative	False Positive	False Negative	Precision	Recall	Accuracy	F-Score
1	238	89	0	149	0	37%	100%	71%	54%
2	192	84	0	108	0	44%	100%	80%	61%
3	136	64	0	72	0	47%	100%	82%	64%
4	3458	75	0	3383	0	2%	100%	86%	4%
5	256	61	0	195	0	24%	100%	80%	38%
6	281	69	0	212	0	25%	100%	80%	39%
7	285	74	0	211	0	26%	100%	74%	41%
8	472	98	0	374	0	21%	100%	75%	34%
9	45	17	0	28	0	38%	100%	75%	55%
10	778	203	0	575	0	26%	100%	77%	41%
11	168	87	0	81	0	52%	100%	89%	68%
12	1346	144	0	1202	0	11%	100%	76%	19%
13	436	114	0	322	0	26%	100%	86%	41%
Overall	8091	1179	0	6912	0	15%	100%	83%	25%
WYT	4633	1104	0	3529	0	24%	100%	79%	38%

The results indicate that the proposed web page division to content blocks solution can identify all content blocks that would be manually labeled. At the same time, it identifies additional content blocks that were ignored during manual labeling. The main reason for ignoring some blocks during manual labeling is their repetitive nature. This repetitiveness can be observed in a couple of ways. First, when a block can have various boundaries while presenting the same content, we use the block's max–min boundary detection to negate the need to label all of the possible combinations of the same block. Another situation with repetitive blocks arises when there are multiple content blocks for the same purpose but with different content. The most basic example of this is the navigation menu. Each menu element has the same structure as all the other elements of the same menu, so users tend to mark only one menu element. We use structural sibling relationships between blocks to detect other menu elements. This allows us to detect all menu items regardless of which menu element was labeled by the user. Sometimes, these two cases of repetitiveness can happen at the same time; for example, menu items can also have multiple boundaries within the max–min range, so both techniques can be used at the same time to determine all other possible labeled block variations.

The obtained results of automated web page division to content blocks comparison to manual labeling results indicate that the solution can identify all manually labeled blocks (directly or indirectly, by using related sibling records). This leads to 100% precision. Currently, the increase in testing data is problematic. This is because the existing datasets of web page segmentation or labeling are not fully adapted to the extended model of web page labeling.

Talking about the accuracy of the proposed method, it could be expressed as 83% (79% WYT) taking into account how many blocks were labeled by person and were present in the dataset of automatically detected blocks, eliminating relevant siblings. These conditions correspond to the ones that were presented for manual labeling—labeling all components for the same purpose. Under the same conditions, the F-score would be 25% (38% WYT).

4.4. Proposed Method Comparison with Existing Segmentation Methods

To compare the proposed method with other existing web page division to content blocks is complicated as there are no exact analogues. However, web page segmentation solutions are very similar by their nature. Those methods are mostly validated by using a commonly used dataset [23]. The labeling of the dataset is not as broad as the proposed method aims to provide. It reflects both in the number of blocks (the average number of blocks in the dataset is 13, while our previously tested web pages had an average of 79 blocks) and details about each block (the dataset has specific block boundaries, while our solutions and previously used web page analysis data has minimum and maximum ranges for each block, as well as relations between siblings, similar blocks). While this dataset has a much higher number of records, web pages usually estimate the method's performance by using this dataset.

This dataset was selected as some existing web page segmentation methods already used it, therefore, there are accuracy metrics for those methods (see Table 1 in Section 2). The precision, recall, accuracy, and F-score were calculated for each record in the dataset, and average values were calculated to summarize the results. With this dataset, our proposed method achieved 11% precision, 100% recall, and 77% accuracy, and the F-score was 19%. The results indicate that our proposed method is not precise (11%), and the F-score (19%) is the lowest among other methods. However, it is related to the fact that the dataset contains just a small portion of labeled blocks and segments, while our solutions aim to find all possible content blocks. Moreover, the numbers are not directly comparable as the other research papers were estimating the accuracy of used segments, not content blocks. However, even taking into account our method of grouping sibling elements into groups, it shows a high accuracy (77%) similar to the web page segmentation methods, while the recall stays constant (100%) because no blocks are removed from the web page, just assigned to one or another block variation or group.

5. Discussion

In the proposed solution, DOM tree and web page similarity estimation are used instead of a visual comparison of the web page. This simplifies its application as no complex models for data clustering are needed.

While our web page division to content blocks method results cannot be compared directly with other research results (because of different purpose, data, and dataset labeling details), they are similar to those obtained by other web page labeling or segmentation methods [12]. As the results can differ depending on the dataset and labeling, the proposed method was compared to a dataset [23] and methods used to segment the same dataset. According to the obtained results, we obtain lower results, but that is due in part to the fact that the dataset had a very limited number of labels, and is adapted to present segments, not all content blocks.

The precision value is among the lowest in comparison to existing research and experiment results. This is affected by the limited number of labeled blocks in the dataset as well, as only the main blocks are included in the dataset but not all small elements were labeled internally. Recall is the other side of it. Our methods achieve 100% recall and outperform any other method. This is because we do not eliminate any of the blocks but group them into variations or sibling groups.

Summarizing the results and limitations of the method, its high potential could be exploited for assistance in manual web page labeling. The method could extract all possible content blocks from the web page and present them to the individual executing the labeling. This would reduce the need for tag/block revision by 90% (70% not taking into account the YouTube case). At the same time, the labeling data will be richer in the sense of relations between blocks. This could be exploited even for more interactive labeling when label assignment to one block automatically generates proposals for the labels of other related blocks.

As more detailed datasets of the extended labeling data become available, the method could be improved to identify or propose the label for the block. This would lead to a full understanding of the web page structure, therefore, the automated integration and transformation of web page content would be possible.

Author Contributions: Conceptualization, K.G. and S.R.; methodology, S.R.; software, K.G.; validation, K.G.; formal analysis, S.R.; investigation, K.G.; resources, K.G.; data curation, K.G.; writing—original draft preparation, K.G.; writing—review and editing, S.R.; visualization, K.G.; supervision, S.R. All authors have read and agreed to the published version of the manuscript.

Funding: This research received no external funding.

Institutional Review Board Statement: Not applicable.

Informed Consent Statement: Not applicable.

Data Availability Statement: The data can be requested from the corresponding author.

Conflicts of Interest: The authors declare no conflict of interest.

References

1. Xie, W.; Zheng, W.; Tang, P.; Ting, Y. Design and Implementation of Web Information Extraction System Based on Crawler. In Proceedings of the 2nd International Conference on Electronic Materials and Information Engineering (EMIE 2022), Hangzhou, China, 15–17 April 2022.
2. Anami, B.S.; Wadawadagi, R.S.; Pagi, V.B. Machine learning techniques in Web content mining: A comparative analysis. *J. Inf. Knowl. Manag.* **2014**, *13*, 10450005. [CrossRef]
3. Cheng, S.C.; Lu, C.A. Retrieving Articles and Image Labeling Based on Relevance of Keywords. In Proceedings of the 2019 International Conference on Machine Learning and Cybernetics (ICMLC), Kobe, Japan, 7–10 July 2019.
4. Hashemi, M. Web page classification: A survey of perspectives, gaps, and future directions. *Multimed. Tools Appl.* **2020**, *79*, 11921–11945. [CrossRef]
5. Abbasi, B.U.D.; Fatima, I.; Mukhtar, H.; Khan, S.; Alhumam, A.; Ahmad, H.F. Autonomous schema markups based on intelligent computing for search engine optimization. *PeerJ Comput. Sci.* **2022**, *8*, e1163. [CrossRef]
6. Escalona, Y.E. Algorithms for Table Structure Recognition. *Ingenius. Rev. Cienc. Tecnol.* **2021**, *25*, 50–61.
7. Dias, S.; Gadge, J. Identifying informative web content blocks using web page segmentation. *Entropy* **2014**, *7*, 37–41. [CrossRef]
8. Win, C.S.; Thwin, M.M.S. Web page segmentation and informative content extraction for effective information retrieval. *Int. J. Comput. Commun. Eng. Res.* **2014**, *2*, 35–45.
9. Cormier, M.; Moffatt, K.; Cohen, R.; Mann, R. Purely vision-based segmentation of web pages for assistive technology. *Comput. Vis. Image Underst.* **2016**, *148*, 46–66. [CrossRef]
10. Zeleny, J.; Burget, R.; Zendulka, J. Box clustering segmentation: A new method for vision-based web page preprocessing. *Inf. Process. Manag.* **2017**, *53*, 735–750. [CrossRef]
11. Sanoja, A.; Gançarski, S. Web page segmentation evaluation. In Proceedings of the 30th Annual ACM Symposium on Applied Computing, Salamanca, Spain, 13–17 April 2015.
12. Kiesel, J.; Meyer, L.; Kneist, F.; Stein, B.; Potthast, M. An empirical comparison of web page segmentation algorithms. In Proceedings of the European Conference on Information Retrieval, Lucca, Italy, 28 March–1 April 2021.
13. Shu, Z.; Li, X. Automatic Extraction of Web Page Text Information Based on Network Topology Coincidence Degree. *Wirel. Commun. Mob. Comput.* **2022**, *2022*, 9220661. [CrossRef]

14. Sun, G.; Zhang, Z.; Cheng, Y.; Chai, T. Adaptive segmented webpage text based malicious website detection. *Comput. Netw.* **2022**, *216*, 109236. [CrossRef]
15. Ghaemmaghami, S.S.S.; Miller, J. Integrated-Block: A New Combination Model to Improve Web Page Segmentation. *J. Web Eng.* **2022**, *21*, 1103–1144. [CrossRef]
16. Kohlschütter, C.; Nejdl, W. A densitometric approach to web page segmentation. In Proceedings of the 17th ACM Conference on Information and Knowledge Management, Napa Valley, CA, USA, 26 October 2008.
17. Xiang, P.; Yang, X.; Shi, Y. Web page segmentation based on gestalt theory. In Proceedings of the 2007 IEEE International Conference on Multimedia and Expo, Beijin, China, 2–5 July 2007.
18. Alcic, S.; Conrad, S. Page segmentation by web content clustering. In Proceedings of the International Conference on Web Intelligence, Mining and Semantics, Sogndal, Norway, 25–27 May 2011.
19. Wu, Y.C. Language independent web news extraction system based on text detection framework. *Inf. Sci.* **2016**, *342*, 132–149 [CrossRef]
20. Sanoja, A.; Gançarski, S. Migrating web archives from html4 to html5: A block-based approach and its evaluation. In Proceedings of the European Conference on Advances in Databases and Information Systems, Nicosia, Cyprus, 24–27 September 2017.
21. Manugunta, R.K.; Maskeliūnas, R.; Damaševičius, R. Deep Learning Based Semantic Image Segmentation Methods for Classification of Web Page Imagery. *Future Internet* **2022**, *14*, 277. [CrossRef]
22. Griazev, K.; Ramanauskaitė, S. Multi-Purpose Dataset of Webpages and Its Content Blocks: Design and Structure Validation *Appl. Sci.* **2021**, *11*, 3319. [CrossRef]
23. Dataset-Popular 2014. A Dataset of Popular Pages (Taken from dir.yahoo.com) with Manually Marked up Semantic Blocks Available online: https://github.com/rkrzr/dataset-popular (accessed on 28 March 2023).
24. Sanoja, A.; Gançarski, S. Block-o-matic: A web page segmentation framework. In Proceedings of the 2014 International Conference on Multimedia Computing and Systems (ICMCS), Marrakesh, Morocco, 12–14 April 2014.
25. Cai, D.; Yu, S.; Wen, J.-R.; Ma, W.-Y. Vips: A Vision-Based Page Segmentation Algorithm. Microsoft Technical Report, MSR-TR-2003-79. Available online: https://www.microsoft.com/en-us/research/wp-content/uploads/2016/02/tr-2003-79.pdf (accessed on 28 March 2023).
26. Xu, Z.; Miller, J. Identifying semantic blocks in Web pages using Gestalt laws of grouping. *World Wide Web* **2016**, *19*, 957–978 [CrossRef]
27. Jiang, Z.; Yin, H.; Wu, Y.; Lyu, Y.; Min, G.; Zhang, X. Constructing Novel Block Layouts for Webpage Analysis. *ACM Trans. Internet Technol.* **2019**, *19*, 1–18. [CrossRef]
28. Ghaemmaghami, S.S.S.; Miller, J. A New Semantic Approach to Improve Webpage Segmentation. *J. Web Eng.* **2021**, *20*, 963–992 [CrossRef]
29. Debnath, S.; Mitra, P.; Giles, C.L. Identifying content blocks from web documents. In Proceedings of the Foundations of Intelligent Systems: 15th International Symposium, ISMIS 2005, Saratoga Springs, NY, USA, 25–28 May 2005; Springer: Berlin/Heidelberg, Germany, 2005; pp. 285–293.
30. Li, Y.; Yang, J. A novel method to extract informative blocks from web pages. In Proceedings of the 2009 International Joint Conference on Artificial Intelligence, Hainan, China, 25–26 April 2009; IEEE: New York, NY, USA; pp. 536–539.
31. Grigera, J.; Gardey, J.C.; Rossi, G.; Garrido, A. Flexible Detection of Similar DOM Elements. In *Proceedings of the Web Information Systems and Technologies: 16th International Conference, WEBIST 2020, Virtual Events, 3–5 November 2020, and 17th International Conference, WEBIST 2021, 26–28 October 2021, Virtual Events*; Revised Selected Papers; Springer International Publishing: Cham, Switzerland; pp. 174–195.
32. Martinez-Rodriguez, J.L.; Hogan, A.; Lopez-Arevalo, I. Information extraction meets the semantic web: A survey. *Semant. Web* **2020**, *11*, 255–335. [CrossRef]
33. Fauzi, F.; Hong, J.L.; Belkhatir, M. Webpage segmentation for extracting images and their surrounding contextual information. In Proceedings of the 17th ACM International Conference on Multimedia, Beijing, China, 19–25 October 2009.
34. Bookstein, A.; Kulyukin, V.A.; Raita, T. Generalized hamming distance. *Inf. Retr.* **2002**, *5*, 353–375. [CrossRef]
35. Kiesel, J.; Kneist, F.; Meyer, L.; Komlossy, K.; Stein, B.; Potthast, M. Web page segmentation revisited: Evaluation framework and dataset. In Proceedings of the 29th ACM International Conference on Information & Knowledge Management, Online, 19–23 October 2020.
36. Algergawy, A.; Nayak, R.; Saake, G. Element similarity measures in XML schema matching. *Inf. Sci.* **2010**, *180*, 4975–4998. [CrossRef]
37. Andrew, J.J.; Ferrari, S.; Maurel, F.; Dias, G.; Giguet, E. Web page segmentation for non visual skimming. In Proceedings of the 33rd Pacific Asia Conference on Language, Information and Computation (PACLIC 33), Hakodate, Japan, 13–15 September 2019.
38. Jayashree, S.R.; Dias, G.; Andrew, J.J.; Saha, S.; Maurel, F.; Ferrari, S. Multimodal Web Page Segmentation Using Self-organized Multi-objective Clustering. *ACM Trans. Inf. Syst.* **2022**, *40*, 1–49. [CrossRef]
39. Manickam, Y.; Rajalakshmi, S.U. Extraction of Information from Web Page Using Content Mining Approach. *Int. J. Sci. Res. Eng. Technol.* **2022**, *2*, 19–22.

70. Amarnadh, S.; Reddy, P.P.; Murthy, N.V.E.S. FreeHand Sketch-based Authenticated Security System using Sequence Matcher. *Int. J. Adv. Sci. Technol.* **2019**, *29*, 6663–6679.
71. Wang, Q.; Fang, Y.; Ravula, A.; Feng, F.; Quan, X.; Liu, D. Webformer: The web-page transformer for structure information extraction. In Proceedings of the ACM Web Conference 2022, Lyon, France, 25–29 April 2022.

Disclaimer/Publisher's Note: The statements, opinions and data contained in all publications are solely those of the individual author(s) and contributor(s) and not of MDPI and/or the editor(s). MDPI and/or the editor(s) disclaim responsibility for any injury to people or property resulting from any ideas, methods, instructions or products referred to in the content.

Article

WSREB Mechanism: Web Search Results Exploration Mechanism for Blind Users

Snober Naseer [1], Umer Rashid [1], Maha Saddal [1], Abdur Rehman Khan [2], Qaisar Abbas [3,*] and Yassine Daadaa [3]

[1] Department of Computer Sciences, Quaid-i-Azam University, Islamabad 45320, Pakistan; snober@cs.qau.edu.pk (S.N.); umerrashid@qau.edu.pk (U.R.); m.saddal@cs.qau.edu.pk (M.S.)
[2] Department of Computer Science, National University of Modern Languages, Lahore 54000, Pakistan
[3] College of Computer and Information Sciences, Imam Mohammad Ibn Saud Islamic University (IMSIU), Riyadh 11432, Saudi Arabia; ymdaadaa@imamu.edu.sa
* Correspondence: qaabbas@imamu.edu.sa

Citation: Naseer, S.; Rashid, U.; Saddal, M.; Khan, A.R.; Abbas, Q.; Daadaa, Y. WSREB Mechanism: Web Search Results Exploration Mechanism for Blind Users. *Appl. Sci.* **2023**, *13*, 11007. https://doi.org/10.3390/app131911007

Academic Editors: Christos Bouras, Jing Zhang, Cangqi Zhou and Jipeng Qiang

Received: 30 August 2023
Revised: 29 September 2023
Accepted: 4 October 2023
Published: 6 October 2023

Copyright: © 2023 by the authors. Licensee MDPI, Basel, Switzerland. This article is an open access article distributed under the terms and conditions of the Creative Commons Attribution (CC BY) license (https://creativecommons.org/licenses/by/4.0/).

Abstract: In the contemporary digital landscape, web search functions as a pivotal conduit for information dissemination. Nevertheless, blind users (BUs) encounter substantial barriers in leveraging online services, attributable to intrinsic deficiencies in the information structure presented by online platforms. A critical analysis reveals that a considerable segment of BUs perceive online service access as either challenging or unfeasible, with only a fraction of search endeavors culminating successfully. This predicament stems largely from the linear nature of information interaction necessitated for BUs, a process that mandates sequential content relevancy assessment, consequently imposing cognitive strain and fostering information disorientation. Moreover, the prevailing evaluative metrics for web service efficacy—precision and recall—exhibit a glaring oversight of the nuanced behavioral and usability facets pertinent to BUs during search engine design. Addressing this, our study introduces an innovative framework to facilitate information exploration, grounded in the cognitive principles governing BUs. This framework, piloted using the Wikipedia dataset, seeks to revolutionize the search result space through categorical organization, thereby enhancing accessibility for BUs. Empirical and usability assessments, conducted on a cohort of legally blind individuals (N = 25), underscore the framework's potential, demonstrating notable improvements in web content accessibility and system usability, with categorical accuracy standing at 84% and a usability quotient of 72.5%. This research thus holds significant promise for redefining web search paradigms to foster inclusivity and optimized user experiences for BUs.

Keywords: blind users; web search; information exploration; usability analysis

1. Introduction

In the contemporary digital age, web search engines have established themselves as critical access points for online information, processing approximately 3.5 billion queries daily, a significant portion of which are centered on exploratory information seeking [1,2]. These exploratory sessions are characterized by users engaging with the search engines with complex, divergent queries aimed at broad-based learning about intricate topics [3]. This interaction typically entails users inputting keyword-based queries and consulting a series of document snippets presented in a linear list by the search engine, ranked according to their relevance to the query [4,5].

This linear interaction paradigm has not been exempted from scholarly criticism, chiefly due to its convergence tendency and a lack of alignment with the needs for diverse content exploration. The central issue lies in the fact that the search results are indexed and optimized based on offline evaluative metrics like precision and recall, which, while gauging relevance, fail to encapsulate subjective user satisfaction, particularly for blind users (BUs) [6,7]. Consequently, recent scholarly endeavors are channeling efforts towards the development of intuitive search engines and evaluative metrics that integrate human-centric considerations [8].

Notwithstanding, the prevailing web search interfaces predominantly cater to the sighted user population, manifesting information in a linear and visually centered fashion [5]. This approach significantly hampers the approximately 75 million BUs globally from accessing and deciphering web content efficiently [7]. The linear representation necessitates BUs to engage in sequential information retrieval, prompting them to devise alternative strategies to navigate accessibility and usability barriers, including utilizing CTRL+F for manual content location, employing screen reader functionalities, or leveraging meta-information to anticipate content [9].

Therefore, it becomes imperative to acknowledge that while existing web search engines are adept at sourcing relevant web-based information, they inadvertently engender accessibility and usability impediments for BUs. The conventional display of the top-ten blue links often results in cognitive overload for BUs. In order to solve this problem, the goal of our research is to come up with a new way for BUs to look for information that takes cognition into account and allows search results to be shown in a better, more organized way. To scrutinize the efficacy of this proposed framework, we enlisted a group of legally blind individuals (N = 25) to gauge its impact on facilitating a more nuanced exploration behavior.

1.1. Major Contributions

The main contribution of the paper is summarized as follows.

1. Formalizing an information exploration framework considering the BU cognitive rule.
2. Categorically organizing the search results space for enhanced BU access.
3. Evaluating the proposed framework from empirical and usability perspectives on legally BUs.

Assistive technologies, such as screen readers and voice assistants, are available to aid BUs in navigating the web. However, not all websites are compatible with these tools, and their limitations may hinder a seamless experience. The cumulative cognitive load of listening to synthesized speech, processing information, and navigating can lead to mental fatigue for BUs. Hence, in this research, we formally investigate a framework that provides BUs with effective access to web content exploration.

BUs encounter a multitude of challenges when attempting to navigate the digital landscape and access online information. The predominant hurdle they face underlies the inherently linear nature of search engine results. These results, presented as ranked snippets, compel BUs to sift through information sequentially, resulting in time-consuming searches and potential disorientation. The struggle intensifies due to the deficiency of navigational aids designed with BUs in mind. Elements like buttons, menus, and images often lack proper labeling or structuring, rendering navigation a complex endeavor. Additionally, much of the online content lacks the necessary accessibility features, such as accurate heading tags, alternative text for images, and semantic markup. Consequently, screen readers—critical tools for BUs—struggle to convey content effectively. Therefore, to provide ease to the BUs, we devise a mechanism to categorically organize the search results space.

Further complicated matters pertaining to deciphering complex user interface elements using screen readers pose their own difficulties and missing labels and improper grouping can render these forms virtually unusable for BUs. Visual elements like charts and graphs—widely used to convey information—pose a significant obstacle to BUs. Without proper alternative representations, the meaning behind these visual aids is lost, hampering comprehensive understanding. Meanwhile, the overwhelming volume of web content exacerbates the challenge and these techniques must be investigated from the BU usability perspectives. Therefore, this research additionally aims to evaluate the formal BU exploration framework from the usability perspectives.

1.2. Paper Organization

The structure of this manuscript is delineated as follows: Section 2 encompasses a critical literature review, examining contemporary strategies prevalent in the domain. Section 3 elucidates the proposed theoretical framework in detail, forming the foundation of this study. Section 4 explains the procedural elements integral to the instantiated framework. Subsequently, Section 5 offers an analytical insight into the empirical and usability metrics applied, along with the resulting data. The penultimate Section 6 hosts an in-depth discussion, paving the way for Section 7, which culminates with concluding remarks and potential future research trajectories.

2. Literature Review

Blindness is a visual impairment that affects individuals' ability to perceive visual information, either partially or entirely. As a significant portion of the population, the BUs face numerous challenges in today's digital landscape. Hence, web accessibility is becoming increasingly crucial to ensure that BUs can access online information seamlessly. Understanding how BUs interact with the web is essential to fostering an online environment that adapts to their diverse needs and allows them to fully participate in the digital world. In this context, exploring the technologies that assist BUs to navigate the web effectively is becoming essential to foster an environment where BUs can participate equally. The traditional interfaces present significant challenges for the BUs when interacting with the web. The subsequent subsections briefly discuss the BU information seeking on the web and the existing accessibility technologies, along with the associated challenges.

2.1. BU Information Seeking

Information searching on the web is a challenging task for BUs [10]. This is due to the enormity of the information on the web and the lack of appropriate navigational support for the BUs. On the contrary, the existing web search engines, being the gateway to accessing information on the web, treat BUs similarly to sighted ones and offer no special assistance in information searching and navigation [10]. Hence, BUs are left at the discretion of navigational support from third-party assistive tools. In such a scenario, the BUs are constrained to use assistive tools [11], such as screen readers and talking software, JAWS, voice assistants, Braille, etc. The screen readers primarily convert text into synthesized speech and use an automated voice to read out the content [12]. Depending on the structure of a document, the voice may provide structural speech, including headings, links, buttons, and text, allowing BUs to navigate and interact with the information. JAWS (Job Access with Speech) is similar to screen readers with the additional functionality of Braille displays, allowing blind users to access information in Braille format [13]. The voice assistants, such as Siri, Google Assistant, Alexa, etc., can help BUs with various web-related tasks, including searching for information, setting reminders, or reading emails [14].

The BUs face a lack of assistive tools and applications. There is an immense need to develop systems that better adapt to the BU's needs and preferences [15]. While the third-party assistive tools provide an interface for accessing the information, they are incapable of effectively rendering the information best suited to the BU's cognitive capabilities. As a result, studies indicate that BUs are hesitant to use assistance due to a lack of trust in such systems.

2.2. BU Accessibility Standards

To overcome the structural difficulties of the content, various accessibility standards are introduced. Firstly, the Web Content Accessibility Guidelines (WCAG) and Authoring Tool Accessibility Guidelines (ATAG) introduced by the World Wide Web Consortium (W3C) provide guidelines and success criteria for making web content more accessible. This includes adding alternate text, making information navigable without a mouse, and establishing structured documents. Section 16 of the Rehabilitation Act requires [16] federal agencies to ensure that their electronic and information technology is accessible by providing appropriate captions and means to skip duplicate content. Accessible Rich Internet Applications (ARIA) ensure that the core navigational features are accessible to the BUs, such as dropdown menus and tab panels, via screen readers [17]. User Agent Accessibility Guidelines (UAAG) from W3C focus on enabling assistive technology conformance with BUs by allowing them to adjust preferences, such as speech rate and Braille display settings, to enhance their browsing experience.

However, studies report that these standards are often overlooked, and most websites do not implement these guidelines [18]. BUs express difficulty in navigating and finding the required information on the web. Moreover, a percentage of the BUs are over the age of 18 [19]. In this regard, there is an immediate need to explore a tool that can structure the content information content that adopts the BU cognitive needs and allows them to explore the information on the web effectively.

2.3. BU State-of-the-Art Tools

Roy et al. [20] developed a voice-activated email prototype, considering the cognitive needs of BUs. Their system operated on three basic commands: send, read, and exit to compose the email, read the inbox, and exit the program, respectively. Fayyaz et al. [21] devised an approach to reduce BU's cognitive load by presenting the summarized information in PDF tables. They used contextual information such as data types, captions, matching sentences, etc., and devised a keyboard-based navigational menu for interaction. Bukhaya et al. [22], Nair et al. [23], and Christopherson et al. [24] leveraged image processing techniques via deep learning to convert the visual information into text for subsequent processing by a text reader. Tucket et al. [25] embedded Near Field Connectivity (NFC) in academic pages preloaded with the speak command.

Zeboudj et al. [26] used the Pigeon algorithm to efficiently find relevant web pages and used resultantly retrieved web documents as pseudo-relevance feedback from the initial query. Subsequently, they extracted keywords via the Frequent Pattern Growth algorithm to determine the optimal query for reformulation. Figueroa-Gutiérrez et al. [27] proposed an architecture considering image processing techniques to automatically extract graphs under an image format, generating a description accessible to users with visual impairments. Meliones et al. [28] used the augmented voice assistance of Alexa to allow elderly BUs to generate voice commands. The system maps the request to relevant services on the web, retrieves the relevant documents, and speaks to the BUs.

However, the existing tools are concerned with enhancing the content for better accessibility by voice assistants. The summarized literature is also presented in Table 1. To the best of our knowledge, a practical investigation to restructure the information presentation mechanism for BUs considering their cognitive capabilities is yet to be undertaken. In the subsequent subsection, we briefly examine the issues and motivation for this research.

Table 1. Summarizing the references, approaches, and limitations of the studies mentioned in the literature review.

Cited	Approach	Limitations
[10]	BUs face challenges due to lack of navigational support	Reliance on third-party assistive tools
[11]	Utilization of screen readers, JAWS, voice assistants	Limited effectiveness of assistive tools
[20]	Voice-activated email prototype	Focused on a specific application (email)
[21]	Reduce cognitive load using summarized information	Limited to information presented in tabular format
[22–24]	Leverage image processing to convert visual information	Relies on image recognition; may not cover all content
[25]	Embed Near Field Connectivity (NFC) for interaction	Limited to specific contexts (academic pages)
[26]	Pigeon algorithm for efficient web page retrieval	Focused on improving search result relevancy
[27]	Image processing for automatic graph description	Limited to content with graphical elements
[28]	Voice assistance augmentation for BUs	Primarily extends voice assistant functionality

2.4. Issues and Motivations

The Internet has become the most ubiquitous technology for seeking information online. Combined with easy access to handheld devices and the ability of the web to interconnect immense amounts of information, the users' information-seeking paradigm is now relying on online information-provider services such as search engines. However, the literature has shown that 81% of Internet BU users still consider accessing online services difficult or impossible [29]. Among them, only 53% of BUs are reported to succeed in their navigation tasks on the web [30]. Hence, the web can then be a cause of exclusion for BUs. These difficulties may be explained by the inherent shortcomings of online information providers. Notably, the information interaction of BU users with online information providers is linear. This presents numerous shortcomings. The BUs has to determine the relevancy of the information content sequentially, which is time-consuming. Subsequently, information seeking in a linear search paradigm is cognitively challenging for BUs, which often results in information disorientation for BUs. Furthermore, the effectiveness of a web service is determined solely by the offline empirical evaluation measures of precision and recall, ignoring the behavioral and usability aspects of designing a search engine.

To overcome the challenges in this research, we are interested in investigating an online web search framework considering the needs of BUs. Mainly, we transformed the online information-seeking paradigm of BUs from linear to hierarchical, considering the cognitive processing capabilities of the BUs. Furthermore, we provided multimodal interaction for enhanced accessibility. Finally, we evaluated the proposed framework from the empirical and usability perspectives to determine its effectiveness by recruiting legally qualified BUs.

3. WSREB Mechanism

We created a WSREB mechanism to address core issues in web document exploration for BUs, i.e., non-linear navigation, accessibility, and cognition load. We instantiated the WSREB mechanism by implementing a tool that facilitates BUs to explore web search documents. Primarily, the WSREB mechanism elaborates formal representations, commencing with tree-based data models and categorical data models, component-based architecture, and SUI design. Moreover, it emphasizes accessibility and navigation of web documents while reducing the cognitive load in a non-linear and integrated way. The WSREB mechanism provides an accessible solution for BUs to explore web search results documents.

3.1. WSREB Approach

The WSREB approach enables the exploration of web search documents utilizing exploratory search principles. The primary goals of the approach are twofold: (i) enable BUs to convey their exploratory needs via multimodal query terms; and (ii) provide web document exploration to enhance accessibility in a non-linear way. Generally, BUs with clear search goals perform lookup activities to reach their required information. However, for exploratory needs, BUs often have ambiguous search goals.

To overcome this challenge, the proposed approach allows BUs to explore and navigate through the retrieved results, as well as refine their query as needed. Figure 1 illustrates the WSREB approach.

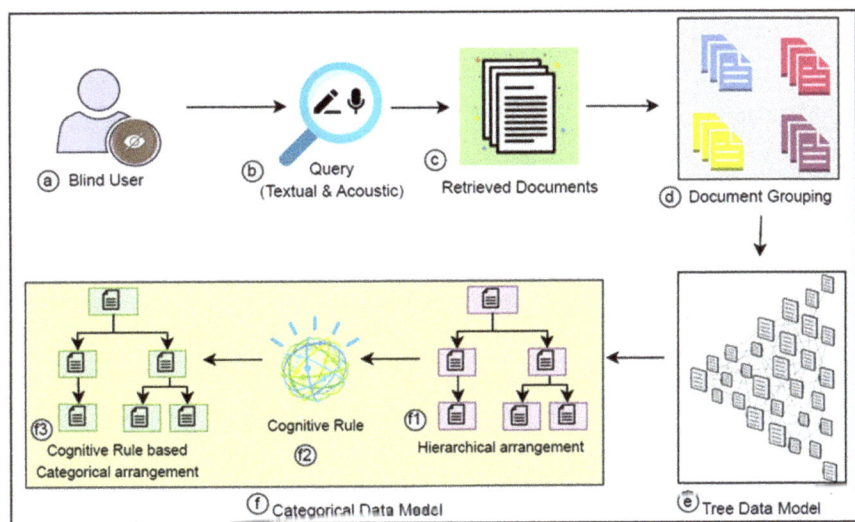

Figure 1. A systematic flow diagram of the WSREB approach.

Our approach allows BUs to express their information needs via multimodal query formulation. The multimodal queries comprise textual and acoustic modalities (Figure 1a,b). The capability to create multimodal queries is critical to fulfilling the exploratory needs of BUs. Textual queries aid in constructing keyword-based queries, while acoustic queries allow users to freely express complete natural language sentences via voice. The SERB system combines complex textual and auditory queries, utilizing Boolean operators (AND, OR, NOT) between the query keywords. Acoustic queries are saved and processed to assist users in the future (as depicted in Figure 1b). Typically, web search engines designed for BUs present query search results linearly, which enhances the search engines' ability to target lookup searches. A set of query-based documents is retrieved depending on the web search engines (Figure 1c). Our approach forms document groups based on the similarities (Figure 1d). These groups are unordered similarity pairs computed via statistical methods.

The mechanism of SERB provides the results in a non-linear form. For this purpose, the tree structure is introduced, which holds the results, and the results are depicted in a hierarchical form so that the exploration activity of the blind user is enhanced. The representation of results in a non-linear form helps the blind user reduce the time spent searching for the required information. The hierarchical structure converts into a categorical form. The interactive categories play a crucial role in exploring the results. Previously, interactive categories were not introduced so that the blind user could interact and search more interactively. In the representation of the categories, the Miller rule is applied, which helps the blind user. In the representation of the categories, cognitive ability is enhanced by using the rule. The blind user can easily search for information within the categories. The blind user, with or without expertise in the domain, can fulfill their information needs. The goal of the approach is to facilitate the blind user by providing a simple, clear structure for the information and a blind-friendly interface, along with interactive categories in the non-linear presentation of the search results. The shortcut keys play a major role in accessibility and interaction with the system. The shortcut keys allow the blind user to access the information; therefore, the shortcut keys are introduced to access the information more conveniently. In this way, the interaction with the blind user is more efficient and effective. The voice-over introduces a guide that guides the blind user to perform the steps and reach the destination. The structure also allows screen readers to serialize the content and read the structure in a minimum amount of time.

3.2. Approach Formal Algorithm Definitions

Definition 1. *Query:*

The BU-based query q retrieves a set of documents $D = \{d_1, d_2 \ldots, d_n\}$, which contains relevant textual information. During the information-seeking journey, the user may issue multiple queries and may refer to the previously issued query. Hence, multiple issued queries can be encapsulated in a set $Q = \{q_1, q_2 \ldots, q_n\}$.

Definition 2. *Multimodal Queries:*

The Q may comprise Textual query Q_t and Acoustic Query Q_a. Both Q_t and Q_a accept multiple keywords as a set $K = k_1, k_2 \ldots, k_n$. Moreover, the query may also incorporate Boolean operators (AND, OR, NOT). Hence, the formation of a query may take the form of $k = k_1 (AND \parallel OR \parallel NOT) k_n$.

Definition 3. *Retrieved Documents:*

The d is considered as a tuple containing associated information $d = t_d, u_d, d_i$, where t_d is the title of a document, u_d is the URL of the document and d_i is the document description. This can be formalized as $\{t_d, u_d, d_i\} \in d \in D$.

Definition 4. *Document Groupings:*

In D, each unordered pair i.e., $\{d_{n-1}, d_n\}$ underpasses through statistical methods to form multiple groups g considering a threshold γ. Let a set of groups $G = \{g_1, g_2, \ldots, g_n\}$ and each g_n is a tuple-containing document $g_n = \{d_1, d_2, \ldots, d_n\}$. However, all g_n documents contains unique d_n; therefore, $g_{n-1} \neq g_n$.

Definition 5. *Tree Data Model:*

Formally, a document tree DT is a pair containing nodes N and edges E given as $T = (N, E)$. In the set of nodes $N = \{n_1, n_2 \ldots, n_n\}$, each n represents the title of documents. For the set of edges $E = \{e_1, e_2 \ldots, e_n\}$, each e represents weighted edges between nodes.

Definition 6. *Categorical Data Model:*

The categorical data model interacts with the k-array tree data model to generate hierarchies $H = \{T_1, T_2 \ldots, T_n\}$. A similarity measure SM^y is applied on each T_n to arrange the hierarchies in descending order of similarity to Q. This can be formalized as $H' = \{\forall (Q, T_n) \| SM^y (Q, T_n) > SM^y (Q, T_{n-1})\}$, where y is a similarity threshold value.

The notable distinction in the proposed categorical model is the prevention of overlapping hierarchies since the existing literature criticizes overlapping as being difficult to interpret, especially when documents belong to multiple branches or categories within the hierarchy [31]. This can make it challenging for users to understand the structure and locate relevant documents [32]. Furthermore, as the hierarchy grows, navigation and management become more challenging [33]. Hence, the decisive hierarchical structure was chosen to ensure that the form hierarchies are easier to interpret, able to handle high-dimensional data, demonstrate simplicity and high speed, good accuracy, and the capability to produce rules for clear and understandable human classification. To further enhance navigation within the proposed model, the cognitive rule is applied to display several categories where $\{\forall T \in H' \rightarrow |T| = 7 \mp 2\}$.

Algorithm 1 Algorithm for querying and retrieving documents.

Input: User Query Q
Output: Retrieved Documents D
Function Query (Q):
    if *modality(Q) != String* **then**
        Q = MultimodalQueries(Q);
    end
    query = extract_keywords(Q);
    documents = fetch_results(query)
    return documents
Function Multimodal Queries (Q_a):
    Q_t = extract_keywords(Q_a);
    return Q_t
Function Retrieved Documents *(documents)*:
    D = [];
    for *document in documents* **do**
        D.append((title, URL, description = extract_metadata (*document*); D.append(tuple(title, URL, description));
    end
return D

3.3. Component-Based Architecture

Architecture is commonly defined as the "fundamental organization of a system embodied in its components, their relationships to each other and to the environment, and the principles guiding its design and evolution" [34]. The eminent feature of a component-based architectural design is the separation of concerns [35]. Therefore, the proposed mechanism employed a component-based architecture, as depicted in Figure 2. The architecture consists of five components: a web component, a query component, an information retrieval component, a tree-ranked component, a categorical component, and a blind exploration component. Each component is restricted to the assigned logic.

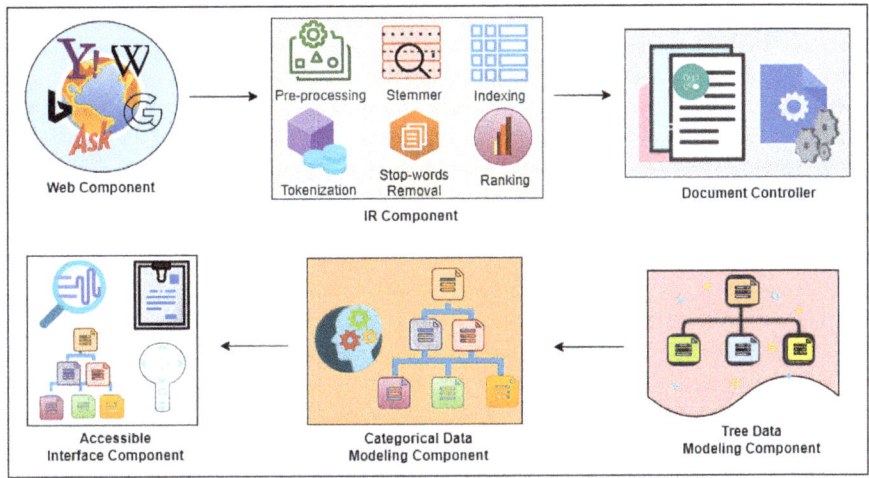

Figure 2. Component-based architectural representation of the proposed mechanism.

The web component accesses the textual objects by exploiting the textual modality. Considering the web documents as textual objects, this component searches the web and archives all the documents. The IR component handles all the information retrieval tasks. The query-based retrieved documents are processed considering their title, content, and URI. The pre-processor performs parsing and term-processing while generating a logical view of the query for searching. The tokenizer creates tokens of words from the documents, which the indexer then uses to create a list by joining the tokens with the keywords. The indexer creates an inverted index while maintaining and mapping the pointers of search keywords to the documents. The indexer and term-processing correlate with the stemmer and stop-word remover. Afterward, the stemmer reduces the inflected words to their base root, while the stop-word remover eliminates the common words, computing their high frequency. Finally, the ranker is triggered, which ranks the retrieved and processed documents based on query relevancy.

Algorithm 2 Algorithm for formation of tree data model.

Input: User Query Q and Documents D
Output: Document Tree TD data model
Function Document Grouping (*documents, query*):
  grouping_threshold = JS(query, documents) + SD(JS);
  document_group = []; **for** *document in documents* **do**
    if *(JS(document) > threshold)* **then**
      document_group.append(document);
    end
  end
  return document_group
Function Tree Data Model (*documents_group, query*):
  tree = k_array();
  _similarity_documents = JS(query, documents_group);
  parent_node_document = sorted_similarity_documents.pop();
  tree.add_parent(parent$_{node\_document}$);
  for *document in* sorted_similarity_documents **do**
    threshold = Mean(sorted_similarity_documents) + SD(JS);
    if *document == parent_node_document* **then**
      tree.append_extra_child(sorted_similarity_documents.pop());
    end
    else if *document > parent_node_document* **then**
      tree.append_left(sorted_similarity_documents.pop());
    end
  Else
  tree.append_right(sorted_similarity_documents.pop());
  end, end
  return tree
Function Categorical Data Model (*tree*):
  min_threshold = 5;
  max_threshold = 9;
  for *branch in tree* **do**
    if *branch.levels() < min_threshold OR branch.levels() > max_threshold* **then**
      tree.remove(branch);
    end
  end
  return tree

Algorithm 3 Algorithm for overall flow of data model.

model. **Input:** User Query Q and Documents D
Output: Document Tree TD data model
Function Main *(Q)*:
   D = Retrieved Documents(Query(Q));
   G = Document Grouping(D, Q);
   DT = Tree Data Model(G, Q);
   C = Categorial Data Model(TD);
return C

The document controller applies multiple statistical computations and thresholding techniques to form groups on the received ranked documents. Each document group is a non-hierarchical group containing distinctive and unique documents. In each document group, a linear list is maintained where the document and group rankings are based on query relevancy and the IR component. The tree data modeling component converts the disjoint document groups into document hierarchies. Each disjoint document group forms a hierarchical structure, developing a parent–child relationship among the documents. This component utilizes several algorithms to form hierarchies and sustain levels of document hierarchies within a group.

The categorical data modeling component is responsible for processing the document hierarchies into categories via cognition. Each group's document hierarchy generates disjoint categories based on the hierarchy's top node and query relevancy. Furthermore, several computations re-arrange the categories in descending order and organize them on a similarity basis. Moreover, a cognitive rule is applied to categories and reorganizes them into more relevant and desired web search documents. Furthermore, each category is divided into sub-categories, and each sub-category contains multiple documents. The accessible interface component directly links with web and categorical data modeling components. The document categories are displayed along with navigational information.

The interface component has direct links with web and categorical data modeling components. The interface visualizes the web search results, highlighting the fact that this interface design is suitable for all kinds of visually impaired users. The visualization aids the other visually impaired users to interact with the web, whereas the blind users can vocally interact with it via assistive technologies. The interface component allows visually impaired or blind users to search the web via multi-modality queries, i.e., textual and acoustic queries. It visualizes the interactive categories received from a categorical component. These categories allow exploration and lookup of web search results, i.e., documents. The navigation panel enhances accessibility, allowing users to navigate and reach the documents based on their information needs.

4. Mechanism Instantiation

A scenario for a blind user to explore web search results instantiates the exploration mechanism. The instantiation process activates the functionality of the proposed approach using a pre-defined structure [36]. The instantiation attains the applicative scenario of the proposed mechanism, eliminating web exploration issues. The following section elaborates on the dataset, instantiation preliminaries, and implementation of the proposed exploration tool.

4.1. Dataset

There are various benchmark datasets available for web search documents, including MSRA, WOS, the Braille dataset (as described in Table 2), and Wikipedia, which have been extensively adopted by multiple researchers [37]. However, Wikipedia is widely used among all the datasets due to its large, consumed source of capturing knowledge. The highly dependable sources during a web search are real-time data. The significance of Wikipedia as real-time data involves progress, data updating, analysis, and dynamic behavior. Therefore, the exploration mechanism is instantiated on a real-time Wikipedia dataset to attain all possibilities of applicative scenarios. The Wikipedia real-time dataset contains a bulk of web documents covering a diverse range of domains and topics.

Table 2. Archive various datasets and Tools utilized for experiments.

No.	URL	Access Date
1. MSRA	https://paperswithcode.com/dataset/msra-td500	12 January 2023
2. WOS	https://paperswithcode.com/dataset/web-of-science-dataset	12 January 2023
3. braille	https://www.kaggle.com/datasets/shanks0465/braille-character-dataset	12 January 2023
4. Wikipedia	https://huggingface.co/datasets/wikipedia	12 January 2023
5. Django	https://www.djangoproject.com/	13 January 2023
6. PyCharm	https://www.jetbrains.com/pycharm/	14 January 2023
7. VoiceAPI	https://www.twilio.com/docs/voice	15 January 2023
8. PyLucene	https://lucene.apache.org/pylucene/	16 January 2023

4.2. Instantiation Preliminaries

Initially, the user issues a query. The keywords are extracted from the query to retrieve the documents along with the metadata (as shown in Algorithm 1). Subsequently, data model processing is performed (as described in Algorithm 2). The categories representing web search results are formulated via similarity values. These similarity values are compared with a threshold, i.e., the highest similar document. The Jaccard similarity, i.e., $J(A, B) = A \cap B, A \cup B$, is applied to attain the textual modality $t = Mean(JS) + SD(JS)$ where t is a textual threshold, mean (JS) is the mean of Jaccard similarity up to I times and $SD(JS)$ is the standard deviation of Jaccard similarity. The textual similarity involves similarity between document keywords, titles, links, and descriptions, generating a set of JS including all nodes. The reasons for choosing Jaccard similarity specifically in this research are numerous. Firstly, Jaccard similarity is robust to outliers since it does not take the shape of the distributions into account and operates on categorical data, which is important in accurate document hierarchy generation. Secondly, the Jaccard similarity forms the hierarchies based on significant overlapping of the documents with minimal preprocessing requirements (e.g., term frequency/inverse document frequency normalization and vector sparsity issues). This facilitates rapid real-time hierarchy generation. Thirdly, Jaccard similarity works closer in spirit to Boolean search than some other text similarity measures. This is primarily because both Jaccard similarity and Boolean search are based on set operations and binary (yes/no) logic. Hence, considering BU needs, Jaccard similarity was deemed a better choice to form the categorical tree data model based on the Miller cognition rule. The overall flow is outlined in Algorithm 3.

4.3. Implementation

A tool-based WSREB mechanism is implemented to allow blind users to explore web search results documents. The tool employed the Django framework and Python libraries via the PyCharm IDE community version 3.7.1, as described in Table 2. The Django web services are utilized for server applications, while the function initiates document and URL mapping. The voice API is exploited for acoustic requests, and Apache PyLucene creates an inverted index of Wikipedia documents.

5. Evaluations

We evaluated the WSREB mechanism to analyze the empirical and usability studies. The empirical evaluation assesses the theoretical aspects, whereas the usability evaluation measures the quality and interactivity of the WSREB mechanism-based tool.

5.1. Empirical Evaluation

The SERB mechanism aims to facilitate the exploration of the categories linear and non-linearly. This mechanism also provides accessibility in activities of web search results. Precision is utilized to measure the effectiveness of search results. Precision is calculated by the relevant search results divided by the retrieved search results. The efficiency and exploration activities are measured with click-through rates. Hence, the efficiency of the SERB mechanism is measured via precision, and the exploration activities are evaluated through click-through rates. Therefore, in the following section, we discuss the participants, experiment procedure, measures, and experiment results.

5.1.1. Evaluation: Category-based Precision

The empirical evaluation was conducted to measure the efficiency of categories and the exploration activities of the documents. The comparison of the efficiency of the categories is based on the two types, which are voice-based categories and text-based categories. The result is analyzed in a better way. This section depicts the evaluation metric, methodology, and results.

5.1.2. Evaluation Metric

The evaluation metric measures the efficiency of categories through precision and comparison of results based on voice and textual queries. The purpose behind the comparison is that, as the user is blind, the blind user queries through voice, while textual queries through a screen reader require effort. The SERB tool provides a voice query as well as a textual query with interactive categories. The proposed structure for the search results for the blind user provides a better analysis. Measuring query-based precision is a division of relevant documents over the retrieved document search results.

5.2. Experimental Setup

The category efficiency measure with the SREB tool is based on retrieved results. The experiments are processed on an Intel(R) Core (TM)i7-4700MQ CPU @ 2.40GHz equipped with 16 GB of RAM and a 64-bit operating system. Textual queries are executed to retrieve the document search results, and data are instantiated in the search results, which are further used in categories and exploration. The formation of the categories is based on the similarity relationship; therefore, the categories show the precision of the relationship as well. The Boolean operators (AND, OR NOT) are also provided for the search. Queries are selected for the comparisons, both voice and textual. The executed queries are based on multiple topics. Table 3 shows the query that is executed. The first keyword depicts the query, and the second keyword depicts the idea or concept of belonging to the first keyword. We conducted multiple experiments, which included five queries to calculate the precision of the textual query-based categories and voice query-based categories. Here, we mentioned that the top 10 (n = 10) results were taken to compute the precision. The $MAPc$ was calculated by performing five experiments. Similarly, the Precision PR, Average Precision APv, and Mean Average Precision (MAP) calculated the correctness of the formation of voice-based categories.

Table 3. Queries selected for the evaluation.

	Operators	Category B
Animals	AND, OR	Sea animals, land animals, vertebrates, reptiles
Corona Virus	AND, OR	Symptoms, cases, countries, vaccine
Imran Khan	AND, OR, NOT	Prime minister, cricketer, education
Plants	AND, OR	Photosynthesis, sunlight, land
Airplanes	AND, OR	Jet fighters, air force
Roses	AND, OR	Red, region
Sports	AND	Games
Wonders of the World	AND	Countries

5.3. Reachability Evaluation

Reachability evaluation is the evaluation of the navigation and exploration activities and the reachability of the results measured via click-through rates (CTRs). The computation of the reachability of blind users is based on the queries. The click-through rate serves as a measure of reachability. Hence, reachability is defined as the number of clicks required to search from the source to the destination. The CTRs calculate the document search results using voice and textual queries. The path of the CTRs is from the source node to the destination node. The formula for the CTRs is calculated by Equation (1).

$$RCTR_e\ (|Si \to Di|) = \text{number of clicks}\ (Si \to Di) \tag{1}$$

In this formula, $RCTR_e$ is the reachability via CTRs of the exploration activities, $|Si|$ is represented as the source node, and $|Di|$ is represented as the destination node in the document search results. The average reachability is measured on the set of the query divided by the total number of queries. The formula of the average reachability is measured as:

$$ARCT_{ex}\ (|Si \to Di|) = \sum_{i=1}^{n} RCT_{ex}\ (|Si \to Di|) \tag{2}$$

Here, the $ARCT_{ex}$ is the average reachability of the exploration activities, i is the ith experiment and N is the total number of the experiments. The $MARCT_{ex}$ is calculated as the number of queries divided by the total number of experiments and calculated by Equation (3) as:

$$MARCT_{ex}\ (|Si \to Di|) = \sum_{i=1}^{n} RCT_{ex}\ (|Si \to Di|) \tag{3}$$

5.4. Usability Evaluation

This questionnaire is utilized to measure the quality of the interface, satisfaction, system usefulness, and information about the system. Nineteen questions are involved to measure the usability, and the scale begins from 1 to 7, which depicts strongly disagreeing to strongly agreeing. The results are shown in Table 4, which summarizes the score of the CUSQ, which covers the interface screen, system information, and terminology, along with the learning and capabilities of the system in a broader range.

Table 4. User's CUSQ Evaluation Overall Satisfaction (Overall), System Usefulness (Usefulness) Information Quality (Info. Qua.) and Interface Quality (Inter. Qua.).

Blind Users	Overall	Usefulness	Info Qua	Inter Qua	Avg	Score
BU1	5.62	5.18	5.62	5.98	5.6	0.8
BU2	5	4.72	5	5.2	4.98	0.71
BU3	5	5.18	5.10	5.13	5.10	0.72
BU4	5.62	5.54	6.9	7.15	6.3	0.9
BU5	5.37	5.18	5.1	5.8	5.3	0.75
BU6	5.25	5.3	5.2	5.4	5.2	0.74
BU7	4.62	4.63	5.0	5.6	4.9	0.7
BU8	4.37	5.1	5	6	5.1	0.72
BU9	5	4.1	4.8	5.1	4.7	0.67
BU10	3.62	3.90	4	5	4.13	0.59
BU11	4.37	4.7	5.1	5.8	4.9	0.7
BU12	5	5	5	6	5.2	0.74
BU13	5.5	4.	3.89	4.5	4.6	0.65
BU14	3.62	5.1	5.0	5.6	4.8	0.68
BU15	5.12	5.5	5.1	5.8	5.3	0.75

Table 4. *Cont.*

Blind Users	Overall	Usefulness	Info Qua	Inter Qua	Avg	Score
BU16	6	5.2	5	6	5.5	0.78
BU17	5.3	5.6	5.3	5.8	5.5	0.78
BU18	5.08	5.3	4.8	5.1	5.0	0.71
BU19	5.6	5.0	4.85	5.2	5.1	0.72
BU20	5.6	5	4.9	5.6	5.2	0.74
BU21	4.6	4.8	4.5	5	4.7	0.67
BU22	5.5	4.8	4.5	5	4	0.57
BU23	5.2	5.6	5.1	5.8	5.4	0.77
BU24	5.2	5.8	5.0	5.6	5.4	0.77
BU25	6.12	5.0	4.58	5.3	5.2	0.74
Avg	5.09	5.0	4.97	5.53	5.08	0.69
Score	0.7	0.71	0.71	0.79	0.72	0.78

The score shows the overall usability of the SERB tool is 78%, which is good. The usefulness of the system is 70%, whereas the information quality is 71%. The interface quality is also at 71%. This shows that the overall usability of the SERB tool for blind users is satisfactory.

6. Results and Discussions

Figure 3 shows the results presented in the categories based on voice and textual queries. In the first experiment, the voice-based categories were more efficient as compared to text-based categories. In the second experiment, the textual queries showed better results than the voice queries. The third experiment depicted that textual-based categories and voice-based categories show a minimal difference. The fourth experiment shows the results are similar, both with textual-based categories and voice-based categories. The fifth experiment shows that the voice-based categories show more efficient results as compared to the textual-based categories. The calculated results of voice-based categories and text-based categories are presented in Table 5. The conclusion of the five experiments is that the category's *MAPc* for the textual-based categories is 84 percent, whereas the voice-based categories *MAPc* is 86%. These results show that blind users can efficiently explore and access the categories with voice. Exploring the categories with voice enables blind users to enhance the search and explore the search results.

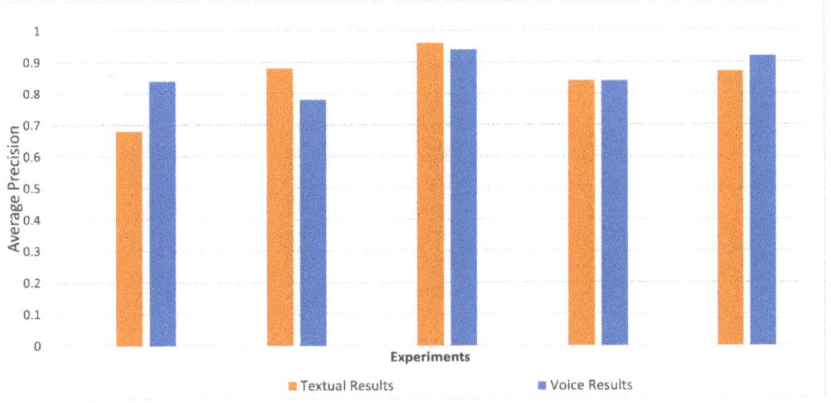

Figure 3. Efficiency comparison of categories based on textual and voice search results.

Table 5. Precision of categories with textual and voice query results (experiments, Query, Categories Precision (Pc), Categories' Average Precision (APc), Voice query Precision (Pv), Voice query Average Precision (APv).

Experiments	Query	P_c	AP_c	P_v	AP_c
1	Qry1	1		0.8	
	Qry2	1		0.4	
	Qry3	1	0.68	1	0.84
	Qry4	0		1	
	Qry5	0.4		1	
2	Qry1	1		1	
	Qry2	1		1	
	Qry3	0.8	0.88	0.6	0.78
	Qry4	0.6		1	
	Qry5	1		0.3	
3	Qry1	1		1	
	Qry2	1		1	
	Qry3	1	0.96	1	0.94
	Qry4	0.84		0.90	
	Qry5	1		0.82	
4	Qry1	1		1	
	Qry2	0.4		0.43	
	Qry3	0.8	0.84	1	0.846
	Qry4	1		1	
	Qry5	1		0.8	
5	Qry1	1		0.90	
	Qry2	1		1	
	Qry3	0.75	0.876	1	0.928
	Qry4	0.63		0.74	
	Qry5	1		1	
MAP			0.84		0.865

The reachability is built on the *CTR* results taken from the source node to the destination node against the query. The raking list is considered from the source node to the destination node of the document search results. Figure 4 shows the average results of the CTR for each experiment that is conducted. The *ARCTR* of the experiments is 6.5, 7, 6.9, 6, and 7.9 to reach the results of the documents at the position that is defined by the exploration mechanism of the SERB tool. The results of the *MARCTRe* of all experiments in numbers are 6.86. It depicts that approximately seven clicks are used to reach the destination results at a certain ranking position. The *ARCTR* of the experiments is 5, 6, 5.9, 6.5, and 6 to reach a certain position of the documents defined by the mechanism of the SERB tool. The *MARCTR* of the experiment is 5.88, which means five clicks are required to reach the destination results of the documents at a certain ranking position. The results depict that the voice query is efficient and reduces the number of clicks that are feasible for reaching the destination. Hence, the proposed approach presents various implications, as provided in Table 6 for BUs. These applications demonstrate the versatility and potential impact of AI-driven content summarization in enhancing BUs' access to information across various domains. By automating the process of distilling essential information, this technology can empower blind BUs to navigate, understand, and engage with online content more effectively.

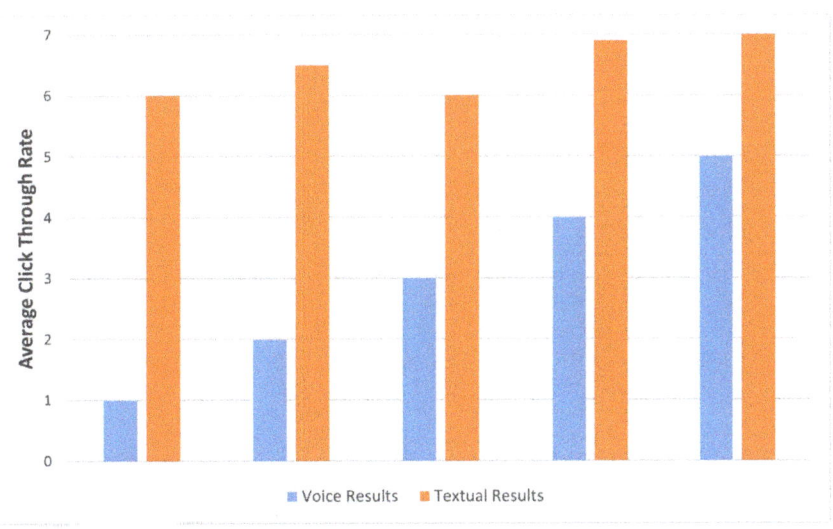

Figure 4. Query-based reachability results.

Table 6. Potential applications of AI-driven content summarization for BUs.

Application	Description
Web Content Summarization	Automatically generate concise summaries of web articles, blog posts, and news articles, aiding BU efficient content consumption.
Academic Material Summarization	Summarize lengthy academic papers, research articles, and textbooks, enabling BUs to grasp key concepts and findings without reading every detail.
Document Summarization	Generate summaries for various document types, including contracts, legal documents, and manuals, making complex information more accessible to BUs.
Email and Communication	Summarize lengthy emails, communication threads, and documents shared electronically, allowing BUs to manage correspondence more effectively.
News and Updates Aggregation	Automatically extract essential details from multiple news sources, presenting BUs with concise and timely updates on current events and topics.
Educational Content Summarization	Summarize educational videos, lectures, and online courses, helping BUs grasp the main concepts and lessons without needing to watch or read the entire content.
Navigational Assistance	Summarize navigational instructions, maps, and directions, providing BUs with concise guidance for travel and navigation.
Technical Documentation	Condense technical manuals, user guides, and documentation for software and hardware, aiding BUs in understanding and troubleshooting complex systems.
Social Media and Posts	Summarize lengthy social media posts, threads, and comments, enabling BUs to engage with online discussions more efficiently.
Personalized News Feeds	Provide BUs with tailored news summaries based on their interests and preferences, helping them stay informed without being overwhelmed by content.

6.1. Computational Analysis

The WSREB mechanism involves several components, including querying, document retrieval, grouping, hierarchical and categorical data modeling, and interface interactions. Each of these components may have its own computational complexity and calculated as follows:

- Querying and document retrieval might have a complexity of $O(n)$ where n is the number of documents retrieved.
- Grouping and statistical methods could contribute additional complexity.

- Hierarchical and categorical data modeling might involve tree traversals, which could be O(log n) for balanced trees, or even O(n) in the worst case if not properly optimized
- The interface interactions may have constant time complexity (O(1)). Considering the interplay of these components, the overall complexity of the WSREB mechanism could be quite complex and not easily reducible to a single Big O notation.

6.2. Theoretical and Practical Implications of the Framework

Traditionally, the existing information systems presented the search results as ranked snippets that compel BUs to sift through information sequentially, resulting in time consuming searches and potential disorientation. The struggle intensifies due to the deficiency of navigational aids designed with BUs in mind. To overcome this challenge, we proposed a theoretical framework that categorically organized the search results space as hierarchies. To determine the effectiveness of the proposed framework, we conducted a thorough empirical and usability evaluation yielding satisfactory results. The proposed approach provided promising results in allowing BUs to effectively browse the relevant information and with each step get closer to the required information logarithmically. The implications of the proposed approach are diverse, especially when augmented with Artificial Intelligence (AI).

Potential applications of AI-driven content are summarized for BUs in Table 6. Specifically, instead of integrating the search results, the proposed framework can incorporate AI-based summarized documents. This especially can aid academic users in summarizing and organizing the academic literature. While the traditional information system can be challenging for BUs to decipher using screen readers, potentially leaving them with an incomplete understanding of the webpage's content, the proposed framework allows BUs to formulate their search journey and navigate via voice commands.

Assistive technologies, such as screen readers and voice assistants, are available to aid BUs in navigating the web. However, not all websites are compatible with these tools and their limitations may hinder a seamless experience. The cumulative cognitive load of listening to synthesized speech, processing information, and navigating can lead to mental fatigue for BUs. In response to these challenges, we devised our approach conforming to the cognitive needs of the BUs. Ultimately, the goal is to create a digital environment that accommodates the diverse needs of individuals, ensuring equal access to information and participation for all, regardless of visual ability.

7. Conclusions

In conclusion, the present era mainly relies on web search as the primary means of accessing information. Within this context, blind users (BUs) constitute a significant portion of web users. Despite recent technological advancements in web search mechanisms, BUs continue to face difficulties in accessing online services, leading to approximately 53% success of the search sessions. These challenges can be attributed to inherent shortcomings in information organization mechanisms on the web. Notably, BUs interact with information linearly, having to sequentially determine the relevance of content, resulting in cognitive strain and time consumption, ultimately leading to information disorientation. Therefore, in this research, we investigated a non-linear information exploration mechanism for BUs. The categorical data model interacts with the tree data model to generate hierarchies based on the similarity threshold. We leveraged the multimodal (textual and voice) interaction of the BUs for searching on the web using the Wikipedia dataset. The efficacy of the proposed mechanism was evaluated from empirical and usability perspectives. The empirical evaluation showed 84% and 86.5% for the categorical precision and voice query precision, respectively. The behavioral analysis showed the accessibility of the search results within five clicks on average. Table 7 describes the potential future directions of the proposed system.

Table 7. Potential future directions for AI-driven content summarization.

Future Work	Description
Enhanced Abstractive Summarization	Develop more advanced abstractive summarization techniques that can generate summaries with higher coherence and readability. Incorporate contextual understanding and style mimicry.
Customizable Summary Length	Allow users, including blind users, to specify the desired length of the summary based on their preferences and reading capabilities.
Multilingual Summarization	Extend AI-driven summarization to support multiple languages, enabling blind users to access content in their preferred language.
Domain-Specific Summaries	Create specialized summarization models for various domains (e.g., scientific literature, news, legal documents) to cater to diverse informational needs.
Adaptive Summarization	Develop algorithms that adapt summarization based on user feedback, continually improving the quality of generated summaries for blind users.
Real-time Summarization	Implement summarization techniques that can generate summaries in real-time, enabling immediate access to key information as blind users navigate the web.
Integration with Assistive Tools	Integrate AI-generated summaries seamlessly with screen readers and other assistive technologies commonly used by blind users.
Cross-Modal Summarization	Explore generating summaries not only in text but also in alternative formats, such as audio summaries, to accommodate varying accessibility preferences.
Evaluation with Blind Users	Conduct thorough user studies and evaluations involving blind users to assess the effectiveness, usability, and impact of AI-driven content summarization.
Privacy-Aware Summarization	Develop techniques that generate accurate summaries while respecting user privacy, ensuring sensitive content is not exposed in the summary.
Hybrid Approaches	Combine extractive and abstractive summarization methods to leverage the strengths of both approaches for improved accuracy and readability.

The usability evaluation covering the interface screen, system information, and terminology, along with the learning and capabilities of the system in a broader range, showed an overall 72.5% usability score. While this research focused on architectural aspects of BU web exploration, in the future, we are interested in investigating the effectiveness of the proposed approach in various instantiation tools such as deep learning and in a standalone service environment that can be embedded in voice-activated assistive technologies. Furthermore, we are also interested in performing a comparative analysis of the existing BU information exploration assistive tools for a detailed investigation of BU information exploration behavior.

Author Contributions: Conceptualization, S.N., U.R., M.S., A.R.K., Q.A. and Y.D.; Data curation, S.N., U.R., M.S. and Y.D.; Formal analysis, U.R., M.S., A.R.K. and Q.A.; Funding acquisition, U.R., Q.A. and Y.D.; Investigation, S.N., M.S. and Y.D.; Methodology, S.N., U.R., M.S., A.R.K., Q.A. and Y.D.; Project administration, Q.A.; Resources, M.S., Q.A. and Y.D.; Software, S.N. and Y.D.; Supervision, U.R. and A.R.K.; Validation, U.R., M.S. and A.R.K.; Visualization, U.R., A.R.K. and Q.A.; Writing—original draft, S.N., U.R., M.S., A.R.K., Q.A. and Y.D.; Writing—review and editing, U.R., A.R.K., Q.A. and Y.D.. All authors have read and agreed to the published version of the manuscript.

Funding: This work was supported and funded by the Deanship of Scientific Research at Imam Mohammad Ibn Saud Islamic University (IMSIU) (grant number IMSIU-RP23122).

Institutional Review Board Statement: Not Applicable.

Informed Consent Statement: Not Applicable.

Data Availability Statement: The datasets generated and/or analyzed during the current study are available from the corresponding author upon reasonable request.

Acknowledgments: This work was supported and funded by the Scientific Research at Imam Mohammad Ibn Saud Islamic University (IMSIU) (grant number IMSIU-RP23122).

Conflicts of Interest: The authors declare no conflict of interest.

References

1. Khan, A.; Khusro, S. Blind-friendly user interfaces—A pilot study on improving the accessibility of touchscreen interfaces. *Multimed. Tools Appl.* **2019**, *78*, 17495–17519. [CrossRef]
2. Anuyah, O.; Milton, A.; Green, M.; Pera, M.S. An empirical analysis of search engines' response to web search queries associated with the classroom setting. *Aslib J. Inf. Manag.* **2020**, *72*, 88–111. [CrossRef]
3. Kulshrestha, J.; Eslami, M.; Messias, J.; Zafar, M.B.; Ghosh, S.; Gummadi, K.P.; Karahalios, K. Search bias quantification Investigating political bias in social media and web search. *Inf. Retr. J.* **2019**, *22*, 188–227. [CrossRef]
4. Rashid, U.; Saleem, K.; Ahmed, A. MIRRE approach: Nonlinear and multimodal exploration of MIR aggregated search results. *Multimed. Tools Appl.* **2021**, *80*, 20217–20253. [CrossRef]
5. Khan, A.R.; Rashid, U.; Saleem, K.; Ahmed, A. An architecture for non-linear discovery of aggregated multimedia document web search results. *PeerJ Comput. Sci.* **2021**, *7*, e449. [CrossRef] [PubMed]
6. Zhang, F.; Liu, Y.; Mao, J.; Zhang, M.; Ma, S. User behavior modeling for Web search evaluation. *AI Open* **2020**, *1*, 40–56. [CrossRef]
7. Khan, A.; Khusro, S. An insight into smartphone-based assistive solutions for visually impaired and blind people: Issues, challenges and opportunities. *Univers. Access Inf. Soc.* **2021**, *20*, 265–298. [CrossRef]
8. Zhang, H.; Park, S.O.; Joo, S.H.; Kim, J.H.; Kwak, S.K.; Lee, J.S. Precisely-controlled, a few layers of iron titanate inverse opal structure for enhanced photoelectrochemical water splitting. *Nano Energy* **2019**, *62*, 20–29. [CrossRef]
9. Bigham, J.P.; Lin, I.; Savage, S. The Effects of" Not Knowing What You Don't Know" on Web Accessibility for Blind Web Users. In Proceedings of the 19th international ACM SIGACCESS Conference on Computers and Accessibility, Baltimore, MD, USA, 20 October–1 November 2017; pp. 101–109.
10. Ullah, A.; Khusro, S.; Ullah, I. Towards a Search and Navigation Platform for Making Library Websites Accessible to Blind and Visually Impaired People. In *Software Engineering Research in System Science*; Silhavy, R., Silhavy, P., Eds.; Springer: Cham, Switzerland, 2023; pp. 595–607.
11. Kim, N.W.; Ataguba, G.; Joyner, S.C.; Zhao, C.; Im, H. Beyond Alternative Text and Tables: Comparative Analysis of Visualization Tools and Accessibility Methods. *Comput. Graph. Forum* **2023**, *42*, 323–335. [CrossRef]
12. Messaoudi, M.D.; Menelas, B.A.J.; Mcheick, H. Review of Navigation Assistive Tools and Technologies for the Visually Impaired. *Sensors* **2022**, *22*, 7888. [CrossRef] [PubMed]
13. Brinkley, J.; Tabrizi, N. A desktop usability evaluation of the facebook mobile interface using the jaws screen reader with blind users. In *Proceedings of the Human Factors and Ergonomics Society Annual Meeting*; SAGE Publications: Los Angeles, CA, USA, 2017; Volume 61, pp. 828–832.
14. Branham, S.M.; Mukkath Roy, A.R. Reading between the guidelines: How commercial voice assistant guidelines hinder accessibility for blind users. In Proceedings of the 21st International ACM SIGACCESS Conference on Computers and Accessibility, Pittsburgh, PA, USA, 28–30 October 2019; pp. 446–458.
15. Alluqmani, A.; Harvey, M.A.; Zhang, Z. The Barriers to Online Clothing Websites for Visually Impaired People: An Interview and Observation Approach to Understanding Needs. In Proceedings of the 2023 ACM Designing Interactive Systems Conference, DIS '23, New York, NY, USA, 10–14 July 2023; pp. 753–764. [CrossRef]
16. Taylor, Z.; Bicak, I. Two-year institution and community college web accessibility: Updating the literature after the 2018 Section 508 amendment. In *Graduate Students' Research about Community Colleges*; Routledge: London, UK, 2021; pp. 125–135.
17. Hristov, H.; Enkov, S.; Bliznakov, M.; Uzunov, A. Method for Designing Accessible Web Content in The Web Space of "Paisii Hilenarski" Plovdiv University. *Int. J. Emerg. Technol. Learn.* **2022**, *17*, 184–196. [CrossRef]
18. Manjari, K.; Verma, M.; Singal, G. A survey on assistive technology for visually impaired. *Internet Things* **2020**, *11*, 100188. [CrossRef]
19. Theodorou, P.; Meliones, A. Gaining insight for the design, development, deployment and distribution of assistive navigation systems for blind and visually impaired people through a detailed user. *Univers. Access Inf. Soc.* **2023**, *22*, 1–27. [CrossRef]
20. Roy, T.S.; Namratha, N.; Malleswari, T.N. Voice E-Mail Synced with Gmail for Visually Impaired. In Proceedings of the 2023 Third International Conference on Artificial Intelligence and Smart Energy (ICAIS), Coimbatore, India, 2–4 February 2023; IEEE: Piscataway, NJ, USA, 2023; pp. 802–807.
21. Fayyaz, N.; Khusro, S. Enhancing Accessibility for the Blind and Visually Impaired: Presenting Semantic Information in PDF Tables. *J. King Saud Univ. Comput.* **2023**, *35*, 101617. [CrossRef]
22. Bhukhya, C.; Bhumireddy, K.; Palakonalu, H.V.R.; Singh, S.K.; Bansod, S.; Pal, P.; Kumar, Y. Virtual Assistant and Navigation for Visually Impaired using Deep Neural Network and Image Processing. *Res. Sq.* **2023**; preprint.
23. Nair, A.K.; Sahoo, J. Edge Eye: A voice assisted campus navigation system for visually impaired. In Proceedings of the 2021 3rd International Conference on Signal Processing and Communication (ICPSC), Coimbatore, India, 13–14 May 2021; pp. 125–129.
24. Christopherson, P.S.; Eleyan, A.; Bejaoui, T.; Jazzar, M. Smart Stick for Visually Impaired People using Raspberry Pi with Deep Learning. In Proceedings of the 2022 International Conference on Smart Applications, Communications and Networking (SmartNets), Palapye, Botswana, 29 November–1 December 2022; pp. 1–6. [CrossRef]
25. Tůcek, D.; Koprda, S.; Magdin, M.; Balogh, Z. Didactic Tool for the Visually Impaired. In *Advances in Information and Communication*; Springer: Cham, Switzerland, 2023. [CrossRef]

26. Zeboudj, M.; Belkadi, K. Designing a Web Accessibility Environment for the Visually Impaired. In Proceedings of the 2022 3rd International Conference on Embedded Distributed Systems (EDiS), Oran, Algeria, 2–3 November 2022; pp. 154–157. [CrossRef]
27. Figueroa-Gutiérrez, S.; Montané-Jiménez, L.G.; Carlos Pérez-Arriaga, J.; Rojano-Cáceres, J.R.; Toledo-Toledo, G. Towards Automatic Interpretation Of Statistical Graphs For The Visually Impaired. In Proceedings of the 2021 9th International Conference in Software Engineering Research and Innovation (CONISOFT), San Diego, CA, USA, 25–29 October 2021; pp. 180–188. [CrossRef]
28. Meliones, A.; Maidonis, S. DALÍ: A digital assistant for the elderly and visually impaired using Alexa speech interaction and TV display. In Proceedings of the 13th ACM International Conference on PErvasive Technologies Related to Assistive Environments, New York, NY, USA, 30 June 2020; pp. 1–9. [CrossRef]
29. Giraud, S.; Thérouanne, P.; Steiner, D.D. Web accessibility: Filtering redundant and irrelevant information improves website usability for blind users. *Int. J. Hum. Comput. Stud.* **2018**, *111*, 23–35. [CrossRef]
30. Xie, I.; Babu, R.; Lee, T.H.; Castillo, M.D.; You, S.; Hanlon, A.M. Enhancing usability of digital libraries: Designing help features to support blind and visually impaired users. *Inf. Process. Manag.* **2020**, *57*, 102110. [CrossRef]
31. IEEE Std 1471-2000; Recommended Practice for Architectural Description for Software-Intensive Systems. IEEE: Piscataway, NJ, USA, 2000.
32. Richards, M. *Software Architecture Patterns*; O'Reilly Media, Inc.: Sebastopol, CA, USA, 2015; Volume 4.
33. Cofer, R.; Harding, B.F. *Rapid System Prototyping with FPGAs: Accelerating the Design Process*; Elsevier: Amsterdam, The Netherlands, 2006; p. 650.
34. Anitha, M.; Kumar, V.D.A.; Malathi, S.; Kumar, V.D.A.; Ramakrishnan, M.; Kumar, A.; Ali, R. A survey on the usage of pattern recognition and image analysis methods for the lifestyle improvement on low vision and visually impaired people. *Pattern Recognit. Image Anal.* **2021**, *31*, 24–34. [CrossRef]
35. Stephany, F.; Braesemann, F. An exploration of wikipedia data as a measure of regional knowledge distribution. In *Proceedings of the International Conference on Social Informatics*; Springer: Cham, Switzerland, 2017; pp. 31–40.
36. Ehrmann, M.; Fratzscher, M. Exchange rates and fundamentals: New evidence from real-time data. *J. Int. Money Financ.* **2005**, *24*, 317–341. [CrossRef]
37. Asheela, E.N. An Intervention on How Using Easily Accessible Resources to Carry Out Hands on Practical Activities in Science Influences Science Teachers' Conceptual Development and Dispositions. Master's Thesis, Rhodes University, Grahamstown, South Africa, 2017.

Disclaimer/Publisher's Note: The statements, opinions and data contained in all publications are solely those of the individual author(s) and contributor(s) and not of MDPI and/or the editor(s). MDPI and/or the editor(s) disclaim responsibility for any injury to people or property resulting from any ideas, methods, instructions or products referred to in the content.

MDPI
St. Alban-Anlage 66
4052 Basel
Switzerland
www.mdpi.com

Applied Sciences Editorial Office
E-mail: applsci@mdpi.com
www.mdpi.com/journal/applsci

Disclaimer/Publisher's Note: The statements, opinions and data contained in all publications are solely those of the individual author(s) and contributor(s) and not of MDPI and/or the editor(s). MDPI and/or the editor(s) disclaim responsibility for any injury to people or property resulting from any ideas, methods, instructions or products referred to in the content.

www.ingramcontent.com/pod-product-compliance
Lightning Source LLC
LaVergne TN
LVHW070640100526
838202LV00013B/849